Migrating your SAP® Data

 PRESS

SAP PRESS is issued by
Bernhard Hochlehnert, SAP AG

SAP PRESS is a joint initiative of SAP and Galileo Press. The know-how offered by SAP specialists combined with the expertise of the publishing house
Galileo Press offers the reader expert books in the field. SAP PRESS features
first-hand information and expert advice, and provides useful skills for pro-
fessional decision-making.

SAP PRESS offers a variety of books on technical and business related topics
for the SAP user. For further information, please visit our website:
www.sap-press.com.

Sigrid Hagemann, Liane Will
SAP R/3 System Administration
2003, approx. 450 pp., ISBN 1-59229-014-4

Helmut Stefani
Archiving Your SAP Data
A comprehensive guide to plan and execute archiving projects
2003, 360 pp., ISBN 1-59229-008-6

Thomas Schneider
SAP Performance Optimization Guide
3rd Edition
2003, 494 pp., ISBN 1-59229-022-1

A. Rickayzen, J. Dart, C. Brennecke, M. Schneider
Practical Workflow for SAP
2002, 504 pp., ISBN 1-59229-006-X

Horst Keller, Joachim Jacobitz
ABAP Objects. The Official Reference
2003, 1094 pp., 2 Volumes and CD Set
ISBN 1-59229-011-6

Michael Willinger, Johann Gradl

Migrating your SAP® Data

The ultimate reference for quick
and easy data migration—
no programming required

Translation Lemoine International, Inc.,
Salt Lake City, UT
Copy Editor Nancy Etscovitz, UCG, Inc.,
Boston, MA
Cover Design department, Cologne, Germany
Printed in the United States of America

ISBN 1-59229-028-0

Contents

4 Batch Input 43

6   Legacy System Migration Workbench   123

1 Introduction

Data migration is hardly a new issue for IT professionals. Rather, it is a never-ending requirement that goes hand-in-hand with each software update. In most cases, however, a successful upgrade doesn't resolve all problems. Changing economic conditions and standard operating procedures within a corporation frequently lead to organizational restructuring, which, in turn, requires reorganization of the datasets in existing IT systems. This fact aside, the major issues inherent in data migration aren't adequately covered in the pertinent literature, which is precisely what motivated us to make them the focus of this book.

In many cases, project managers underestimate the quantity of resources that data migration can tie up for the duration of a project. This frequently results in staffing bottlenecks and, therefore, financial ones as well. One primary reason why such staffing bottlenecks arise is that data migration usually requires programmers—individuals with detailed technical knowledge—and because programmers are responsible for all the applications in an installation, this merely contributes to and exacerbates the staffing problem.

Staffing Bottleneck: Data Migration

Keeping this programmer staffing issue in mind, you would benefit from having in place data migration techniques that can be implemented not only by programmers, but by consultants as well, that is, those without highly technical skills. Ideally, the user departments—those departments that supply the data—should have the ability to trigger data transfers and migration projects, and model them in the IT systems. Reaching this goal, however, demands that migration techniques be easy to learn and require very little programming.

Programming-Free Data Migration

Nonetheless, we are well aware that there will always be situations in which specific project requirements are so complex that some minimal programming is still unavoidable. Still, we'd like to consider programming as a last resort, a recourse that should be used only when all other data migration techniques fail to achieve the required results. Therefore, this book will focus less on techniques for programming data migration and more on methods that enable you to avoid programming entirely.

When a legacy system is replaced with SAP R/3, these programming-free techniques are supplied by SAP. The procedures provided aren't limited to specific R/3 applications, either; they can be used in a wide range of applications—accounting, logistics, and even Human Resources Management. Regardless of which application is used, the general procedure remains

Applicability

the same. Moreover, the type of data that has to be migrated is immaterial. For example, it is just as easy to migrate master data from Human Resources (HR) as it is to migrate transaction data from Financial Accounting (FI).

The particular charm of this method is that it is not limited merely to the traditional R/3 applications, but is also available for some of the latest products that build on the SAP R/3 technology, such as SAP CRM (Customer Relationship Management) and SAP APO (Advanced Planner and Optimizer, the technical foundation of mySAP SCM—Supply Chain Management). Regardless of the specific application, the procedures themselves are so flexible that they permit the optional integration of any customer-specific ABAP coding required for the migration, which makes them almost universally applicable. The availability of these methods in the individual SAP applications is discussed in the upcoming chapters.

Intended Audience
Because custom programming should remain the exception, however, this book is primarily intended for individuals who don't necessarily require programming skills themselves, but who might have to use programming, directly or indirectly, in the course of their work. This includes *SAP consultants* hired to implement a data migration for a customer or within their own organizations, as well as *project managers* who need an overview of the individual methods available in order to make qualified decisions. This subject is also relevant for *SAP developers* who want to learn about efficient migration techniques to save time and money. The methods described in this book could make the need to write and test custom programs for data migration, so-called "throwaway programs," a thing of the past. Experience also shows that the simplicity of the data migration procedures enables the *user departments* to migrate data themselves, rounding out our intended audience. Consequently, the role of user departments is no longer limited to that of data supplier. With their knowledge of the data migration methods on the one hand and their years of experience with the legacy IT system on the other hand, the user departments will most certainly play an active role in data migration projects.

Prerequisites
Because our intended broad audience cannot be expected to have an equivalent skill base, we have chosen the explanations and case examples in this book to be comprehensible and practical for readers both with and without a detailed technical knowledge of the SAP system. We must assume, however, that readers have a basic understanding of SAP R/3, Windows 98/2000/NT, and common Microsoft Office products such as Word, Excel, and Access in order to define the scope of this book.

Although readers will find that knowing some of the business contexts is beneficial for certain issues, it is not a prerequisite for understanding the descriptions in this book. The terms *data migration* and *data transfer* are used synonymously in this book. The data source can be any legacy IT system, assuming an initial data transfer is involved, in addition to a live SAP R/3 system, if the dataset must be modified to meet organizational changes.

The data migration itself is frequently underestimated and not perceived as a fully qualified, independent subproject within the overall project. Therefore, **Chapter 2** addresses the preparatory measures for data migration, which are critical to the success of any project. These measures include selection of the project team, definition of the project schedule, and issues regarding which data will be transferred and how it will be translated into the SAP terminology. These processes should represent the starting point of any data migration project, regardless of which specific methods are used.

Data Migration as a Subproject

Chapter 3 deals with the basics of data migration. It introduces the basic terms that are used repeatedly throughout the rest of the book. It also describes the steps that are involved in every data migration, along with a brief overview of the data migration techniques supplied by SAP.

Data Migration Basics

Once Chapters 2 and 3 have familiarized you with the basics, **Chapter 4** introduces the conventional method for migrating data to R/3: *the batch input technology*. In addition to a general introduction, this chapter introduces both the standard batch input programs for data migration supplied by SAP and custom batch input programs that are relatively easy to write. Because the latter require programming, however, which we want to avoid wherever possible, the batch input technology is discussed here in combination with Microsoft Word mail merge processing, which makes programming-free data migration possible.

Batch Input Technique

This theme of avoiding programming continues throughout Chapters 5 and 6. **Chapter 5** introduces the *Computer Aided Test Tool* (CATT), a tool that was originally developed to test business processes, but that also can be used for data migration. In addition to introducing the CATT, this chapter discusses how this tool can be used for data migration, which is illustrated by using two detailed case examples from the enterprise accounting area.

CATT

For cases in which the requirements of a data migration prove to be too complex for the CATT, the *Legacy System Migration Workbench* (LSM

LSMW

Workbench or LSMW) introduced in **Chapter 6** is much more flexible than the CATT, although the similarities between the two tools are unmistakable. The LSM Workbench lets you transfer data from non-SAP systems to an SAP R/3 system with minimal programming required. This tool is the right choice whenever the structure of the legacy data differs significantly from the structure of the data in the SAP R/3 system—making data conversion unavoidable—or when the legacy data must be augmented with data already in the SAP R/3 system.

Avoiding Programming

If you have read through to Chapter 6 and you still think you will have to resort to programming for your own data migration, we highly recommend that you read **Chapter 7**. This chapter uses numerous examples to show how the migration dataset can be prepared with Microsoft Excel or Microsoft Access, for example, using the described programming-free method instead of a custom-written program to migrate the data to the SAP R/3 system.

Rating Migration Techniques

After the individual data migration methods have been introduced, **Chapter 8** looks at each of these methods with a critical eye. In particular, this chapter describes the advantages and disadvantages of each technique and attempts to pinpoint the best procedure for a given situation.

Migrating Fixed Assets with Microsoft Excel

Chapter 9 is a special case, because the data migration method described here, in contrast to the procedures covered in the previous chapters, is not application-independent, but instead can be used only in Asset Accounting. In addition to the necessary Customizing settings for the migration, a case example in this chapter illustrates how you can use Microsoft Excel to transfer both asset master data and the corresponding transaction data to SAP R/3, provided this data has the required format.

Outlook and Related Areas

In closing, **Chapter 10** informs you of recent developments and areas related to data migration—such as *eCATT, the Data Conversion and Migration Workbench*, and data extraction from live SAP R/3 systems.

Appendices A and B

As mentioned, datasets within existing IT systems must also be adapted to changing framework conditions over the course of time. **Appendix A** provides you with a module-specific overview of selected R/3 tables that typically must be processed during a restructuring. Familiarity with these tables will help you find the relevant data in the system, via accelerating the overall process. In addition, all the relevant terminology for this book is listed and defined in a glossary in **Appendix B**.

The structure of this book makes it possible for you to jump directly to the chapter that interests you without having to read all the previous chapters.

All the same, this book is also intended as a comprehensive project manual for data migration. Once you have read it in its entirety, you will be able to plan, judge, and execute your own migration projects. Detailed case examples, illustrated with numerous screenshots, will help you to achieve this goal.

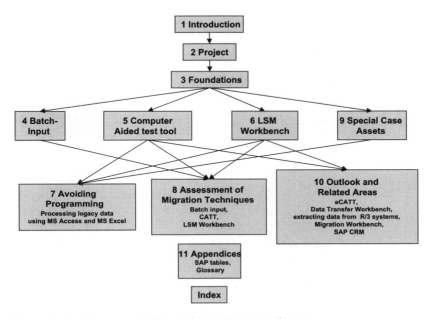

Figure 1.1 Book Structure and Dependencies Between Chapters

We owe a particular debt of thanks to Katja Ohliger, who gave us critical support during the editing of this book, pointed out several minor mistakes, and made many suggestions that significantly contributed to making this book more invaluable. We would also like to thank Mitra Bakhshaee, who wrote the original version of the Visual Basic program introduced in Chapter 9.

Acknowledgments

We trust that you will enjoy reading this book and find it most helpful in your data migration endeavors and responsibilities.

Walldorf, Germany   April 2004
Michael Willinger and **Johann Gradl**

2   Managerial Foundations for Migrating Data to SAP R/3

In order for data migration to deliver the desired results, it should be discussed at an early stage. Furthermore, it has to qualify as a subproject within the overall implementation project. Lastly, sufficient project resources must be reserved for migration activities.

2.1   Data Migration as a Subproject

Frequently, data migration does not get the attention it deserves. All too often, project managers fail to realize that, depending on the project scope, data migration can tie up staffing resources and financial resources as well. Staffing bottlenecks will occur whenever the data migration technique restricts the migration activities to a select group of individuals. Because custom data transfer programs are often used, programmers are the primary cause of the bottlenecks. As we mentioned in Chapter 1, the objective of this book is to introduce migration techniques that are easy to learn, guarantee data security, and—in the ideal situation—don't require any custom programming. Consequently, data migration is no longer the sole responsibility of programmers. Because individuals who don't possess complex programming skills can be involved in the migration process as well, the likelihood of staffing bottlenecks is significantly reduced.

Staffing Bottleneck

The need to manage limited project resources is not the only factor that qualifies data migration as an independent subproject within an overall implementation project. Another aspect that you should not underestimate is the information conveyed within the migrated data, that is, the data quality. It is indisputable, for example, that the open items in the legacy system must correspond to those items in SAP R/3—both individually and accumulated—in order to guarantee data consistency between the systems. This alone is far from sufficient, however. Because data migration is the foundation for all subsequent business processes in SAP R/3, you must also migrate information that may not appear to be relevant, but that may be the control data that ensures smooth handling of downstream processes.

Foundation for Business Processes

Therefore, it is not enough to simply ensure that the migrated data is quantitatively complete. You must also investigate whether the migrated data can handle the operative transactions in the new system, and whether it has the necessary information for the decision-making processes. In the example of the open items, this means that besides verifying that the amounts are correct, you must also ensure that the due dates are calculated properly, because they can have a direct impact on an enterprise's liquidity planning. Missing or incorrect information can steer decision-making processes in an entirely unintended direction.

Data Migration as an Iterative Process

For this reason, we recommend that you design your data migration project as an iterative process. This means you can begin testing the data migration as soon you have extracted the first data from the legacy system and customizing in SAP R/3 permits the data migration (the latter will be dealt with in detail later in this book). Based on the initial results, you then check in a subsequent step whether all the information required for smooth handling of the downstream processes is available. This involves comprehensive system testing and potential changes to the configuration. If information is missing, you must first determine where to obtain it, and repeat the data migration until you achieve the results that you want. Note that you can never execute data migration or test business processes in isolation; these two tasks are inextricably paired with one another.

System Comprehension

Again, this last aspect emphasizes the importance of data migration in an overall implementation process. In this context, the individuals who are responsible for the data migration are well advised to deal with the processes in the legacy system early on, and to examine how these processes can be modeled in SAP R/3, especially when the new system is being implemented, a *business reengineering* is required. Because no one knows the legacy IT system better than the user department staff, they should be involved in the processes from the start, in order to prevent staffing bottlenecks in this area as well. With this approach, the user department staff will become familiar with the philosophy of the SAP R/3 system step by step, and will be better able to determine which data must be provided to ensure a smooth system migration.

2.2 Preliminary Considerations

At the start of the project, you can determine the preliminary considerations that will shape the subsequent migration project based on the legacy system, without requiring detailed knowledge of the SAP R/3 system.

2.2.1 Defining the Dataset for Migration

The data to be migrated can be divided into the following categories:

▶ **Master data**

Master data is data that remains unchanged over a long period of time. Relevance It involves information that you always need for the same purpose. Of course, it makes sense to migrate only the master data that is actually used. Dormant data (see Section 2.2.2), data without any operative use, should be flagged as such in the legacy system to exclude it from the migration process.

▶ **Transaction data**

Transaction-based data has a short lifecycle and can be assigned to spe- Line Items or Balances cific master data. It is sometimes also referred to as "posting documents." In this case, you must clarify just how detailed a history of the legacy system should be modeled in SAP R/3. Specifically, you must decide whether you want to migrate the individual posting documents, or line items, or need only the accumulated, updated values, namely, the balances. If you decide to migrate the line items, you must determine the number of items in the past fiscal years that you want to migrate, and which role the cleared items (for information purposes only) have to perform. If you decide to migrate the balances, the legacy system must remain available to provide detailed information, at least during the transition phase.

Past experience shows that most migration projects use a combination of line items and balances. Many managers decide to migrate all the line items for customers and vendors and use them to continue the business processes in SAP R/3. Conversely, the line items are not integral to balance sheet accounts and income statement accounts. The specific situation is what determines which data has to be migrated.

2.2.2 Identifying Dormant Data

You should always think of a change to a new IT system as an opportunity Analyzing the Legacy Dataset to examine your legacy data and eliminate data that, while still stored in the legacy system, has no operative use now or in the future. Your time investment in this task will more than pay off, as it will ensure a consistent, orderly data basis in the new system. In addition, this procedure can significantly reduce the data volume for migration and, therefore, lessen the overall time required for the data transfer.

The issue here is how to identify this dormant data. The following examples describe several methods.

▶ **Master data**

If the legacy system can analyze which master data has not been used actively for a longer period (two years, for example), this analysis can be the starting point for deciding whether the identified data will be needed in the future. If not, you can flag the data as not relevant for migration, excluding it from further migration steps.

You will frequently encounter situations in which identical master data exists several times in a legacy system. While this data is saved under different identification numbers, its contents are identical or nearly so. In this case, an analysis can help you discover whether this situation exists in your system. If so, the redundant data can also be flagged as not relevant, to exclude it from further migration steps.

The situation becomes somewhat more complex when transactions are based on the redundant master data. In such situations, you will have to change the identified postings in the legacy system or auxiliary external system (such as Microsoft Excel) before you can eliminate the redundant master data. If you do not do this, migrating the transaction data will cause errors, because the transaction data will not have the corresponding master data in the new system.

Regardless of the issues that we just addressed, the affected user departments should always investigate whether the current operative master data will continue to be used in the same manner in the new system, or whether the history should start anew with the successor system. Classic examples include charts of accounts that have grown over time and yet consist of many individual accounts. In this case, you must ask yourself, "Is all the master data really needed, or would it be more expedient for information and control purposes to consolidate the master data and reduce it to a more manageable amount?" If you decide on the latter, posting changes will be required.

▶ **Transaction data**

You may discover that your legacy system contains transactions that the SAP R/3 system cannot identify as such. Such cases involve postings with zero values. To avoid problems with the subsequent migration from the start, you should search your legacy dataset for such transactions and eliminate any such items found.

What do you want to do with transactions that can be allocated to the same master data record, but which balance to zero when added together? Is there a reason for this situation that justifies identifying the items separately, or has someone simply forgotten to clear the items in the legacy system? Analysis in the legacy system will help you to answer these questions. If the analysis indicates that balancing the items would be beneficial, you can do so directly in the legacy system, or in an auxiliary system. This step will have a direct impact on the migration data volume.

2.2.3   Measures for Reducing Data Volume

The question as to how detailed duplication of the legacy system's history will be in the successor system has a major influence on the data volume. But even if you decide to migrate the line items, several measures can help you to reduce the numbers of these items prior to migration:

▶ If processes can be closed, they should not be set to a status such as "Open" or "Partially complete"; set these processes to "Completed." Depending on the application, items with this status may be excluded from the data migration.

Close Processes

▶ If your economic situation and company policy permit it, you might consider paying outstanding vendor invoices before executing the data migration in order to take advantage of cash discounts. This will not only shrink the volume of data to be migrated (assuming paid items aren't relevant for the migration), but will also help to reduce your expenses.

Payment Before the Due Date

▶ Another possible approach is to adjust your payment pattern to keep credit memos to a minimum.

2.2.4   Preparatory Measures for Extracting the Legacy Data

As long as the user departments or other individuals responsible for extracting the legacy data are not sufficiently familiar with processes in the SAP R/3 system, it makes little sense for them to provide an initial data extract for testing the legacy data transfer in this early project phase. Nonetheless, you should check at the start of the project whether the legacy system can collect all the information contained in the master and transaction data and export it to one or more files. One question that is most relevant here is whether the legacy system has standard functions for creating such data extracts, or whether custom programming will be required. In the latter case, you must clarify whether in-house expertise is available, or whether you will have to bring in external consulting resources—which will have to be scheduled accordingly.

How Do I Extract the Data?

2.2.5 Addendum: Accounting Considerations

If you want to migrate transaction data, you must deal directly with accounting issues that have to be solved prior to the data migration. Hopefully, we will have presented this rather dry and sometimes menacing subject—as far as it affects the data migration—in an easily comprehensible manner. The information below will help you to better understand Chapters 4 and 5, which are both dedicated to the migration of transaction data. Here, the main issue is *how* the transaction data, such as open credit items, will be migrated to R/3.

Migration Account   It is clear that the gross amounts from invoices and credit memos will have to be identified in the credit and debit columns of the corresponding vendor accounts. But what about the corresponding offsetting postings? One option is to configure a *migration account* in the general ledger (G/L) that transfers only the open items and receives all the offsetting entries from the data migration. To document the special status of this account, the account number "9xxxxx" is usually selected. The following example illustrates this option.

Example 1   Vendor 1 has two open invoices (I) in the amounts of $100.00 and $200.00, and a credit memo (C) in the amount of $50.00. Vendor 2 has an outstanding invoice in the amount of $150.00.

From an accounting perspective, the following vendor accounts are displayed:

Vendor 1		Vendor 2	
Debit	Credit	Debit	Credit
C $50	I $100	Balance $150	I $150
Balance $250	I $200		

The following migration account is displayed:

Migration Account	
Debit	Credit
I $100	C $50
I $200	Balance $400
I $150	

As this example shows, the balance of the migration account is the exact sum of the balances of the vendor accounts to be migrated. This means that the migration account is ideal for an initial comparison of the totals between the legacy system and the SAP R/3 system. If the totals are identical in both systems, you can simply check a random sampling of the vendor accounts to confirm their accuracy.

In most cases, the migration account is not assigned to a balance sheet item, which means it is identified as a non-assigned account under the bottom line. If you migrate your data at the start of a fiscal year and use only one migration account for the vendor data, open sales items, and figures from the remaining balance sheet accounts, this account will balance to zero—assuming the data migration runs without errors. In this case, you can consider the migration account as an account that mirrors all the postings to be transferred from all accounts. You can draw parallels to an *opening balance sheet account*, which mirrors all the opening balances of the *opening balance sheet* and also balances to zero. In contrast to an opening balance sheet account, which contains only opening balances (one balance per account), the migration account can also explain the reason for these balances, as it lists the corresponding line items.

Attributes of the Migration Account

But, what does "transferring the remaining balance sheet accounts" mean? These are all the accounts listed in the financial statements, provided they don't represent *reconciliation accounts*. Here, a reconciliation account is a general ledger account that records the transactions from *subledger accounting*, such as accounts payable and accounts receivable. You cannot post directly to the reconciliation accounts. Instead, they receive all the values automatically as soon as a corresponding posting is created in the subledger. Generally, several accounts from subledger accounting—several vendor accounts, for example—point to a shared reconciliation account. This identifies the subledger transactions in general ledger accounting for the financial statements. Because the corresponding vendors and customers are posted to directly during the migration of the vendor/customer open items—that is, the posting takes place in the subledgers—the integration of the general ledger and the subledgers indicates that no further postings to the reconciliation account are needed, therefore, you can exclude the reconciliation accounts entirely from the data migration process.

Reconciliation Accounts

When *asset values* must be migrated, the situation differs. Here, integration of the general ledger and the asset subledger is not ensured for the duration of the legacy data transfer. Therefore, after the data migration,

Migrating Assets

you must manually post to the reconciliation accounts in Asset Management. Because direct postings to reconciliation accounts aren't supported in the application menu for Financial Accounting, however, the corresponding functions are located in Customizing for Asset Management. The special features associated with the migration of asset values are described in detail in Chapter 9.

Migrating Profit and Loss (P&L) Accounts

Like the migration of balance sheet accounts, the migration of the *P&L accounts* must also be clarified. If you migrate the data at the *start of a fiscal year*, the decision is clear. Because all the P&L accounts transfer their balances to the *retained earnings account*, which you define in Customizing for Financial Accounting, at the end of the fiscal year, they all have a zero balance at the start of the new fiscal year. This, in turn, means that they don't contain any transactions from the current year and therefore can be excluded from the data migration. If you migrate your data in *mid-year*, however, transactions may have taken place in the P&L accounts, and, therefore, will have to be migrated. In the latter case, note that the P&L accounts have not yet passed their postings on to the retained earnings accounts, which is identified in the financial statements. This means the assets and liabilities are not directly equal; the profit or loss currently in the P&L accounts still must be added. Thus, the migration account will have a balance after the migration of the balance sheet accounts, which corresponds exactly to the amount of profit or loss. The following example illustrates this situation.

Example 2

Fixed assets (FA) show a balance in the amount of $1,000 and current assets (CA) show a balance in the amount of $500. In addition, the opening balance of stockholders' equity (SE) was $500, which means the P&L account now shows a profit (PROF) of $500 that has not yet been transferred to the retained earnings account. Therefore, this amount is not allocated to SE yet in the financial statements. If you take into account the current payables (PAYB) in the amount of $500, the following table results are displayed.

Financial Statement	
Assets	**Liabilities**
FA 1,000	SE 500
CA 500	PAYB 500

Profit and Loss Statement	
Debit	Credit
	PROF 500

Note that the value for the payables comprises a large number of G/L accounts and line items, for example, and also contains the open credit items, which are represented by the vendor reconciliation account. As just described, all of these line items will result in an appropriate offsetting posting in the migration account. To present a simple, easy to follow financial statement, however, we have chosen to omit a breakdown of FA, CA, SE and PAYB into G/L accounts and their line items. We used the same strategy with the identification of the profit in the profit and loss statement.

Given these basic assumptions, and after migrating the balance sheet accounts (including subledgers), you would see the following migration account displayed:

Migration Account	
Debit	Credit
SE 500	FA 1,000
PAYB 500	CA 500
Balance 500	

Therefore, the balance in the migration account, after the migration of the balance sheet accounts, corresponds exactly to the amount of the profit or loss—the amount of revenues in the preceding example—that has to be migrated. Once the revenues have also been migrated to SAP R/3, the following migration account is displayed:

Migration Account	
Debit	Credit
SE 500	FA 1,000
PAYB 500	CA 500
PROF 500	

Summary: The Balance of the Migration Account Is Always Zero

To summarize, the following rule applies. After a successful data transfer, the migration account must always have a balance of zero, regardless of whether the data migration was performed at the start of a fiscal year or in mid-year. If the data is migrated at the start of a fiscal year, the migration account doesn't have any P&L components, and, therefore, shows only the transactions in the subledgers and other balance sheet accounts. If the data is migrated in mid-year, however, the migration account may also contain P&L components. It should also be apparent that the migration account always represents all the transactions to be migrated as a mirror image of the postings to the G/L accounts, or the postings in the subledgers.

One or More Migration Accounts

Alternatively, you can work with multiple migration accounts. For example, you can have one migration account for vendors, another migration account for customers, and still another for fixed assets, as well as other balance sheet and P&L accounts. In this constellation of accounts, the balances of the different migration accounts will add up to zero after an error-free migration. There is no general recommendation as to how many migration accounts you should use; it depends primarily on your personal preferences. It is definitely not advisable, however, to define vast numbers of migration accounts in order to make it easier to localize errors later on. You can achieve the same results if you use only one migration account, but different *document types*—depending on the situation—that you can then select for the migration account.

Posting Keys

Once you have settled on which migration account to use, you can concentrate on the next subject, which is directly related to the migration of the accounting documents, namely, the *posting key* (PK). This is a two-digit numeric key that controls the recording of document items. Among other things, the posting key defines the account type, that is, whether a vendor account, a customer account, a G/L account posting, or a posting from Asset Management is involved. The posting key also indicates whether the specified account is posted to in credit or in debit. Posting keys are used whenever you use documents for posting, such as open credit items, in the standard R/3 transactions for document entry, especially Transaction FB01.

Reference to Example 1

Returning to Example 1 above, typically, a data transfer document consists of two items. In addition to the vendor accounts (vendor 1, vendor 2), G/L accounts (migration account) are also included. Debit postings to G/L accounts must be assigned account key 40, and credit postings to G/L accounts must be assigned posting key 50. You can differentiate further between debit and credit postings to vendor accounts; that is, you can choose from different debit and credit posting keys. We recommend using the standard R/3 posting keys for vendor invoices (31) and vendor credit memos (21), which would result in the following vendor invoice:

Vendor Invoice		
PK 40	Migration Account	100
PK 31	Vendor 1	100 (-)
Vendor Credit Memo		
PK 21	Vendor 1	50
PK 50	Migration Account	50 (-)

In the process, the SAP R/3 system assigns a minus sign (-) to every credit posting, independently of the account type, so the document items always balance to zero when they are entered correctly. Therefore, the posting key controls whether an entered amount is interpreted as positive or negative.

Lastly, you must transfer customer open items and G/L account postings in a similar manner.

Customer Invoice		
PK 01	Customer 1	100
PK 50	Migration Account	100 (-)
Customer Credit Memo		
PK 40	Migration Account	50
PK 11	Customer 1	50 (-)
G/L Account Posting in Credit		
PK 40	Migration Account	200
PK 50	G/L Account	200 (-)
G/L Account Posting in Debit		
PK 40	G/L Account	100
PK 50	Migration Account	100 (-)

2.3 The Data Migration Process from the Project Perspective

Once you have finalized the considerations discussed in Section 2.2, you can begin to prepare for the actual data migration.

2.3.1 Basic Customizing

First, Customizing in SAP R/3 must have progressed enough to enable execution of the basic processes that follow the data migration.

2.3.2 System Presentations in SAP R/3

Theoretical and System Presentations

Before they can provide the files with the necessary data from the legacy system, the involved user departments must become familiar with and understand the process flows in the SAP R/3 system. One way to impart this knowledge is to give theoretical presentations of the R/3 structures, their mutual dependencies, and the data flow that these structures create in an integrated system. This theoretical background makes it easier to understand and classify subsequent presentations in a live or simulated SAP R/3 system.

Ideally, after this initial meeting, the participating user departments will already be able to roughly determine which data has to be extracted from the legacy system in order to achieve the desired results in SAP R/3.

2.3.3 Business Reengineering

Paradigm Shift

A far more difficult situation arises when the SAP R/3 system and the legacy system are based on different application logic and, therefore, the legacy system data cannot be migrated directly to SAP R/3. In such a situation, the data must be processed prior to the transfer in order to enable its subsequent use in SAP R/3. This process can be extremely time-consuming. If such data transformations are required within the scope of your project, you will have to allocate the necessary resources. The SAP R/3 system often requires information to model the business processes—called *required entry fields*—that does not necessarily exist in this form in the legacy system. Conversely, the legacy system may contain information in its data records that SAP R/3 does not require due to differing application logic and possible organizational structures.

Organization Follows Software

The system knowledge described in Section 2.3.2 is particularly important in this framework, because, for the participating user departments, it is the foundation on which they can restructure and redesign their business processes. Therefore, the organization and data structures follow the demands of the new software. Because this *business reengineering* can take on extremely complex dimensions, you may once again want to discuss the extent to which you want to model the legacy system's history in the successor system (see Section 2.2.1).

2.3.4 Simulating the Data Migration

Once you have held the initial SAP R/3 system presentations, and the user departments understand the logic of the SAP R/3 system, you can intensify your focus on the activities associated with the data migration itself:

▶ Identify the R/3 transactions that you want to use to migrate the legacy data to SAP R/3.

▶ Run these identified transactions manually in SAP R/3 with test data from the legacy system and note which fields are required. There may be required entry fields that have no corresponding data fields in the legacy system.

Once the SAP transactions and the fields to be maintained are known, you can continue with the *mapping* phase.

2.3.5 Mapping (Field Matching)

The field texts in the legacy system agree with the corresponding terminology in the SAP R/3 system only in the rarest of cases. If different naming conventions are used, the respective texts must be recorded and assigned accordingly—theoretically at first, on a piece of paper. This procedure is usually called *mapping*.

Mapping

In the simplest case, the field texts will be identical, which means the following equation applies:

1:1 Relationships

Field text (legacy system) = Field text (SAP R/3)

If the fields differ only in their terminology, but not their content, this relationship still holds true.

If different designs are involved, however, the fields from the legacy system must be transformed beforehand—because SAP R/3 does not recognize them in their source format—and then assigned to the corresponding fields in R/3. The legacy system doesn't necessarily have to work with posting keys, which are control parameters from Financial Accounting that control the account type, among other things, and determine whether a debit posting or a credit posting is involved. Similarly, you may discover

Transformations

that the legacy system uses different logic to categorize its postings. In such cases, the individual fields of the legacy system, which control whether the postings to the respective accounts are listed under credits or debits, must be transformed to the appropriate posting keys in keeping with the R/3 philosophy.

In general, the following applies:

Field texts (legacy system) → Transformation → Field texts (SAP R/3)

Example 3   First, consider the example of the posting keys. If you assume that the legacy system generally flags invoices with "I" and credit memos with "C," the following transformation process is required:

	Flag in Legacy System	Posting Key in SAP R/3 system
Vendor Invoices and Credit Memos	I	31
	C	21
Customer Invoices and Credit Memos	J	01
	C	11

Required Entry Fields   If a field is mandatory in SAP R/3 (*required entry field*), but the legacy system doesn't have an equivalent field, the existing structures in the legacy system will have to be reworked—in an auxiliary system such as Microsoft Excel, for example—and adapted to meet the requirements of the new system landscape (see Section 2.3.3). Alternatively, you can set the field to a constant (solely for the data migration), or change the field to an optional entry field in Customizing.

At the end of this step, every R/3 field that is required for data migration must be assigned a corresponding field from the legacy system, either by direct assignment or via a transformation process.

2.3.6   Data Extraction from the Legacy System

Text Files   Once the legacy system fields have been mapped to the corresponding R/3 fields, at least theoretically (see Section 2.3.5), the next step involves extracting all the fields that are required to model the business processes in SAP R/3 and their contents from the legacy system.

When extracting the data from the legacy system, you should ensure that the data is provided in one or more text files; this makes it much easier to postprocess the data manually with a spreadsheet program (see Section 2.3.7).

2.3.7 Manual Postprocessing of the Extracted Data

Only rarely will the field mapping between the legacy system and the SAP R/3 system deliver results that don't require manual postprocessing of the extracted data. In most cases, the data records must be adapted or transformed—due to a changed system landscape or business reengineering—to enable their processing in the SAP R/3 system.

Therefore, your objective in this manual postprocessing is to create a file that the SAP R/3 system can process without any further transformations or adjustments. This file is the result of the mapping performed in a previous step (see Section 2.3.5). Here, you amend the extracted data from the legacy system according to the rules defined in Section 2.3.5 to create a proper file. The elimination of data that is no longer needed is also part of this process (see Section 2.2.2) .

Conventional spreadsheet programs such as Microsoft Excel will help you to achieve this objective, with their various calculation, filtering, and replacement functions. If your intention is to *avoid programming*, you must ensure that this step is properly addressed within the process chain. As we mentioned previously, because one of our book's main goals is to show you how to enable data migration without using custom programming, in Chapter 7, we describe several ways in which you can format your dataset in advance to avoid time-intensive programming during the subsequent migration phase.

Using Spreadsheet Programs

2.3.8 Selecting a Data Migration Technique

When selecting the migration techniques, you must weigh your data security needs against the speed with which the data has to be migrated to the SAP R/3 system. You should be aware that speed always comes at the expense of data security; it is almost impossible to achieve both goals simultaneously.

Speed versus Security

After you learn about the individual methods for data migration, in Chapter 8 we will assess the various techniques and indicate which procedures are optimal for certain situations. Chapter 9 contains a similar assessment of the various techniques for migrating asset values.

2.3.9 Uploading the Data in SAP R/3

Upload According
to Migration
Technique

The data upload to R/3 is a strictly technical process that you perform according to the selected migration procedure (see Section 2.3.8). Chapters 4 to 6 describe which preparation steps are required in SAP R/3.

Troubleshooting

Problems that occur during the data upload are usually the direct result of an insufficient or erroneous data basis (see Section 2.3.7). Should the upload process terminate, you will have to analyze the data basis in depth and adjust it accordingly, and then repeat the upload. Any changes made to the database in the interim will have to be undone to avoid falsifying the results, which is yet another reason to pay particular attention to the activities described in Section 2.3.7.

Unfortunately, not all the application areas in the SAP R/3 system provide functions for deleting specific data. In such cases, you will have to back up your data prior to migration and restore the backup if your initial migration fails.

Dependencies and
Order of Activities

To be thorough, you should take into account many dependencies during the migration. These dependencies require you to perform certain activities in a specific order, for example:

▶ Master data before transaction data

▶ General ledger before subledger (e.g., reconciliation account before vendor)

▶ Purchase orders before goods receipt postings

▶ Material master data before material bills of material (BOMs)

2.3.10 Testing the Business Processes in SAP R/3

Quantitative
Completeness

Once you have transferred your dataset to the SAP R/3 system—without program terminations—you must ensure that the migrated data is quantitatively complete. If transaction data is involved, you can compare the totals between the data in the upload file and the results in SAP R/3 for an initial assessment. If no variances are detected, you can then analyze several random data records to ensure that all the fields in SAP R/3 have been filled as expected according to the mapping (see Section 2.3.5). If differences occur between the expected and actual results, however, we recommend localizing the difference through a targeted analysis in R/3. This will help you to determine whether the data basis was insufficient, or whether the problems are due to a systematic error related to the selected migration procedure. Depending on the result, you will have to analyze the data basis or the selected data migration procedure again and change it if necessary.

However, verifying that the data is quantitatively complete won't suffice. You must ensure that the data contains all the information required to model the subsequent business processes in SAP R/3. To do so, the migrated data must be processed further in the SAP R/3 system, because this data is used as the foundation for testing the business processes. As you can see, you can't look at a data migration in isolation; you always have to see it in the context of system tests as well.

Testing the Business Processes

If the data basis fails this system test because required information is missing, you will have to migrate additional fields from the legacy system to SAP R/3. Consequently, you will have to revise the mapping that you developed in Section 2.3.5. This new information then serves as the foundation for extracting and postprocessing the data again, as described in Sections 2.3.6 and 2.3.7, and then importing it into SAP R/3 (after you have deleted the old, incorrect dataset). You have to continue this iterative process until you achieve the desired results in SAP R/3.

Iterative Process

Figure 2.1 shows an overview of the full data migration process, as described in this section.

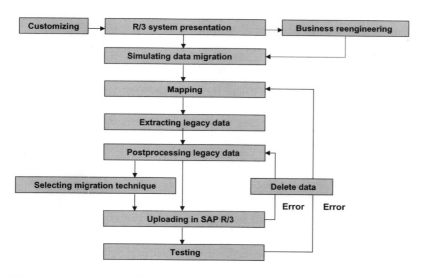

Figure 2.1 Process Flow of Data Migration

3 Technical Basics for Migrating Data to SAP R/3

This chapter introduces you to the basic concepts that you need to understand during any data migration, regardless of which technique you select. It also describes—from a technical perspective—the major process steps involved in data migration.

3.1 Basic Terminology

The following basic terms will appear throughout the book.

▶ **Data migration, migration**
The term *data migration* refers to the transfer of business data (master and transaction data) from any application system to an SAP R/3 system. The term *migration* is used as a synonym. Please note that this term is also used in other contexts, such as migrating from one technical platform to another; however, this is not the intended meaning here. Data migration is sometimes also referred to as *data transfer*.

▶ **SAP R/3 system**
The term *SAP R/3 system* refers to a system that is based on the SAP R/3 technology, such as SAP R/3, SAP APO, or SAP CRM.

▶ **Legacy system**
The application system that contains the data to be transferred before the migration is referred to as the *legacy system* (or *source system*).

▶ **Legacy data**
The data that is to be migrated from a legacy system to the SAP R/3 system is referred to as *legacy data* (or *source data*).

▶ **Data object, business data object, business object**
A data migration is usually based on *data objects*. A data object is a business data unit such as a customer master, material master, financial document, and so on. Such objects are sometimes called *business data objects* or simply *business objects*.

▶ **Data migration object, object**
When data objects are mentioned in the context of data migration, the terms *data migration object* or simply *object* refer to a data object that has additional attributes that are relevant for data migration, for example, the structure of the data object in the legacy system and the SAP R/3 system, along with the mapping that connects the two structures.

► **File, text file, table-like file, sequential file**

All of the data migration techniques described in this book assume that the legacy data is available in one or more *files*. These files are usually *text files*, or files divided into several lines. The structure of these lines is differentiated as follows. If all the lines in a file have the same structure, the file is called a *table-like file*. In this case, the sequence of the lines in the file is usually not important for data migration. If all the lines in a file don't have the same structure (header and item records, for example), the file is called a *sequential file* (see Section 6.2.9).

► **Frontend, SAP application server**

In the SAP R/3 system, files can be saved in one of two places: either on a *frontend*, that is, the end user's workstation, or on an *SAP application server*, the computer that runs the application logic of the SAP R/3 system (or a storage medium accessible to the SAP application server).

3.2 The Data Migration Process from a Technical Perspective

Regardless of which migration procedure you select, every data migration project involves certain basic technical steps. The following five steps are characteristic of nearly every data migration procedure.

3.2.1 Exporting the Data

First, the data that you want to transfer to the SAP R/3 system—that is, the legacy data—has to be exported from the legacy system. This step is also called *extracting* or *unloading* the legacy data.

Data Extraction Is the Responsibility of the Legacy System

The data migration procedures introduced in this book don't provide any support for exporting the legacy data from legacy systems. You will need to determine whether your legacy system offers functions for this purpose. If not, you will need to write suitable programs for data extraction in the legacy system.

In the process of exporting data, you must define how you want to store the legacy data. In particular, you must decide whether you want to group all the legacy data together in one file or divide it into several smaller files. You'll also need to define whether you want to write the legacy data to table-like files or to sequential files.

3.2.2 Reading the Data

Technically speaking, the legacy data exported from a legacy system can be saved in different files (see Section 6.2.9). It may therefore make sense initially to transform the data to a technically standardized format. However, most of the data migration procedures don't support this option. Instead, it is assumed that the legacy data will be provided in a predefined format.

Transforming the Data to a Technically Standardized Format

Of all the data migration procedures introduced in this book, only the Legacy System Migration Workbench (LSM Workbench) offers this option. In this case, the files, which can exist in different formats, are merged in a single sequential file. For more details on this process, see Section 6.2.9.

3.2.3 Converting the Data

Application systems can model business data in many ways. You cannot assume that the data you export from a legacy system can be easily imported into an SAP R/3 system without additional processing. Consequently, you usually have to convert the exported data to the appropriate format.

Converting the Legacy Data to SAP Format

The term *convert* is used synonymously with *transform*. The terms *data conversion* and *data transformation* are also used in this context, as well as *mapping* and *field mapping*.

The data conversion can be as complex as is necessary. The effort required depends on how different are the source and target formats. However, in order to make the work less cumbersome, you can define typical conversion tasks that must be performed repeatedly.

► *Value conversion* involves translating a known set of possible field values to a different set of values. This can apply to the country codes, for example, if the legacy data stores this information in a one-place field ("D" for Germany, "U" for the U.S., "I" for Italy, and so on), while the SAP R/3 system uses ISO codes that can be up to three places long ("DE" for Germany, "USA" for the U.S., "IT" for Italy, and so on). In this case, the following conversion has to be defined:

Value Conversion

  ► D → DE

  ► U → US

  ► I → IT

  ► And so on

This process is also referred to as *translation*.

Converting Field Attributes

▶ The *conversion of field attributes* involves changing the representation of certain field contents. Assume, for example, that your legacy system saves date values in the format DDMMYY (such as 311295), while the SAP R/3 system expects these values in the format YYYYMMDD (such as 19951231). You must convert these values accordingly. You can do so with custom programming, or by using a tool that supports such standard cases at the touch of a button.

Default Field Values

▶ You may also need to define default values for certain field values. You should always keep the following fact in mind: The data objects in the SAP R/3 system are usually quite extensive. In most cases, your legacy system will contain only a fraction of the fields that are available in the SAP R/3 system for a given data object. Frequently, you'll encounter situations in which the SAP R/3 system expects a value for a field, but your legacy system doesn't have an equivalent for that field; for example, in the SAP R/3 system is the company code—a variable that is unknown in many legacy systems.

There are two basic ways of dealing with such situations:

▶ If the desired value can be derived from other available data, then you can fall back on a simple conversion of values (translation).

▶ If the desired value is always constant (or at least for long periods), you can set it to a constant. The technique of using *fixed values*, which provides a greater degree of flexibility than working with constants, is introduced in Chapter 6, together with the LSM Workbench (see Section 6.2.8).

Converting Structures

▶ In some cases, you must not only convert field contents and field attributes on the way from the legacy system to the SAP R/3 system, but also change the overall structure of the data object.

Assume, for example, that a legacy system can save a maximum of three contact persons for a customer. Assume also that these (maximum) three contact persons are saved in the header record of the customer master record. You can define any number of contact persons in the SAP R/3 system. A separate table record is created for each contact person. Therefore, in this case, you must convert the structure as shown in Figure 3.1.

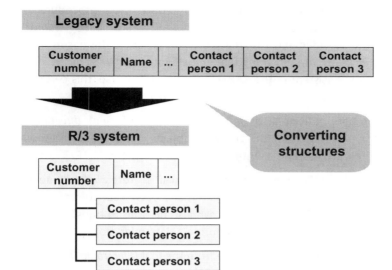

Figure 3.1 Converting Structures — Example

3.2.4 Importing the Data

All the previous steps serve to successively convert the legacy data into a format that the SAP R/3 system can process. The next logical step is to transfer this converted legacy data to the database of the SAP R/3 system. In addition to *importing data*, the term *loading data* is also used, as well as *uploading to SAP R/3*. There are generally two options for importing data.

If you fully understand how the structure of database tables works in the SAP R/3 system, you can use an ABAP program to write the legacy data directly to the database tables, at least theoretically. When it comes to throughput—the number of data records processed in any given time unit—this method is unbeatable. However, we don't recommend using this procedure because of the incalculable risk involved, namely, if this technique is used, the database of the SAP R/3 system could contain data that is inconsistent according to the rules of the SAP application. As a result, you might not be able to process it further—or even display it—in the SAP R/3 system. **Direct Writing to the Database**

All the procedures introduced here employ a different method. They are based exclusively on the interfaces provided in the SAP R/3 system. In the following sections, these interfaces are called *standard R/3 interfaces*. The standard R/3 interfaces used in this book are outlined below. **Using Standard R/3 Interfaces**

Batch Input *Batch input* refers to both a standard R/3 interface and a procedure for data migration. This mature, proven technology "feeds" dialog transactions with the provided data (usually in the background). This ensures that all input checks are run, ensuring that all data imported with batch input is correct and consistent in the SAP R/3 system. Of course, this certainty has its price: The data checks reduce throughput.

Direct Input Because throughput from batch input is not always sufficient, *direct input programs* have been written for some data objects. In a sense, direct input involves the controlled, direct writing to the database of the SAP R/3 system.

BAPI *Business Application Programming Interfaces* (BAPIs) were originally developed to open the SAP R/3 system for external access. Data objects usually have read and write BAPIs. The latter can also be used to transfer data to the database of the SAP R/3 system during a data migration.

IDoc *Intermediate Documents* (IDocs) come from the EDI (*Electronic Data Interchange*) environment. The challenge here is to transfer documents (such as purchase orders) electronically from one application system to another, possibly very remote, system. To do so, the structures of these documents first had to be defined for business purposes. This resulted in the development of IDocs, or more precisely, *IDoc types*. Secondly, a technique for processing these documents in the SAP R/3 system had to be developed— *inbound processing*. As you will see in Chapter 6, you can also use this technique for data migration.

Connection Between BAPI and IDoc An important connection exists between BAPIs and IDocs. At a touch of the button, you can generate an IDoc type from a BAPI in the SAP R/3 system. SAP already supplies the generated IDoc types for some BAPIs. In general, inbound processing of IDocs involves the following sequence. The data received in an IDoc is passed on to the corresponding BAPI, which updates the data in the SAP R/3 system. This process is described in more detail in Chapter 6.

3.2.5 Verifying the Data

No Blanket Solution Of course, once the legacy data has been imported into the SAP R/3 system, you want to ensure that the process is complete and accurate. Unfortunately, there is no blanket solution for measuring the success of a data migration.

Ultimately, you will have to rely on random samples and plausibility checks, such as comparing key figures (balances, for example), or comparing the number of records between the legacy system and the SAP R/3 system.

3.3 Overview of Technical Procedures for Data Migration

This chapter concludes with a summary of the major data migration techniques introduced in this book.

3.3.1 Batch Input

As mentioned in Section 3.2.4, *batch input* is both a type of standard R/3 interface and a procedure for data migration. Batch input can be used for data migration in two ways:

▶ **Standard batch input programs**
The SAP R/3 system contains various batch input programs that transform prepared legacy data into a format that dialog transactions can process. These programs are called *standard batch input programs*.

▶ **Batch input recording**
In addition to the standard programs, the SAP R/3 system enables you to record the process flow of a dialog transaction and generate an ABAP program from this recording at the touch of a button. While these generated programs theoretically work just like standard batch input programs, they lack the flexibility to react to changing screen sequences. The clear benefit of a batch input recording is that you deal only with the input fields of a dialog transaction that are relevant for your specific case. You can ignore all other input fields.

3.3.2 Computer Aided Test Tool

The *Computer Aided Test Tool* (CATT) is a tool that was originally developed to test business processes. Technically, a business process always consists of a sequence of dialog transactions. To avoid having to enter each transaction manually, the CATT enables you to automate transaction processing and supply the transactions with appropriate values. Ultimately, the data generated in this manner forms the foundation for the system, integration, and mass tests that are essential to every R/3 implementation project.

Migrating Data with the Test Tool

But, where is the connection to data migration? Data migration also involves creating data records with a specific transaction—such as FK01, *vendor create*—and copying them automatically to SAP R/3. If you use the CATT for data migration, you aren't interested in whether the dialog transactions respond accordingly with your expectations; you simply assume that this is where things are at this point in the migration process. At this point, you are concerned only with transferring the legacy data to SAP R/3 automatically, simply, and reliably.

3.3.3 Legacy System Migration Workbench

The *Legacy System Migration Workbench* (*LSM Workbench*) is an R/3-based tool for the one-time or periodic transfer of data from legacy systems to SAP R/3 systems. It provides easy-to-use functions to convert legacy data and import it into the SAP R/3 system, using standard R/3 interfaces. The LSM Workbench is based on the following principles:

Principles of the LSM Workbench

▶ Business data objects are migrated, not individual tables or field contents.

▶ The most frequent conversion tasks (see Section 3.2.3) are predefined and available at the touch of a button. Conversions can be added via the suitable ABAP statements.

▶ No ready-made conversion programs are provided. Instead, the conversion programs are generated from the defined conversion rules.

▶ Quality and consistency of the data imported into the SAP R/3 system are more important than speed and throughput. Therefore, only the standard R/3 interfaces are used.

▶ Conversion rules that have been defined once can be reused.

These three techniques are introduced in detail in the following chapters.

4   Batch Input

This chapter introduces you to one of the basic techniques for data entry in the SAP R/3 system. Using this technique, you can copy the data to be entered in the screen templates of an SAP transaction. You'll also learn several ways in which you can use this technique for data migration.

4.1   What Is Batch Input Processing?

Batch input processing is a term and technique derived from the early days of mainframe computing.

In the initial releases of SAP R/3, batch input processing was the only technique available to transfer external data to the SAP R/3 system. Eventually, other techniques (BAPIs, IDocs) also became available. Yet, even today, batch input processing is still the most frequently used method for data migration. The reasons include the obvious similarities between batch input and dialog transactions, as well as the wide range of support available to users in the SAP R/3 system. Both aspects are discussed in more detail in the next sections.

The Most Frequently Used Method for Data Migration

The basic principle of batch input processing is to "feed" the input fields in the screen templates (dynpros) of R/3 dialog transactions with the provided data in the background. This ensures that the same input checks and authorization checks that would occur during manual entry are performed. Therefore, data imported via batch input is guaranteed to be just as accurate and consistent as the manually entered data.

Basic Principle

4.2   How Does Batch Input Work?

4.2.1   What Is a Batch Input Session?

The main object in batch input processing is the *batch input session*. A batch input session consists of one or more calls of SAP transactions and the data to be processed by the transaction. The value for each field is specified for each transaction call, screen template, and input field. You can think of a batch input session as an ordered sequence of instructions for the SAP R/3 system: "Supply value A to field X in screen template Y of transaction Z." In other words, a batch input session lets you control the SAP R/3 system.

In the SAP R/3 system, batch input sessions are saved according to ABAP Dictionary structure BDCDATA. This structure has the following composition:

1. PROGRAM: This field contains the name of the ABAP program to which the current dynpro (screen) belongs.
2. DYNPRO: This field contains the four-digit number of the current screen; i.e., it is saved here.
3. DYNBEGIN: This field indicates whether a new screen template (value "X") or a new transaction (value "T") starts.
4. FNAM: This field contains the technical name of the input field.
5. FVAL: This field contains the input value.

The following table, which shows an excerpt of a batch input session, gives you an idea of the structure. In the example, SAP Transaction FK01 (*Create Vendor*) is called and supplied with data.

No.	PROGRAM	DYNPRO	DYNBEGIN	FNAM	FVAL
01		0000	T	FK01	BS
02	SAPMF02K	0105	X		
03		0000		BDC_CURSOR	RF02K-KTOKK
04		0000		BDC_OKCODE	/00
05		0000		RF02K-LIFNR	34567
06		0000		RF02K-BUKRS	1000
07		0000		RF02K-KTOKK	0001
08	SAPMF02K	0110	X		
09		0000		BDC_CURSOR	LFA1-LAND1
10		0000		BDC_OKCODE	=VW
11		0000		LFA1-ANRED	Company
12		0000		LFA1-NAME1	Smith Jones Inc.
13		0000		LFA1-SORTL	WG
14		0000		LFA1-STRAS	123 Main St.
15		0000		LFA1-ORT01	Anytown
16		0000		LFA1-PSTLZ	55555

Table 4.1 Excerpt from a Batch Input Session

No.	PROGRAM	DYNPRO	DYNBEGIN	FNAM	FVAL
17		0000		LFA1-LAND1	USA
. . .					
18	SAPMF02K	0130	X		
19		0000		BDC_CURSOR	LFBK-BANKS(01)
20		0000		BDC_OKCODE	=VW
21	SAPMF02K	0210	X		
22		0000		BDC_CURSOR	LFB1-FDGRV
23		0000		BDC_OKCODE	=UPDA
24		0000		LFB1-AKONT	196300
25		0000		LFB1-FDGRV	A1

Table 4.1 Excerpt from a Batch Input Session (continued)

In detail, lines 01 to 25 mean the following:

No.	Explanation
01	Transaction FK01 is called.
02	Screen 0105 from program SAPMFK02 is called.
03	The cursor is positioned on field RF02K-KTOKK (account group).
04	Function code (OK code) 00 is triggered. This is equivalent to pressing the **Enter** key.[1]
05	The value 34567 is entered in field RF02K-LIFNR (vendor).
06	The value 1000 is entered in field RF02K-BUKRS (company code).
07	The value 0001 is entered in field RF02K-KTOKK (account group).
08	Screen 0110 from program SAPMFK02 is called.
09	The cursor is positioned on field RF02K-LAND1 (country).
10	Function code (OK code) VW (continue) is triggered.
11	The value Company is entered in field LFA1-ANRED (form of address).
12	The value Smith Jones Inc. is entered in field LFA1-NAME1 (name).

Table 4.2 Explanation of the Batch Input Session from Table 4.1

---

1 Of course, the function code (OK code) is not triggered until the input fields of the screen have been supplied with value, that is, after line 07.

No.	Explanation
13	The value WG is entered in field LFA1-SORTL (sort key).
14	The value 123 Main St. is entered in field LFA1-STRAS (street).
15	The value Anytown is entered in field LFA1-ORT01 (city).
16	The value 55555 is entered in field LFA1-PSTLZ (zip code).
17	The value USA is entered in field LFA1-LAND1 (country).
18	Screen 0130 from program SAPMFK02 is called.
19	The cursor is positioned in the table in line 01 and column LFBK-BANKS (bank key).
20	Function code (OK code) VW (continue) is triggered.
21	Screen 0210 from program SAPMFK02 is called.
22	The cursor is positioned on field LFB1-FDGRV (cash management group).
23	Function code (OK code) UPDA (save) is triggered.
24	The value 196300 is entered in field LFB1-AKONT (reconciliation account).
25	The value A1 is entered in field LFB1-FDGRV (cash management group).

Table 4.2 Explanation of the Batch Input Session from Table 4.1 (continued)

You now have an idea of what a batch input session can do and how it is structured. Next, we come to the following two important questions:

▶ How do you create a batch input session?

▶ How do you process a batch input session?

Let's start with the simpler of the two questions, "How do you process a batch input session?"

4.2.2 How Do I Process a Batch Input Session?

Modes for Batch Input Processing

In addition to *process*, the terms *run* and *play* are sometimes used in the context of processing batch input sessions. The SAP R/3 system offers three different options (modes) for processing or running a batch input session.

▶ **Process in foreground**

In this mode, each screen is displayed with its configured data. You press the **Enter** key to go to the next screen. Any incorrect transactions can be corrected interactively. Use OK code /n to exit the current transaction and go to the next one. Use OK code /bend to cancel processing of the batch input session and resume it later (if desired).

It should be apparent that this mode is not suitable for large numbers of transactions.

▶ **Display errors only**
This mode is similar to the foreground processing mode, with one exception: transactions that are free of errors aren't processed interactively; instead, they are processed in the background. If an error occurs, background processing is interrupted and the screen where the error occurred is displayed. Once the error is corrected, processing switches from dialog back to background processing and remains there, until the next error occurs or the batch input session is processed.

▶ **In the background**
In this mode, batch input sessions are scheduled for processing in the background.

The following basic principles apply to the processing of a batch input session (see Figure 4.1):

Principles of Batch Input Processing

▶ Transactions that are processed successfully are removed from the batch input session.

▶ Incorrect transactions remain in the batch input session and must be corrected manually and processed again.

▶ Once all the transactions in a batch input session have been processed successfully, the entire batch input session is deleted.

When you create a batch input session, you can indicate that you want that session to be *retained*. In this case, the batch input session remains in the overview even after it is processed successfully. This can be useful for documentation purposes. However, even in this case, every batch input session can be processed only once.

▶ The processing of a batch input session is recorded in a detailed log.

The status of a batch input session tells you the state of its processing at a glance. The following status values are possible:

Status

▶ **New**
Batch input sessions with this status are ready for processing, but have not been processed yet.

▶ **Error**
If a batch input session has this status, this means processing either couldn't be performed completely due to incorrect transactions, or was cancelled prematurely in foreground processing, that is, **Process in foreground** or **Display errors only**.

▶ **Processed**

As previously mentioned, successfully processed batch input sessions are usually deleted. If the Retain Session option is set for a batch input session, however, and that session is processed successfully, it is assigned this status. Processed batch input sessions are retained in the SAP R/3 system until they're deleted by a perodic reorganization run. These reorganization runs don't affect erroneous batch input sessions.

▶ **In process**

Batch input sessions have this status while they're being processed.

▶ **In background**

Batch input sessions have this status while they're being processed in the background.

▶ **Blocked**

This status means that you can block a batch input session to protect it against unintended processing.

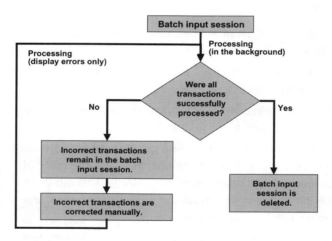

Figure 4.1 Processing Batch Input Sessions

More Options

Additional control options, which are available for processing batch input sessions, are briefly described here:

▶ **Processing batch input sessions automatically**

When you migrate data to the SAP R/3 system regularly—every night, for example, within the framework of a periodic data transfer—the batch input sessions created by the corresponding programs should generally be processed automatically. This automatic processing of one or more batch input sessions is achieved via a call of ABAP program RSB-DCSUB. You can set the following selection parameters for the program:

- Name(s) of the batch input session(s)
- Creation date and time
- Status (ready for processing or error)

▶ **Deleting batch input sessions**

If you no longer need a batch input session in the list, you can delete it manually. You should not delete batch input sessions that still have unprocessed transactions, however, that is, sessions with status **New** or **Error**. In such cases, you must correct the transactions first and then continue processing, or enter the transaction data in the SAP R/3 system in some other way.

▶ **Blocking and releasing batch input sessions**

You can block a batch input session to prevent the system from processing it before a specified date.

These (and other) functions involving batch input sessions are located in Transaction SM35 (batch input overview). You can also reach this transaction via menu path **System · Services · Batch Input · Sessions**.

Transaction SM35

Let us now turn to the more difficult of the two questions we asked regarding batch input sessions.

4.2.3 How Do I Create a Batch Input Session?

There are three basic ways in which to create a batch input session.

▶ You can use the SAP transaction recorder to record transaction flows. These are called *batch input recordings* or simply *recordings*. You can use these recordings to create a batch input session at the touch of a button. This option is described in more detail in Section 4.5.

Batch Input Session from Recording

▶ You can use any suitable ABAP program to create batch input sessions. We differentiate between two different types of programs:

Batch Input Session from Program

  ▶ The SAP R/3 system offers an option for generating an ABAP program from a batch input recording at the touch of a button. Programs created in this manner usually must be revised manually. This technique is introduced in Section 4.4.

  ▶ In addition, the SAP R/3 system comes with various *standard batch input programs*. These programs are described in detail in the next section.

The three procedures for generating batch input sessions are contrasted in Figure 4.2.

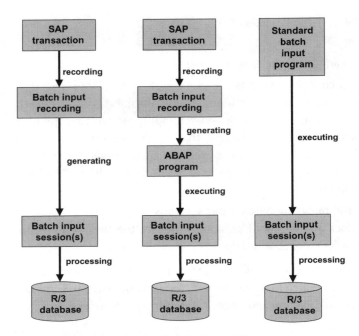

Figure 4.2 Procedures for Creating Batch Input Sessions

4.3 Standard Batch Input Programs

The SAP R/3 system comes with a variety of batch input programs, which are called *standard batch input programs*.

Manual Programming Standard batch input programs aren't generated automatically; they're programmed manually, and they're usually much more complex than automatically generated batch input programs for the following reason.

A program generated from a recording models the process flow of that recording precisely. SAP transactions, however, can respond differently to different input data. This means the screen sequence is not always identical; instead, it frequently depends on the selected input data. A generated batch input program supports only the screen sequence from the recording. Conversely, a standard batch input program can generate the suitable screen sequence for a given set of input data, enabling it to be processed without errors.

Specially Structured File as Input Standard batch input programs usually expect input files to have a special structure. From the data migration perspective, the trick is to transform the existing data from the legacy system to this required format. Tools such as the Legacy System Migration Workbench (LSM Workbench), which is described in detail in Chapter 6, can help you with this task.

The most important standard batch input programs are introduced briefly below. For more detailed information, please refer to the online documentation for each program.

4.3.1 RFBIDE00 — Customer Master

Batch input program RFBIDE00 supports the following functions:

▶ Create customer master data, including credit limit data and bank master data (Transaction XD01)

▶ Change customer master data, including credit limit data and bank master data (Transaction XD02)

▶ Block and unblock customers (Transaction XD05)

▶ Set and reset deletion flag for customers (Transaction XD06)

▶ Maintain credit limit (Transaction FD32)

Any lock fields or deletion indicators passed on during the create (XD01) and change (XD02) customer master data transactions are also processed.

This program is the foundation of the detailed example used in Chapter 6.

4.3.2 RFBIKR00 — Vendor Master

Batch input program RFBIKR00 supports the following functions:

▶ Create vendor master data (Transaction XK01)

▶ Change vendor master data (Transaction XK02)

▶ Block and unblock vendors (Transaction XK05)

▶ Set and reset deletion flag for vendors (Transaction XK06)

Any lock fields or deletion indicators passed on during the create (XK01) and change (XK02) vendor master data transactions are also processed.

4.3.3 RFBISA00 — G/L Account Master

Batch input program RFBISA00 supports the following functions:

▶ Create G/L account master data (Transaction FS01)

▶ Change G/L account master data (Transaction FS02)

▶ Block and unblock G/L accounts (Transaction FS05)

▶ Set and reset deletion flag for G/L accounts (Transaction FS06)

4.3.4 RFBIBL00—Financial Documents

Batch input program RFBIBL00 supports the following functions:

▶ Post document (Transaction FB01)

▶ Foreign currency valuation (Transaction FBB1)

▶ Enter accrual/deferral document (Transaction FBS1)

▶ Park document (Transaction FBV1)

▶ Post with clearing (Transaction FB05)

This program is primarily intended to create batch input programs. However, you can also use the **Type of Data Transfer** parameter to create documents immediately with call transaction (see Section 4.4.5) or direct input.

4.3.5 RCSBI010, RCSBI020, RCSBI030, RCSBI040—Material BOMs

Batch input program RCSBI010 supports the creation of BOMs (bills of material) without long texts. You can create document structures, equipment BOMs, material BOMs, standard objects, and BOMs for functional locations. The following transactions are supported:

▶ Create document structures (Transaction CV11)

▶ Create equipment BOMs (Transaction IB01)

▶ Create material BOMs (Transaction CS01)

▶ Create standard objects (Transaction CS51)

▶ Create BOMs for functional locations (Transaction IB11)

Batch input program RCSBI020 permits changes to BOMs without long texts. You can change document structures, equipment BOMs, material BOMs, standard objects, and BOMs for functional locations. The following transactions are available:

▶ Change document structures (Transaction CV12)

▶ Change equipment BOMs (Transaction IB02)

▶ Change material BOMs (Transaction CS02)

▶ Change standard objects (Transaction CS52)

▶ Change BOMs for functional locations (Transaction IB12)

Two other batch input programs, RCSBI030 and RCSBI040, which let you create variant BOMs without long texts and BOMs with long texts (respectively) and support the same transactions as RCSBI010, are also available.

4.3.6 RM06BBI0—Purchase Requisitions

Batch input program RM06BBIO enables you to create purchase requisitions in the SAP R/3 system.

You don't have to select a transaction for this program because it is automatically selected by the program.

4.3.7 RM07MMBL—Material Documents

You can use program RM07MMBL to create batch input sessions for goods movements. The data used to create the batch input session must have the same structure as ABAP Dictionary structure BMSEG.

4.4 Batch Input Recording: General Approach

The following sections describe how you can use the batch input technique to migrate legacy data to SAP R/3, based on the example of open debit items. The procedure can be divided into the following steps:

Steps for Data Migration

▶ Identify the transaction that you want to use to transfer the legacy data to the SAP R/3 system.

▶ Implement this transaction with a typical data record and record it with the R/3 transaction recorder.

▶ Use the recording to create the ABAP source code with the appropriate pushbutton.

▶ Although the ABAP program created in this manner is the foundation for the data migration, you will still have to customize it to meet specific requirements.

4.4.1 Creating the Batch Input Recording

Once you've decided which transaction you want to use to migrate your open debit items to SAP R/3—Transaction FB01 in this case—you can simulate the data migration with a sample data record. To do so, use the transaction recorder. You can access it via menu path **System · Services · Batch Input · Sessions** (Transaction SM35). Then, choose **Recording** and then **New Recording**. The dialog box shown in Figure 4.3 opens.

Create the Recording

Enter a name for the recording along with the transaction code that you want to use to transfer the open debit items to SAP R/3 (Transaction FB01). To make it easier to manage your various recordings, we recommend that you include the transaction code in the name of the recording in some way (for example, Z_FB01). After you've maintained both fields, click the **Start Recording** button to start entering a sample data record. Immediately, you'll see the same screen template that you otherwise see in the first screen for document entry in Transaction FB01. You can maintain the document header data here (see Figure 4.4).

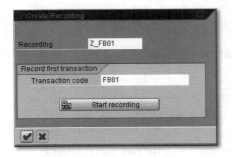

Figure 4.3 Creating a Recording

Maintaining Data During data entry, you should maintain all the mandatory fields—or *required entry fields* in the SAP terminology—and all the fields that you want to provide for the data migration in your input file. Using this approach, you can ensure that the recording will contain all the information required for the data migration.

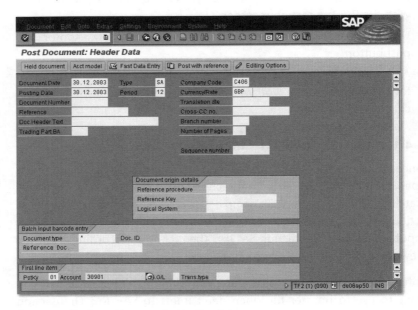

Figure 4.4 Posting a Document—Header Data

To avoid confusion, you should note that a recording with the transaction recorder is almost identical to dialog processing. This means that you must navigate through the respective entry templates for the transaction as usual and make your entries, which you complete by posting. The session does not merely simulate a transaction; the update triggers a change in the database. The only difference with strict dialog processing is that the data entry is recorded in the transaction recorder simultaneously. Its activities are documented by occasional messages in the status bar.

Change in the Database

Once you've specified your entries in the document header, set posting key 01 to indicate that the next account to be posted to, account 10101, is a customer account, that a debit posting is involved, and that it represents an invoice. When you press **Enter**, the screen shown in Figure 4.5 is displayed.

Customer Item

To keep things simple, maintain only the **Amount** field, which reflects the gross amount of the sales invoice. The offsetting posting is made in credit to G/L account 900001, which was configured especially for the data migration, as indicated by posting key 50 (see Section 2.2.5). Pressing **Enter** displays the screen from Figure 4.6, where you also have to maintain the **Amount** field. Because this is the last line item, you can enter "*" instead of the amount. The SAP R/3 system calculates the remaining amount automatically in this case.

G/L Account Item

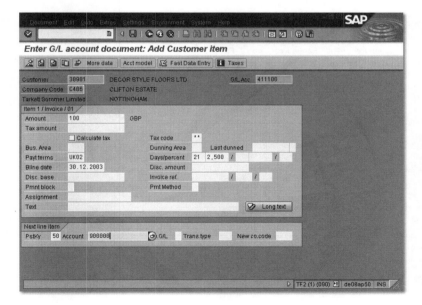

Figure 4.5 Posting a Document—Customer Item

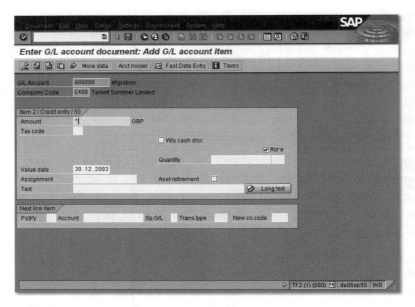

Figure 4.6 Posting a Document—G/L Account Item

The **Post** button triggers both a change to the database and the end of the recording. You go directly to the editor of the transaction recorder, which is shown in Figure 4.7.

	Program	Screen	St...	Field name	Field value	
1			T	FB01		
2	SAPMF05A	0100	X			
3				BDC_CURSOR	RF05A-NEWKO	
4				BDC_OKCODE	/00	
5				BKPF-BLDAT	30.12.2003	
6				BKPF-BLART	SA	
7				BKPF-BUKRS	C406	
8				BKPF-BUDAT	30.12.2003	
9				BKPF-MONAT	12	
10				BKPF-WAERS	GBP	
11				FS006-DOCID	*	
12				RF05A-NEWBS	01	
13				RF05A-NEWKO	30901	
14				BDC_SUBSCR	SAPMF05A	1300APPL_SUB_T
15				BDC_SUBSCR	SAPLSEXM	0200APPL_SUB
16	SAPMF05A	0301	X			
17				BDC_CURSOR	RF05A-NEWKO	

Figure 4.7 End of Recording—Transaction Recorder

The editor provides information on the program used for the transaction that you just recorded and which screens (dynpros) were processed during the transaction. You also see a list of all the table fields with their corresponding content that you maintained during the recording.

Editor

If you compare this recording with the batch input session introduced in Section 4.2.1, you should immediately recognize a likeness—which also explains why, at the mere touch of a button, you can create a batch input session from a recording.

If you want to conduct the data migration later, in the same client in which you made the recording, you must cancel or delete the data record that you just created in order to avoid falsifying the results of the data migration.

Cancel

There are several rules that you should follow when recording transactions:

Rules for Recording

▶ Before you start the recording, ensure that you know how the transaction works.

▶ Don't toggle unnecessarily between screens.

▶ Don't double-click on lists.

▶ Don't trigger any error messages during the recording.

▶ Once you've finished the recording, don't make any customizing changes that alter the screens or their sequence within the transaction.

Once you've pressed **Save** to save your recording, you can generate the ABAP source code in the next step.

Generating the Program

4.4.2 Generating an ABAP Program from a Batch Input Recording

To do so, press **F3** to return to the recording overview and then choose **Create** (see Figure 4.8).

Enter a **program name**, such as Z_FB01_PROGRAM in this case.

The **Field Contents** section offers two options:

Options for Field Contents

▶ **Read from file**
The field contents from the recording can be replaced by the technical R/3 field texts.

▶ **Transfer from recording**
The field contents from the recording can be used in the program to be generated.

To make the connection between the recording and the programming immediately apparent, the option **Transfer from recording** was selected here, even though the other option may involve less manual intervention during the subsequent revision of the program.

In the next dialog boxes, you are prompted to enter a **Title**, a **Development Class**, and a **Transport Request** for the program.

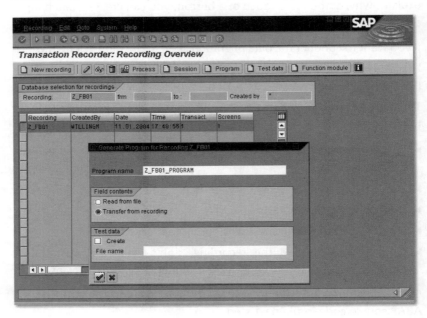

Figure 4.8 Generating a Program from a Recording

ABAP Program

The result is a program with the following logic:

```
1  REPORT z_fb01_program NO STANDARD PAGE HEADING
   LINE-SIZE 255.
2  INCLUDE bdcrecx1.
3  START-OF-SELECTION.
4  PERFORM open_group.
5  PERFORM bdc_dynpro      USING 'SAPMF05A' '0100'.
6  PERFORM bdc_field       USING 'BDC_CURSOR'
7                                'RF05A-NEWKO'.
8  PERFORM bdc_field       USING 'BDC_OKCODE'
9                                '/00'.
10 PERFORM bdc_field       USING 'BKPF-BLDAT'
11                               '16.03.2003'.
12 PERFORM bdc_field       USING 'BKPF-BLART'
```

```
13                              'SA'.
14 PERFORM bdc_field     USING 'BKPF-BUKRS'
15                             '1000'.
16 PERFORM bdc_field     USING 'BKPF-BUDAT'
17                             '16.03.2003'.
18 PERFORM bdc_field     USING 'BKPF-WAERS'
19                             'EUR'.
20 PERFORM bdc_field     USING 'RF05A-NEWBS'
21                             '01'.
22 PERFORM bdc_field     USING 'RF05A-NEWKO'
23                             '10101'.
24 PERFORM bdc_dynpro    USING 'SAPMF05A' '0301'.
25 PERFORM bdc_field     USING 'BDC_CURSOR'
26                             'RF05A-NEWKO'.
27 PERFORM bdc_field     USING 'BDC_OKCODE'
28                             '/00'.
29 PERFORM bdc_field     USING 'BSEG-WRBTR'
30                             '100'.
31 PERFORM bdc_field     USING 'RF05A-NEWBS'
32                             '50'.
33 PERFORM bdc_field     USING 'RF05A-NEWKO'
34                             '900001'.
35 PERFORM bdc_dynpro    USING 'SAPMF05A' '0300'.
36 PERFORM bdc_field     USING 'BDC_CURSOR'
37                             'BSEG-WRBTR'.
38 PERFORM bdc_field     USING 'BDC_OKCODE'
39                             '/00'.
40 PERFORM bdc_field     USING 'BSEG-WRBTR'
41                             '100'.
42 PERFORM bdc_field     USING 'BDC_OKCODE'
43                             '=BU'.
44 PERFORM bdc_transaction USING 'FB01'.
45 PERFORM close_group.
```

Listing 4.1 Z_FB01_PROGRAM—ABAP Program Generated from a Recording

This automatically generated program already contains most of the commands and subroutines required for the subsequent data migration. Therefore, we recommend that you use this fragment as the foundation for the actual data migration program and adapt it accordingly. What does this program logic do?

Foundation for Data Migration

PERFORM **open_group**	Simply put, the `PERFORM open_group` command in line 4 opens a batch input session. Later in the program, this batch input session is filled with the screens (dynpros) and field contents that resulted from the prior recording of Transaction FB01. To underscore this fact, analyze program lines 5, 10, and 11 more precisely.
PERFORM **bdc_dynpro**	`PERFORM bdc_dynpro USING 'SAPMF05A' '0100'` initially means that a subroutine named `bdc_dynpro` is called with the `PERFORM` command. The `USING` supplement passes the two parameters in single quotation marks to subroutine `bdc_dynpro`. This involves screen 0100 (see Figure 4.4) of program SAPMF05A. Program SAPMF05A is the main Financial Accounting program and the foundation for Transaction FB01. You have now defined which screen template has to be processed, along with the corresponding field contents.
PERFORM **bdc_field**	`PERFORM bdc_field USING 'BKPF-BLDAT' '16.03.2003'` calls another subroutine, `bdc_field`, which is also assigned two parameters. The first parameter is the document date field, BLDAT, which appears in document header table BKPF and can be referenced using BKPF-BLDAT. The second passed parameter is the format of the document date resulting from the recording—16.03.2003 in this case.
	The situation in program lines 12 and 13 is analogous: `PERFORM bdc_field USING 'BKPF-BLART' 'SA'` dictates that the open item should be posted with document type "SA".
PERFORM **bdc_dynpro and** **PERFORM** **bdc_field**	As you can see from this brief explanation, the interaction between `PERFORM bdc_dynpro` and `PERFORM bdc_field` ultimately determines which screen (dynpro) and which fields are assigned values. Program lines 5 through 23 all refer to screen 0100, the document header. The information for the customer item (see Figure 4.5) is determined in program lines 24 through 34. The last screen to fill, 0300, is the G/L account line item (see Figure 4.6) and is determined by program lines 35 through 43.
PERFORM **bdc_transaction**	Once all the document information is known, `PERFORM bdc_transaction USING 'FB01'` calls a subroutine named `bdc_transaction`, which uses Transaction FB01 to post the document passed on in the parameters. Therefore, `PERFORM bdc_transaction` concludes the transaction with a posting and is *de facto* the last statement in the batch input session (see program line 44).
PERFORM **close_group**	Before you can process a batch input session, however, you must first close the open session. You do this with `PERFORM close_group`, which

doesn't require any parameters because the currently opened session is closed automatically (see program line 45).

Now that you have read the above, you may be wondering exactly what the individual subroutines do. So far, all you know is that these subroutines—also called *form routines*—are assigned parameters. Simply put, these form routines themselves consist of *function modules*, subroutines with a clearly defined interface that can be called by any ABAP program. These function modules continue to process the parameters previously passed onto the form routine in order to enable their subsequent placement in an executable batch input session.

Program Logic

The advantage of this approach is that you don't have to worry about any of these technical details. The flow logic of all the form routines and the function modules they use is summarized in program line 2: INCLUDE bdcrecx1 calls the additional ABAP code of program bdcrecx1, which is responsible for the overall batch input control. Among other things, this program defines how the data records will be processed. When the program starts, for example, you can choose whether you want to create a batch input session, which will then be processed with Transaction SM35, or whether you want to process the data records with the *call transaction* procedure, which posts the data records directly. Chapter 8 addresses the advantages and disadvantages of both procedures.

INCLUDE bdcrecx1

Because INCLUDE bdcrecx1 is not considered essential, it isn't discussed in any detail. For more information, you can examine this program in greater detail in the SAP R/3 system.

You can summarize your activities up to this point as follows. The automatically generated ABAP program can apply the batch input method to create a batch input session, which can then be processed. Alternatively, processing can also take place using the *call transaction* procedure.

Conclusion

This program, however, cannot be used for data migration in its current form for the following reasons:

Modifying the Program

▶ It can process only a single data record.
▶ It permits only the constant values from the recording.

Because both the number of data records and the instances of the field contents are variable during data migration, however, the program logic must be modified accordingly to take these factors into account.

4.4.3 Modifying the Generated ABAP Program

Data Transfer File

Before you modify the coding of the program from Section 4.4.2 to meet the requirements of data migration, you should first create a table-like file containing the open debit items that you want to migrate. Because you maintained only the required entry fields when recording Transaction FB01 in Section 4.4.1, this information should be available for all the data records you have to migrate. This file, opened with Microsoft Excel, could resemble Figure 4.9.

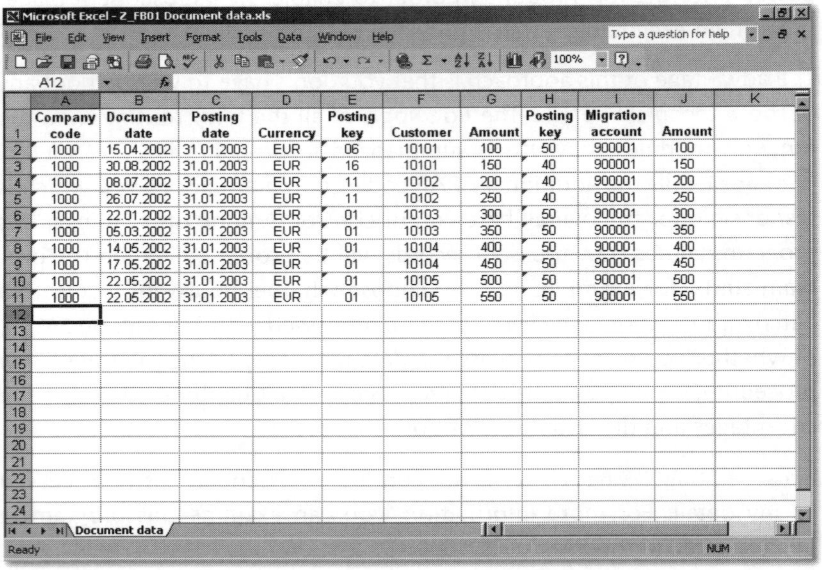

Company code	Document date	Posting date	Currency	Posting key	Customer	Amount	Posting key	Migration account	Amount
1000	15.04.2002	31.01.2003	EUR	06	10101	100	50	900001	100
1000	30.08.2002	31.01.2003	EUR	16	10101	150	40	900001	150
1000	08.07.2002	31.01.2003	EUR	11	10102	200	40	900001	200
1000	26.07.2002	31.01.2003	EUR	11	10102	250	40	900001	250
1000	22.01.2002	31.01.2003	EUR	01	10103	300	50	900001	300
1000	05.03.2002	31.01.2003	EUR	01	10103	350	50	900001	350
1000	14.05.2002	31.01.2003	EUR	01	10104	400	50	900001	400
1000	17.05.2002	31.01.2003	EUR	01	10104	450	50	900001	450
1000	22.05.2002	31.01.2003	EUR	01	10105	500	50	900001	500
1000	22.05.2002	31.01.2003	EUR	01	10105	550	50	900001	550

Figure 4.9 Requirements of the Supplied Data

Missing Data

In other situations, it is entirely possible that you won't be able to provide values for every field in every data record you maintained during the recording. Consider the phone numbers during a master data migration, for example. In such situations, you must supply the field contents that are required during the recording (required entry fields). If necessary, you can also change the attribute of the respective fields from required entry to optional entry in Customizing, and then change it back after the migration.

Data Requirements

The task at hand is to import the data shown in Figure 4.9 into the SAP R/3 system and process it there. To do so, a local file should already be saved on your computer. Because the SAP R/3 system can process text files more easily than other formats, you should save the data transfer file in **Text**

(Tab-Delimited) (*.txt) format. To avoid complicating the program unnecessarily, make sure that the file does not contain any blank lines, as special program logic would be required to deal with the resulting exception situations. The same applies to the first line of the file, which is usually reserved for the field texts. Delete this line to ensure that all the data records have the same structure; therefore, the program won't have to handle any one line differently (see Figure 4.10).

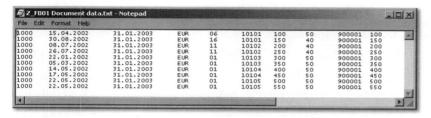

Figure 4.10 Text File for Upload

How can you load a text file into the SAP R/3 system? Once again, we recommend that you use the subroutine technique to provide for a clear program structure. A subroutine (form routine), `load_data`, which is assigned the path of the data transfer file on your PC as a parameter, is responsible for loading the data to the SAP R/3 system and adheres to the following logic.

Subroutine load_data

```
1  FORM load_data USING file.
2  CALL FUNCTION 'UPLOAD'
3       EXPORTING
4            filename          = file
5            filetype          = 'dat'
6       TABLES
7            data_tab          = itab
8       EXCEPTIONS
9            conversion_error  = 1
10           invalid_table_width = 2
11           invalid_type      = 3
12           no_batch          = 4
13           unknown_error     = 5
14           others            = 6.
15 ENDFORM.
```

Listing 4.2 Subroutine LOAD_DATA with Function Module UPLOAD

Function Module UPLOAD

As program line 2 indicates, this subroutine uses CALL FUNCTION 'UPLOAD' to call a function module named UPLOAD[2], which, in turn, is assigned various parameters for processing with EXPORTING. Specifically, these parameters are the file name, represented by the file placeholder, and the file format, 'dat', which is the SAP-specific name for the **Text (Tab-Delimited) (*.txt)** format of the data transfer file.

In addition, the function module uses TABLES to pass on the name of an internal table, itab.

The logic of the function module now places the data transfer file, file, in internal table itab, which is then accessed later on in the program.

Internal Table itab

To ensure proper results, itab must have the same structure as the data transfer file. Specifically, this means the company code, which is contained in the first column of the data transfer file (see Figures 4.9 and 4.10), must also be displayed in the first column of the internal table. Similarly, the document date and posting date, which appear in columns 2 and 3 of the data transfer file, must also be displayed in columns 2 and 3 of the internal table. The same applies to the remaining fields. If you declare internal table itab as shown below, you will have a one-to-one match with the data transfer file, ensuring the correct transformation of the field contents:

```
DATA:
  BEGIN OF itab OCCURS 0,
    bukrs  LIKE bkpf-bukrs,
    bldat  LIKE bkpf-bldat,
    budat  LIKE bkpf-budat,
    waers  LIKE bkpf-waers,
    bschl1 LIKE bseg-bschl,
    kunnr  LIKE bseg-kunnr,
    wrbtr1(8),
    bschl2 LIKE bseg-bschl,
    hkont  LIKE bseg-hkont,
    wrbtr2(8),
  END OF itab.
```

Listing 4.3 Declaration of Internal Table itab

Defining Amount Fields as Characters

The field texts of internal table itab are based on the respective field names in the SAP R/3 system and their *data types* are assigned accordingly, except for the amount fields wrbtr1 and wrbtr2. These fields are defined

---

2 This function module is obsolete in SAP Basis Release 6.10 and later. Its successor is called GUI_UPLOAD.

as eight-place character fields, because batch input processing would not fill the amount fields if the declaration were LIKE bseg-wrbtr, which means the migration data could not be processed.

As you can see from program lines 8 to 14, the function module can also deal with exceptions. An exception occurs whenever the function module has calls with parameters that cause an error. The *exceptions* enable the function module to catch such errors and inform the calling program of their cause. This helps you avoid runtime errors. Because your data migration program does not support error handling, this component of the function module is not discussed here.

Error Detection

With the modifications you have made, you can now load your dataset into SAP R/3. To process it, however, you will need to make further changes to the automatically generated program from Section 4.4.2.

As previously mentioned, this program can process only data records whose values are constant and determined by the underlying recording. You now have to replace these fixed values with *variables* in order to process a number of different data records.

Replacing Constants with Variables

After the upload, all of the data records to be migrated are already contained in internal table itab, which you now have to process sequentially, that is, data record by data record. Therefore, itab has to be included in a *loop* that reads all the data records in sequence and places them in a batch input session accordingly. You can process an internal table in the SAP R/3 system with the statement LOOP AT itab ... ENDLOOP.

Including the Internal Table in a Loop

```
LOOP AT itab.
  PERFORM bdc_dynpro      USING 'SAPMF05A' '0100'.
  PERFORM bdc_field       USING 'BDC_CURSOR'
                                'RF05A-NEWKO'.
  PERFORM bdc_field       USING 'BDC_OKCODE'
                                '/00'.
  PERFORM bdc_field       USING 'BKPF-BLDAT'
                                itab-bldat.
  PERFORM bdc_field       USING 'BKPF-BLART'
                                'SA'.
  PERFORM bdc_field       USING 'BKPF-BUKRS'
                                itab-bukrs.
  PERFORM bdc_field       USING 'BKPF-BUDAT'
                                itab-budat.
  PERFORM bdc_field       USING 'BKPF-WAERS'
                                itab-waers.
```

```
PERFORM bdc_field        USING 'RF05A-NEWBS'
                               itab-bsch11.
PERFORM bdc_field        USING 'RF05A-NEWKO'
                               itab-kunnr.
PERFORM bdc_dynpro       USING 'SAPMF05A' '0301'.
PERFORM bdc_field        USING 'BDC_CURSOR'
                               'RF05A-NEWKO'.
PERFORM bdc_field        USING 'BDC_OKCODE'
                               '/00'.
PERFORM bdc_field        USING 'BSEG-WRBTR'
                               itab-wrbtr1.
PERFORM bdc_field        USING 'RF05A-NEWBS'
                               itab-bsch12.
PERFORM bdc_field        USING 'RF05A-NEWKO'
                               itab-hkont.
PERFORM bdc_dynpro       USING 'SAPMF05A' '0300'.
PERFORM bdc_field        USING 'BDC_CURSOR'
                               'BSEG-WRBTR'.
PERFORM bdc_field        USING 'BDC_OKCODE'
                               '/00'.
PERFORM bdc_field        USING 'BSEG-WRBTR'
                               itab-wrbtr2.
PERFORM bdc_field        USING 'BDC_OKCODE'
                               '=BU'.
PERFORM bdc_transaction USING 'FB01'.
ENDLOOP.
```

Listing 4.4 LOOP Statement for Processing Internal Table itab

Loop Processing   The coding listed above is nearly identical to the coding from Section 4.4.2. The only difference is that the constant field values—such as "16.03.2003" for the document date and "1000" for the company code—have now been replaced by the variable contents of internal table itab: itab-bldat and itab-bukrs. Consequently, you can process different field values from the itab table during each loop pass. To reiterate: Passing the loop once fills all the screens—document header, customer line, and G/L account line item—with the current field values of table itab and places them in the open batch input session. Each pass is concluded with the statement to post the document with Transaction FB01. Therefore, the number of loop passes determines the number of documents to be posted. Once the last data record in itab has been processed, the batch input session can be closed.

Before you see the complete data migration program, you should first learn about several special details that you have to deal with when testing the program:

▶ **Document date and posting date**

If you transfer the contents of `itab-bldat` and `itab-budat` directly to fields `bkpf-bldat` and `bkpf-budat`, a number of exotic date formats will be passed on—but probably not the right one. Therefore, you should configure the date formats explicitly prior to the final transfer. You can format the document date as indicated below:

```
CONCATENATE        itab-bldat+6(2)
                   itab-bldat+4(2)
                   itab-bldat+0(4) INTO bldat1.
```

If `itab-bldat` has the R/3-internal format 20030316, for example, this statement will set the format of variable `bldat1` to 16032003, which can then be transferred to field `bkpf-bldat`. The same applies to the posting date.

▶ **Cursor position**

When you record a transaction with the transaction recorder, the cursor position in the current screen is always recorded as well. Because the cursor position is irrelevant for the data migration in this example—even though it can have a negative impact in rare cases—the relevant passages have been commented out (with *) in the program.

```
REPORT z_fb01_program.
********************Declarations ******************
TABLES: bseg,bkpf.
INCLUDE bdcrecx1.
DATA  : bldat1 LIKE sy-datum,
        budat1 LIKE sy-datum.
DATA: BEGIN OF bdc_data OCCURS 0.
        INCLUDE STRUCTURE bdcdata.
DATA: END OF bdc_data.
DATA: BEGIN OF itab OCCURS 0,
      bukrs  LIKE bkpf-bukrs,
      bldat  LIKE bkpf-bldat,
      budat  LIKE bkpf-budat,
      waers  LIKE bkpf-waers,
      bschl1 LIKE bseg-bschl,
      kunnr  LIKE bseg-kunnr,
      wrbtr1(8),
```

```abap
      bsch12 LIKE bseg-bschl,
      hkont  LIKE bseg-hkont,
      wrbtr2(8),
      END OF itab.
********************** Initializations **************
START-OF-SELECTION.
  CLEAR bdc_data.
  REFRESH bdc_data.
********************** Upload ********************
  PERFORM load_data USING
  'C:\Willinger\data_for_FB01.txt'.
**** Batch input processing—Extended form routine *****
    PERFORM open_group.  "Open batch input file
  LOOP AT itab.
    CONCATENATE    itab-bldat+6(2)
                   itab-bldat+4(2)
                   itab-bldat+0(4) INTO bldat1.
    CONCATENATE    itab-budat+6(2)
                   itab-budat+4(2)
                   itab-budat+0(4) INTO budat1.
    PERFORM bdc_dynpro    USING 'SAPMF05A' '0100'.
*   PERFORM bdc_field     USING 'BDC_CURSOR'
*                               'RF05A-NEWKO'.
    PERFORM bdc_field     USING 'BDC_OKCODE'
                                '/00'.
    PERFORM bdc_field     USING 'BKPF-BLDAT'
                                bldat1.
    PERFORM bdc_field     USING 'BKPF-BLART'
                                'SA'.
    PERFORM bdc_field     USING 'BKPF-BUKRS'
                                itab-bukrs.
    PERFORM bdc_field     USING 'BKPF-BUDAT'
                                budat1.
    PERFORM bdc_field     USING 'BKPF-WAERS'
                                itab-waers.
    PERFORM bdc_field     USING 'RF05A-NEWBS'
                                itab-bschl1.
    PERFORM bdc_field     USING 'RF05A-NEWKO'
                                itab-kunnr.
    PERFORM bdc_dynpro    USING 'SAPMF05A' '0301'.
```

```
*     PERFORM bdc_field        USING 'BDC_CURSOR'
*                                    'RF05A-NEWKO'.
      PERFORM bdc_field        USING 'BDC_OKCODE'
                                     '/00'.
      PERFORM bdc_field        USING 'BSEG-WRBTR'
                                     itab-wrbtr1.
      PERFORM bdc_field        USING 'RF05A-NEWBS'
                                     itab-bschl2.
      PERFORM bdc_field        USING 'RF05A-NEWKO'
                                     itab-hkont.
      PERFORM bdc_dynpro       USING 'SAPMF05A' '0300'.
*     PERFORM bdc_field        USING 'BDC_CURSOR'
*                                    'BSEG-WRBTR'.
      PERFORM bdc_field        USING 'BDC_OKCODE'
                                     '/00'.
      PERFORM bdc_field        USING 'BSEG-WRBTR'
                                     itab-wrbtr2.
      PERFORM bdc_field        USING 'BDC_OKCODE'
                                     '=BU'.
      PERFORM bdc_transaction USING 'FB01'.
    ENDLOOP.
    PERFORM close_group.
*********************** Form routines **************
FORM load_data USING file
    CALL FUNCTION 'UPLOAD'
        EXPORTING
              filename           = file
              filetype           = 'dat'
        TABLES
              data_tab           = itab
        EXCEPTIONS
              conversion_error   = 1
              invalid_table_width = 2
              invalid_type       = 3
              no_batch           = 4
              unknown_error      = 5
              OTHERS             = 6.
ENDFORM.
```

Listing 4.5 Z_FB01_PROGRAM—Final Version for the Data Migration

If you run this program via menu path **System · Services · Reporting** (or, alternatively with Transaction code SE38 or SA38), you can determine whether you want to use the batch input technique or call transaction (see Figure 4.11).

Before a selection screen like the one shown in Figure 4.11 (with the corresponding selection texts) is displayed, however, you have to maintain them. To do so, choose menu path **Goto · Text Elements · Selection Texts** and enter the necessary texts.

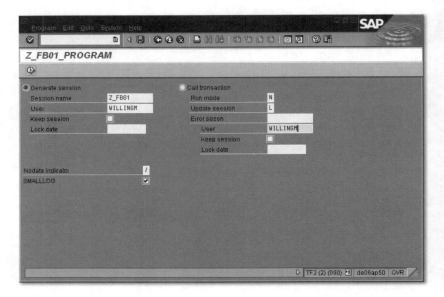

Figure 4.11 Selection Screen of Program Z_FB01_PROGRAM

4.4.4 Creating and Processing the Batch Input Session

If you use the batch input technique to process the data, only the left side of the selection screen from Figure 4.11 is relevant.

Therefore, select **Create Session** and choose a session name for the generated session. As soon as program Z_FB01_PROGRAM is finished, the session will appear with this name—Z_FB01 in this case—in the session overview (Transaction SM35). In the **User** field, enter the name of an SAP user whose authorizations you want to use to process the session. This field is set to your user name by default, but can be overwritten. If you want to retain correctly processed sessions in the SAP R/3 system—for logging purposes, for example—set the **Retain Session** checkbox. If you enter a date in the **Lock Date** field, the session cannot be processed before the specified date. This flag can help you organize large data migration projects with multiple batch input sessions because you can prevent the sessions from being processed before the final data transfer is complete. Use the **nodata indicator** to define which character will be written to the batch input session when the system identifies missing data. The "/" character is proposed by default. You can then select whether you want a small log, or summary log, of the data transfer.

Once you have set all the parameters, pressing **Execute** immediately generates a batch input session, which appears in the batch input overview (Transaction SM35) under the folder name you specified previously, Z_ FB01. When you select this session and press **Execute**, in the dialog box that subsequently opens, you can select the processing options.

Generating the Batch Input Session

Because the duration of batch input processing is primarily determined by the data volume, you should always select background processing for sessions involving 1,000 or more data records. When smaller data volumes are involved, you can interactively correct any errors that occur immediately, which is supported in the **Display errors only** mode. Here, the **Process in foreground** mode is not recommended. You should use this mode only if you want to test the data migration with a few example data records. The process described above is illustrated schematically in Figure 4.12.

Processing the Batch Input Session

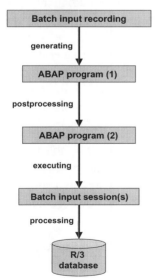

R/3 system

Batch input recording

generating

ABAP program (1)

postprocessing

ABAP program (2)

executing

Batch input session(s)

processing

R/3 database

Figure 4.12 Data Migration with the Batch Input Procedure

4.4.5 Call Transaction and Batch Input Session in Case of Error

If you choose the call transaction method for performance reasons, the right side of the selection screen from Figure 4.11 is relevant. Chapter 8 assesses the various techniques and reviews the advantages and disadvantages of these methods.

Selection Fields
First, choose the **Call Transaction** option. Then, select the **processing mode**, which determines whether the session will be processed in dialog or in the background. Three options are available:

▶ "A" means display all. Because every screen template is displayed, this option is feasible for testing only individual data records. It isn't a practical alternative for data migration.

▶ Processing mode "E" displays only the errors in dialog, while error-free transactions are run in the background. Background processing continues until an error is encountered. If an error is encountered, the call transaction procedure changes to dialog processing in order to enable the error to be corrected manually. Once the data is corrected, the system switches back to background processing and continues until the next error occurs, or processing is complete.

▶ Mode "N" is pure background processing without any dialog.

Update Mode
In the next step, you define the settings for the **update mode**; that is, you define how the data will be updated. "S" stands for synchronous update, "A" for asynchronous update, and "L" for local update. If you want to update error-free transactions with **Call Transaction**, but place erroneous transactions in a batch input session for subsequent processing—which is explicitly recommended for background processing—you must enter a name in the **Error Session** field with which you can identify and process the error session in the folder overview (Transaction SM35).

Meaning of the Error Session
If you don't specify an error session here, the system won't be able to collect erroneous transactions or present them for subsequent interactive processing. Instead, error-free transactions will be posted as expected. Erroneous data records are merely recorded in the log, however, and are excluded from the data migration.

The fields **User**, **Lock Date**, and **Session** were introduced in Section 4.4.4 and have the same meanings here.

72 Batch Input Recording: General Approach

The following parameters are recommended for data migrations based on the call transaction procedure: **processing mode** "N," **update mode** "L," **error session** "X," **user** "Y."

Setting the Parameters

Once you have maintained the selection fields, press **Execute** to start updating the data with **Call Transaction**.

Figure 4.13 shows a schematic diagram of the call transaction procedure.

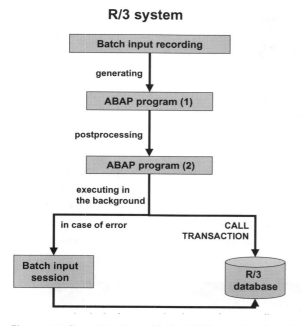

Figure 4.13 Data Migration with the Call Transaction Procedure

4.5 Batch Input Recording Combined with Microsoft Word Mail Merge Processing

In Section 4.4, you learned how to use a batch input recording to generate an ABAP program, which you then revise, import as a local file from the PC, and process as a batch input session. This procedure requires programming skills, however—a direct contradiction to the objectives of this book—and therefore should be avoided whenever possible.

Avoiding Programming

The following sections introduce you to a procedure that will enable you to reach the same objective in a much more user-friendly manner. In this approach, a batch input recording is combined with mail merge functions, which you know from Microsoft Word. The result is a batch input session that you can process using Transaction SM35.

Batch Input Recording Plus Mail Merge

Example: FB01   To illustrate this procedure, let's return to the example of the open debit items that you want to post to the SAP R/3 system with Transaction FB01. The first part, creating the recording, is identical to Section 4.4, and is repeated here for the sake of completeness.

First, choose menu path **System · Services · Batch Input · Sessions** (Transaction SM35), and then press **Recording**, and then **New Recording**. The dialog box that is displayed in Figure 4.14 opens.

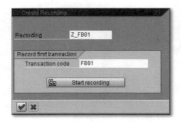

Figure 4.14 Creating a Recording

Create the Recording   Enter a name for the recording and transaction code that you want to use to transfer the open debit items to SAP R/3 (Transaction FB01). For structuring purposes, we suggest that you include the transaction code in the name of the recording in some way (for example, Z_FB01). Once you have maintained the two fields, press the **Record** button to create your recording (see Figures 4.15 to 4.18).

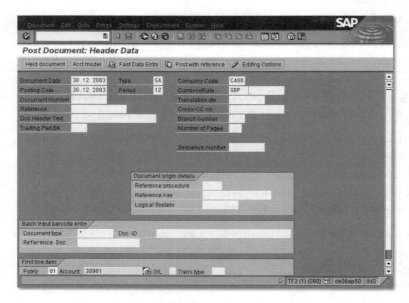

Figure 4.15 FB01—Document Header

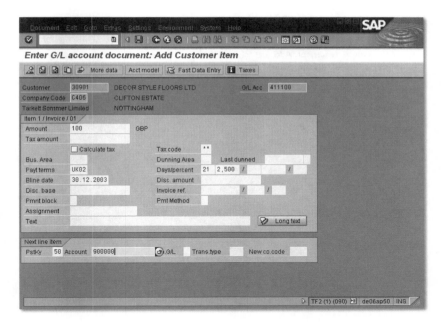

Figure 4.16 FB01—Line Item 1

Maintain the fields in Figure 4.15 as if you were using regular online processing, without the transaction recorder in the background. Press the **Enter** key to go to the next screen template (see Figure 4.16), where you can enter the information for the first line item.

Document Header

The next line item contains a balance sheet account (see Figure 4.17) that was created exclusively to migrate the transaction data, and which accepts all the open debit items accordingly.

Customer Line

You can usually set the **Amount** field of the last line item to "*". The SAP R/3 system then calculates the remaining amount automatically. The **Post** button ends the recording, creates a document in the database, and returns you to the transaction recorder screen (see Figure 4.18).

G/L Account Line

Now, you see information on the program used for the transaction that you just recorded and which screens (dynpros) were processed during the transaction. You also see a list of all the table fields, with their corresponding content that you maintained during the recording.

Result of the Recording

Use menu path **Recording · Export** (or, alternatively, the **Export** button) to export the transaction you just recorded (see Figure 4.19).

Exporting the Recording

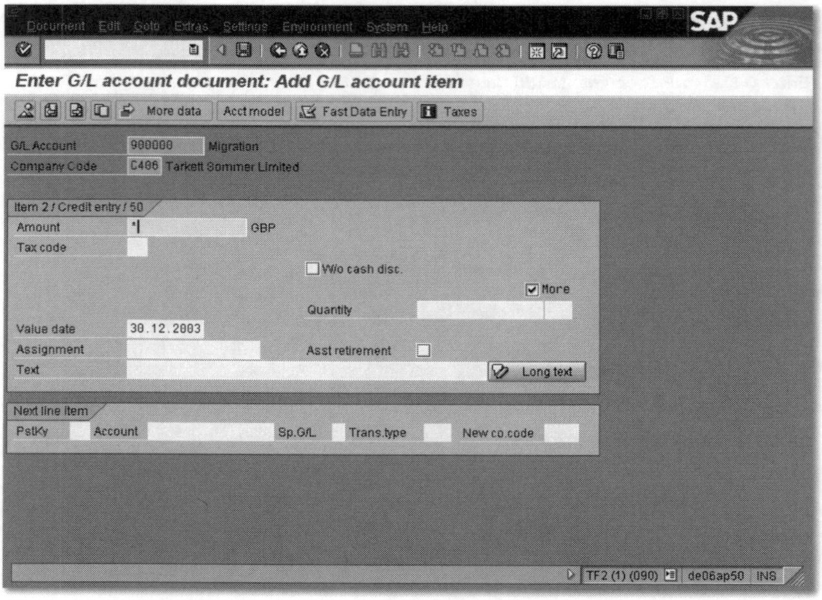

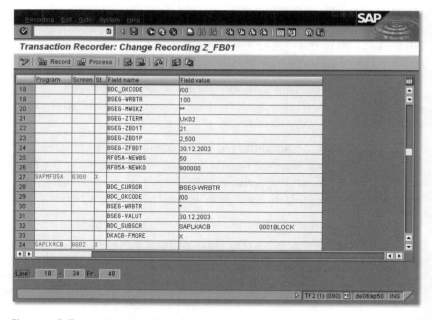

Figure 4.17 FBO1—Line Item 2

Figure 4.18 Transaction Recorder—Result of the Recording

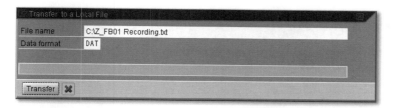

Figure 4.19 Exporting the Recording

Choose a file name and file format "DAT," which corresponds to **Text (Tab-Delimited) (*.txt)** format.

As a result, the text file you just generated contains the same data record you created during the recording of Transaction FB01 (see Figure 4.20).

Concurrently, prepare the open debit items that you want to migrate—preferably with Microsoft Excel (see Figure 4.21). Here, the order of the columns is not important.

The Excel file must consist of a single worksheet. You also must have one table row for each data record, with row 1 of the table reserved for the field texts. To improve clarity, we recommend that you set the field texts to the corresponding names. Then, you can arrange the field contents for migration starting in row 2, according to the field texts from row 1.

Format of the Excel file

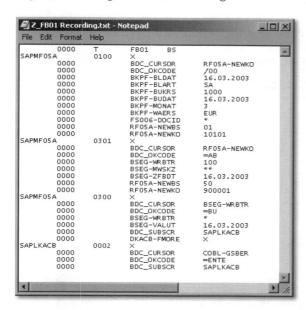

Figure 4.20 Viewing the Recording as a Text File in a Text Editor

Company code	Document date	Posting date	Reference	Document header text	Currency	Posting key	Customer	Amount	Posting key	Migration account	Amount
1000	15.04.2002	31.01.2003	6000001	Reference 6000001	EUR	06	10101	100	50	900001	100
1000	30.08.2002	31.01.2003	6000002	Reference 6000002	EUR	16	10101	150	40	900001	150
1000	08.07.2002	31.01.2003	6000003	Reference 6000003	EUR	11	10102	200	40	900001	200
1000	26.07.2002	31.01.2003	6000004	Reference 6000004	EUR	11	10102	250	40	900001	250
1000	22.01.2002	31.01.2003	6000005	Reference 6000005	EUR	01	10103	300	50	900001	300
1000	05.03.2002	31.01.2003	6000006	Reference 6000006	EUR	01	10103	350	50	900001	350
1000	14.05.2002	31.01.2003	6000007	Reference 6000007	EUR	01	10104	400	50	900001	400
1000	17.05.2002	31.01.2003	6000008	Reference 6000008	EUR	01	10104	450	50	900001	450
1000	22.05.2002	31.01.2003	6000009	Reference 6000009	EUR	01	10105	500	50	900001	500
1000	22.05.2002	31.01.2003	6000010	Reference 6000010	EUR	01	10105	550	50	900001	550

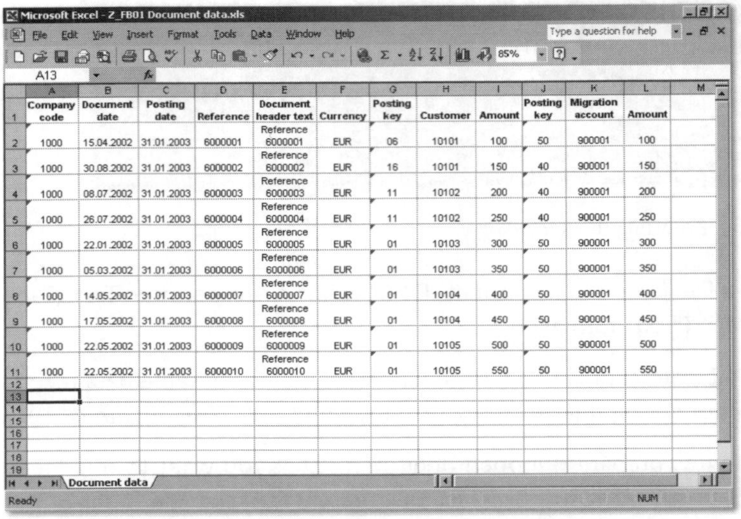

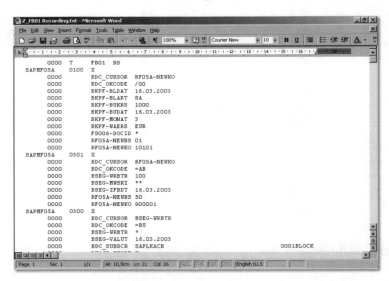

Figure 4.21 Document Data in Microsoft Excel

Note that you should avoid using lines and columns in the worksheet where you have no data. However, you can fill a line or column for individual records, but not for each record.

Mail Merge Once you have completed the preparations for the data migration, you can now open the text file you generated from the recording (see Figure 4.20) with Microsoft Word (see Figure 4.22).

```
       0000  T     FB01  BS
SAPMF05A     0100  X
       0000        BDC_CURSOR  RF05A-NEWKO
       0000        BDC_OKCODE  /00
       0000        BKPF-BLDAT  16.03.2003
       0000        BKPF-BLART  SA
       0000        BKPF-BUKRS  1000
       0000        BKPF-BUDAT  16.03.2003
       0000        BKPF-MONAT  3
       0000        BKPF-WAERS  EUR
       0000        FS006-DOCID *
       0000        RF05A-NEWBS 01
       0000        RF05A-NEWKO 10101
SAPMF05A     0301  X
       0000        BDC_CURSOR  RF05A-NEWKO
       0000        BDC_OKCODE  =AB
       0000        BSEG-WRBTR  100
       0000        BSEG-MWSKZ  **
       0000        BSEG-ZFBDT  16.03.2003
       0000        RF05A-NEWBS 50
       0000        RF05A-NEWKO 900001
SAPMF05A     0300  X
       0000        BDC_CURSOR  BSEG-WRBTR
       0000        BDC_OKCODE  =BU
       0000        BSEG-WRBTR  *
       0000        BSEG-VALUT  16.03.2003
       0000        BDC_SUBSCR  SAPLKACB                    0001BLOCK
```

Figure 4.22 Opening the Recording with Microsoft Word

To use the mail merge functions for the data migration, choose **Tools ·
Mail Merge ...** in the open document in Microsoft Word (see Figure 4.23).
When you press **Create** and select **Form Letters ...**, the dialog box shown
in Figure 4.24 opens. If you choose **Active Window**, the result should look
like the dialog box displayed in Figure 4.25.

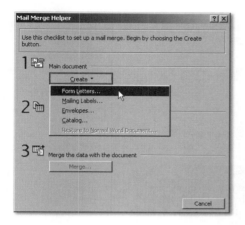

Figure 4.23 Microsoft Word—Mail Merge Wizard (1)

Figure 4.24 Microsoft Word—Mail Merge Wizard (2)

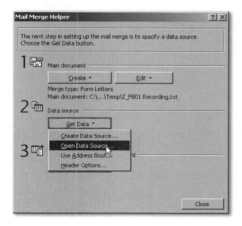

Figure 4.25 Microsoft Word—Mail Merge Wizard (3)

Importing the Data You can now press **Get Data** and **Open Data Source ...** to import your previously prepared Excel file (see Figure 4.21) into the text file open in Word, that is, import the recording.

Click **OK** to confirm the next dialog box (see Figure 4.26).

Figure 4.26 Microsoft Word—Mail Merge Wizard (4)

Figure 4.27 Microsoft Word—Mail Merge wizard (5)

If you click **Edit Main Document** again (see Figure 4.27), an additional button will appear in your active window: **Insert Merge Field**. This field contains all the field texts from the previously opened Excel file, as defined in row 1 (see Figure 4.28).

Setting the Parameters You now have to replace all the constants that resulted from your original recording with the corresponding field texts, wherever the field contents of the Excel file can vary. For example, you must replace the document date, 16.03.2003, which has a variable character, with the field text **Document Date**. If you proceed accordingly with the other fixed values from the recording, your results should resemble those displayed in Figure 4.29.

Starting the Mail Merge Now, you're ready to process the data records from the Excel file in a mail merge document. To do so, choose menu path **Tools · Mail Merge ...** and then select **Execute ...** and **Merge**.

This action will modify every data record according to the structure of the exported recording (see Figure 4.29), thus, enabling the SAP R/3 system to process it. Save the file again as a text file (**Text Only (*.txt)**) and close the file.

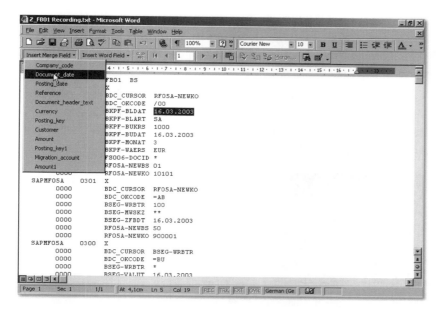

Figure 4.28 Microsoft Word—Mail Merge Wizard (6)

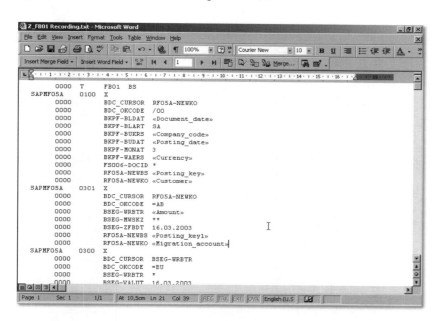

Figure 4.29 Microsoft Word—Mail Merge Wizard (7)

Now that the data is available in a format supported by SAP R/3, you can switch back to the SAP R/3 system and start Transaction SM35 there. Click the **Recording** button to display a list of all the recordings and then select

Importing the Recording

the relevant one. If you press **Change,** the recording editor is displayed (see Figure 4.18). Now, choose menu path **Recording · Import** to import the recording that you modified with the mail merge function back into the SAP R/3 system.

Generating the Batch Input Session
Save the modified recording and press **F3** to return to the recording overview. Select your recording and then choose **Edit · Create Session** to create a batch input session called Z_FB01 from recording Z_FB01 (see Figure 4.30), which you can then process.

Figure 4.30 Creating the Batch Input Session

You should activate the **Retain Session** option for logging purposes.

As soon as you press **Enter** to confirm your entries, the SAP R/3 system creates a batch input session and displays it in the batch input session overview (Transaction SM35, see Figure 4.31).

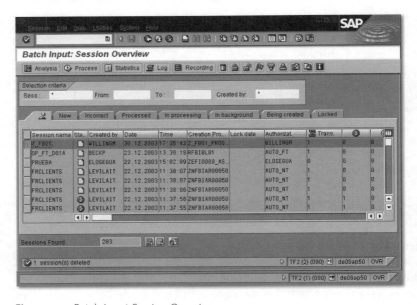

Figure 4.31 Batch Input Session Overview

You can now use the familiar processing modes to process your new session Z_FB01 (see Figure 4.32).

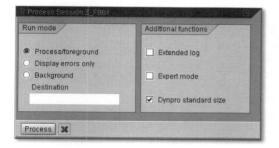

Figure 4.32 Processing the Batch Input Session

Lastly, the data migration procedure utilizing Microsoft Word mail merge processing is summarized in a schematic diagram (see Figure 4.33).

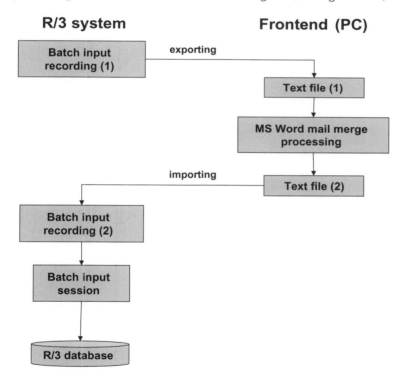

Figure 4.33 Data Migration with Microsoft Word Mail Merge Processing

5   Computer Aided Test Tool

This chapter describes how you can use a tool—the Computer Aided Test Tool (CATT) that was originally developed to test business processes—for data migration. The major benefits of the CATT are that it can be used in nearly all applications and enables you to avoid programming entirely during data migration.

5.1   What Is the CATT?

As its name implies, the *Computer Aided Test Tool* (CATT) is a tool that supports the testing of business processes. Because testing is an essential activity, but a time-consuming and cost-intensive process as well, many users asked for a way to reduce the amount of time required for testing, while simultaneously maintaining the quantity and quality of the tests. The answer to these demands was to automate test scenarios with the CATT. At the same time, the CATT also made it much easier to document and analyze the test results. Ultimately, using the CATT proved to significantly increase productivity during the testing phase. **Purpose and Objective**

With the CATT, you only have to develop and record a test for a specific transaction in the SAP R/3 system once, and can then run it again at any time, as required. Note that the term *test case* is used in the remainder of this chapter instead of *test*; this is merely to conform to the exact SAP R/3 terminology. There is no intrinsic difference between the two terms. **Test Case**

When you create a test case for a transaction, it doesn't take any longer than it does to perform a single, manual transaction in the SAP R/3 system. This is because you simply execute the transaction to be tested within the CATT, running through the same dynpros (screen templates) as you would when performing the transaction in the conventional manner. When you click on **Enter**, all the entries you make are recorded in a transaction recorder. The recorded transactions form the test cases, which are saved and suitable for functional and regression tests, because they can be reused at any time. When you execute test cases, the recorded transaction is actually performed, testing the system in its current configuration. You can either run the CATT in full automatic mode, or assume partial or complete control of the execution yourself. In either case, the result is a log, in which the test program run is documented, and a corresponding update is saved in the database. **Transaction Recorder**

Starting Test Cases Test cases are cross-client and can generally be created in any defined client. You use the client table, T000, to define whether or not test cases can be started in a specific client (see Figure 5.1).

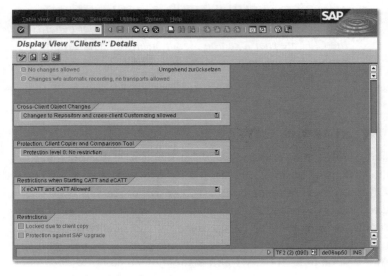

Figure 5.1 Display Clients—Details

To do so, choose **Tools · Administration · Administration · Client Administration · Maintain Client**s or, alternatively, enter transaction code SCC4.

Make sure the flags **eCATT and CATT Allowed** are selected in the detail view of the client, in group **Restrictions for Starting CATT and eCATT** (see Section 10.1).

Test Cases in Productive Clients In general, if you want to use the CATT exclusively to test business processes, you should prohibit CATT runs in production clients. The test master and transaction data created as a result of the CATT would inevitably cause errors in a production system.

If you want to use the CATT functions for data migration projects, however—as described in the sections below—you must allow CATT runs in all clients involved in the data migration, including production systems. Once the data migration is complete, you must reset the option **eCATT and CATT Allowed** in the production clients.

Functions for Data Migration This book is not intended to describe the full range of functions available in the CATT. Instead, it will focus on the functions that are required during CATT-supported data migration. If you need more detailed information on the CATT, please refer to the pertinent documentation from SAP.

5.2 How Does the CATT Work?

The functionality of the CATT can be best demonstrated by using a simple example: creating vendor master data. Because the procedure is always identical, regardless of which application you want to test with the CATT, the example can be applied to other R/3 modules. To better understand the case example in Section 5.3, you might find it helpful to familiarize yourself with the basic concept of the CATT.

Case Example: Create Vendor

5.2.1 Recording a Test Case

Three options are available to access the initial screen of the CATT (see Figure 5.2):

CATT: Initial Transaction

▶ System · Services · CATT · Record
▶ Tools · ABAP Workbench · Test · Test Workbench · CATT
▶ Transaction code SCAT

You assign a name for the new test case in this initial screen. Remember that the name has to start with Y, Z, or your namespace prefix in the customer namespace. To help you structure your test cases later, we recommend that you include the transaction code of the relevant transaction in the name of the test case, for example, you could call a test case for creating vendors ZFK01. With this approach, you can use the search help to check whether a test case already exists for the transaction you want to test. If this is so, you must clarify whether you can use this test case as is, or whether you need to adapt it to fit a different test situation (the latter case is discussed in more detail later).

Name Assignment

Once you have defined the name of the test case, choose **Record Transaction**. In the process, a transaction recorder records all the input and triggered functions within a transaction flow.

Recording a Transaction

You use the dialog box in Figure 5.3 to specify the transaction code of the transaction to be tested. If you do not know the transaction code, you can use the **F4** input help. You can also navigate to the transaction through the menu tree. Position the cursor on the corresponding menu and select **Adopt**.

Entering the Transaction Code

If you know the transaction code, you can begin with the actual recording of the transaction. To do so, click on **Record** (first icon on left) in Figure 5.3. You go to Transaction FK01—*Create Vendor* (see Figure 5.4).

Creating a Vendor

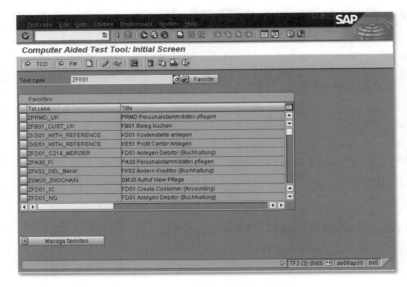

Figure 5.2 Computer Aided Test Tool—Initial Screen

Figure 5.3 Recording a Transaction

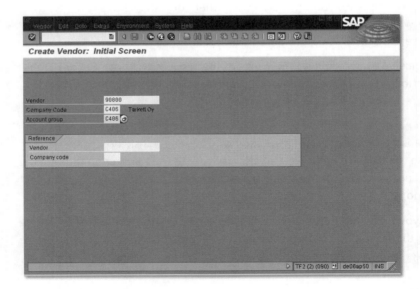

Figure 5.4 Create Vendor—Initial Screen

You now have to enter your values and navigate through the appropriate screens exactly as if you were performing the transaction manually, without the CATT. The only indications that the CATT is active and that the transaction recorder is recording the input in the background are the occasional messages in the status bar, which appear whenever you confirm your entries with **Enter** or execute certain functions within the transactions.

The example assumes that a vendor with external number assignment and account group C406 is involved, who has to be created in company code C406. In addition, his address and phone number, VAT registration number, the reconciliation account, the terms of payment, and the payment method should be entered.

Fields to Fill

Accordingly, enter the account number, the account group, and the company code in the initial screen.

When you click on **Enter**, the address data in Figure 5.5 is displayed, which you can maintain accordingly.

Address Data

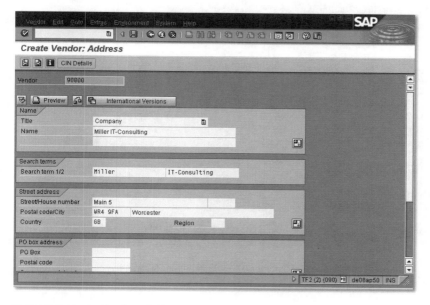

Figure 5.5 Create Vendor—Address

Click on **Enter** or the **Next Screen** button to reach the control data, as shown in Figure 5.6.

Tax Data

Once you have maintained the general data for the vendor, you can continue with the company code-specific values (see Figures 5.7 and 5.8).

Company Code-Specific Fields

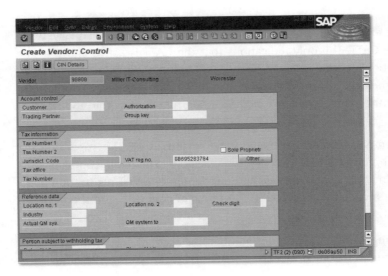

Figure 5.6 Create Vendor—Control Data

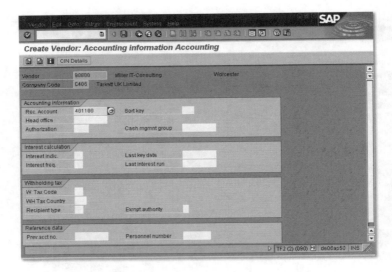

Figure 5.7 Create vendor—Accounting Information, Accounting

Ending the Transaction

Once you have entered all the data, click on the **Save** button to finish creating the vendor. Clicking on **Save** always ends the current transaction and saves the processed data record in the database. If you want to use the CATT for data migration, you must delete the first data record that you created during the recording in order to avoid falsifying the migration results. A dialog box opens (see Figure 5.9), prompting you to record another transaction or exit the recorder.

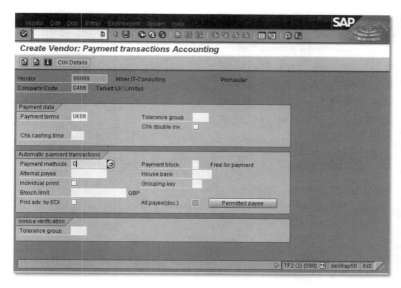

Figure 5.8 Create Vendor—Payment Transactions Accounting

Figure 5.9 Recording Another Transaction

Recording one transaction will suffice in data migration using the CATT, so you can press **Exit Recording** to exit the transaction.

You then see a screen template (see Figure 5.10) where you have to maintain the attributes of the test case.

Default values are already proposed for a majority of the fields and you can use them unchanged: The name of the current test case appears in the **Test Case** field and a short description of the test case appears in the **Title** field. The person who created the test case is automatically entered in the **Responsibility** section. If the person who created the test case is not the contact person, change this entry. The **Component** field (not visible in Figure 5.10)—which is a required entry field and does not have a default value—contains the corresponding SAP R/3 application component where the transaction you want to test is located. You can use a matchcode to find this component.

Maintaining the Test Case Attributes

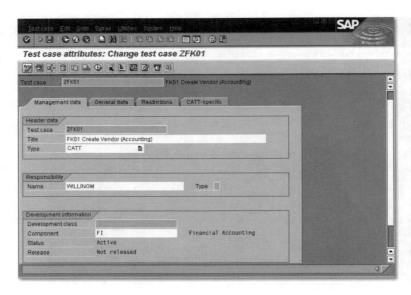

Figure 5.10 Test Case Attributes—Change Test Case ZFK01

Once you have finished maintaining the attributes, you can save the test case (see Figure 5.11).

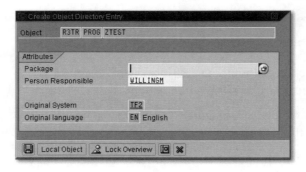

Figure 5.11 Create Object Directory Entry

Development Class and Transport Request

If you want to transport the test case to other systems, you must select a development class that supports this, along with a transport request. If you want the test case to be available only in the current client, save it as a local object.

This was the last activity involved in recording a test case. Up to this point, the procedure is identical, whether you plan to use the test case to generate test data, or to migrate data.

5.2.2 Executing a Test Case

Once the test case has been created, you can execute it immediately. From the initial screen of the CATT (Transaction SCAT), you can specify the test case to execute and then click on the **Execute** button. This takes you to the screen template shown in Figure 5.12.

Execution

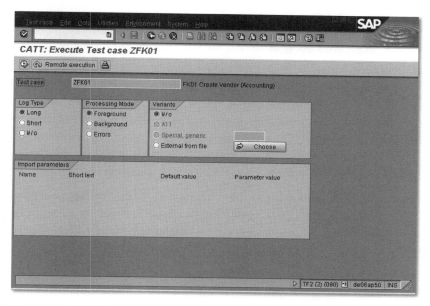

Figure 5.12 CATT—Execute Test Case ZFK01

In the **Log Type** section, you can first decide which type of log you want the CATT to generate. Three options are available:

Type of Log

▶ **Long**
All screen templates and input fields are recorded under this option; the input fields show the assigned values from the recording. If an error occurs, a long log is generated automatically beginning with the incorrect module. This is the case even if you select the No log option in the initial screen.

▶ **Short**
If no errors occur, the short log contains information only about the functions called in the test case and the parameter contents. The major attributes of the parameters are described in detail in Section 5.3.1.

▶ **W/O**
No log

In the **Processing Mode** section, you define how you want to process the test case. Again, three different options are available:

Foreground
The test case is executed fully in dialog. In the process, you can change field inputs to influence the test results. Click on **Enter** to get to the next screen.

▶ **Background**
The transactions are executed in the background, without any dialog.

▶ **Errors**
In this case, the transactions continue to be processed in the background until the first error or termination occurs. When an error occurs, the system switches to dialog mode, enabling you to change incorrect entries. Once you click on **Enter** to confirm the corrected entry, the system switches back to background processing and continues until the next error occurs or processing is complete.

Variants

You can initially ignore the options contained in the **Variants** section, which apply to variant processing. You can leave the default setting, **No Variant**. Section 5.3.3 will discuss variants in the context of using the CATT functions for data migration.

Foreground Processing

Once you have decided on a log type and a processing mode, you can start the test case with the **Execute** button (**F8**). If the **Foreground Processing** function is selected, for example, you will see the screens illustrated in Figures 5.13 to 5.18, which you can confirm with **Enter**.

Problems with External Number Assignment

At the start of this exercise, we defined that the vendors should have external number assignment. Because recording the test case caused a change in the database, vendor 90800 already exists. As a result, if you execute the test case now, the system would attempt to create the vendor again under the same number, which is not possible. To migrate all the recorded data anyway, you have to choose a vendor number that does not yet exist, which is easy in foreground processing with its interactive change options.

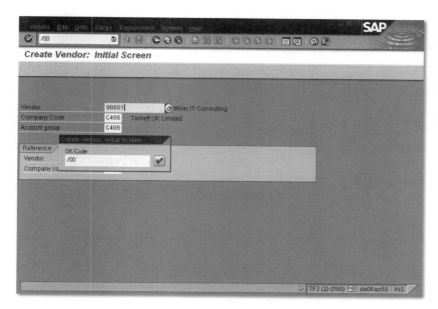

Figure 5.13 Create Vendor—Initial screen

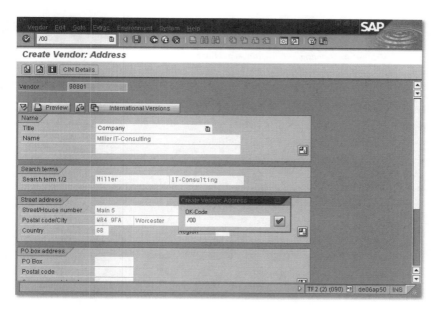

Figure 5.14 Create Vendor—Address

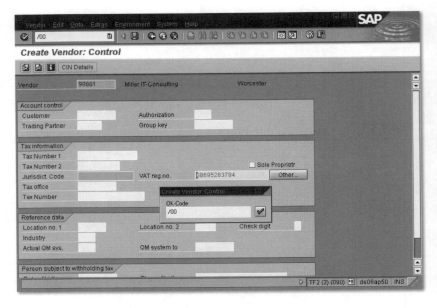

Figure 5.15 Create Vendor—Control

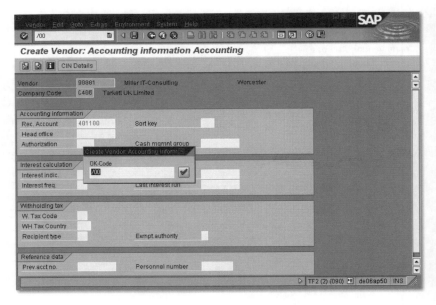

Figure 5.16 Create Vendor—Accounting Information, Accounting

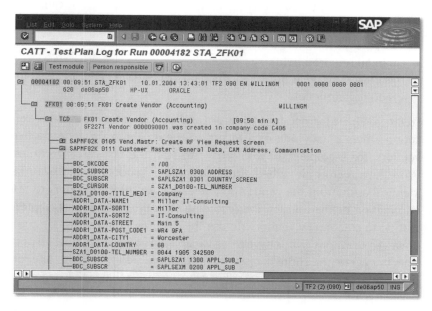

Figure 5.17 Create Vendor—Payment Transactions, Accounting

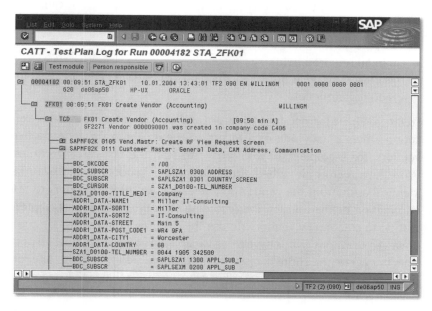

Figure 5.18 CATT Test Log

The last screen template (see Figure 5.18) always displays a log of the last   Log
performed test case in a hierarchical structure. The example shown here
uses a long log. The header section—which contains, among other things,

the executing client, date, time, and platform—forms the top hierarchy level. The next level lists the test case used, ZFK01, which is broken down further into the called transaction, FK01, the executed programs and screens, SAPxxxxx, the inputs made, and the messages generated by the CATT.

You should recognize the obvious similarities with the batch input recording shown in Chapter 4.

Frequent Error Messages Ultimately, the log indicates whether the test case was executed successfully. If an error occurred, the responsible components are highlighted in red in the log; however, in our example, this is not the case.

Examples of frequently occurring error messages include the following:

▶ **Batch input data not available for screen ...**
The reason for this error can be an incorrectly maintained screen sequence or a missing screen in the test case. An unexpected dialog box during execution of the test case can also cause this error message.

▶ **Field <table-field_name> does not permit input**
An output field was assigned values, not an input field. The cause for this could be incorrect parameterization of the input fields. This possibility is discussed in detail later on (see Section 5.3.1).

▶ **Fill in all required fields**
This error message is displayed when no values have been specified for a required entry field.

Summary and Outlook So far, you have learned how to record and execute a test case. Each execution writes exactly one data record to the database. To generate five vendors, for example, you would have to start the test case five times. With the structure described above, these five vendors would even be identical aside from the vendor number, because the CATT refers to the information defined during the recording each time and uses this information to create new vendors. To use the CATT as a data migration tool, however, the input values have to be variable. In addition, it must be possible to migrate the entire dataset—that is, all the creditors—with one run of the test case. Section 5.3 describes how you can achieve this degree of flexibility.

5.3 How Can You Use the CATT for Data Migration?

This section focuses on answering the preceding question. In it, you will build on and expand the example for creating vendors automatically that you read about in Section 5.2.

Case Example: Creating a Vendor

5.3.1 Parameterization for Input Fields

In all the business processes that you want to model in test cases, you must first enter the data in the R/3 input templates and fields. This data can be used to create master data, for example—as illustrated in Section 5.2—or to generate transaction data. To make the test cases flexible—which is an essential prerequisite if you want to use them for data migration—we recommend that you parameterize the input fields instead of using fixed values. This gives the input fields a variable character, enabling them to process different values for the migration. This section clarifies how you can achieve this parameterization.

Flexibility through Parameterization

In the initial screen of the CATT (Transaction SCAT), first enter the test case that you want to edit, ZFK01, and choose **Change**. The screen shown in Figure 5.19 opens.

Function Editor

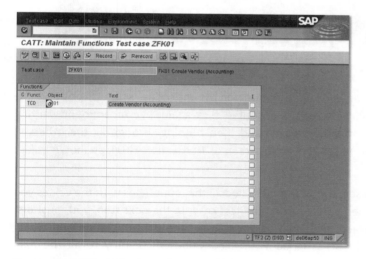

Figure 5.19 CATT—Maintaining Functions for Test Case ZFK01

You see the *function editor* of the CATT, which uses function listing TCD to define the transaction that will be run in the test case. In our example, this is Transaction FK01, which is used to create vendors. The numerous editing and control commands available in the function editor aren't described in any detail here. Instead, the function editor will focus on the functions that are needed and used within the data migration framework. For more information on the function editor, please refer to the official SAP documentation.

When you double-click to navigate to the detail view of this transaction (see Figure 5.20), you see a list of all the screen templates from Transaction FK01 that you processed during your recording.

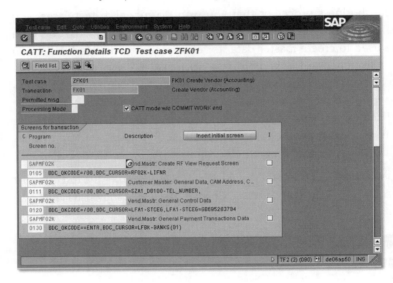

Figure 5.20 CATT—Details of Function TCD

Each Line Corresponds to One Screen — To display detailed information for the individual screens, position the cursor within a screen and double-click again. We recommend starting with the first screen, 0105, and then running through all the others in sequence. You see the initial screen of Transaction FK01, as shown in Figure 5.21.

Screen Details — As you can see, the system has filled all the input fields with the values you entered when you recorded the test case. In the next step, you must distinguish which fields will be variable for the data migration and which fields should be assigned with fixed values that apply to all the data records for migration. To make the test case as flexible and universally applicable as possible, we recommend that you parameterize as many fields as possible. This procedure is extremely simple. Position the cursor on a field whose contents you want to define variably and double-click (or choose **Details**). If you choose the **Account Group** field, for example, a dialog box like the one shown in Figure 5.22 opens.

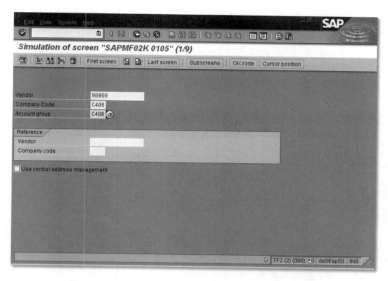

Figure 5.21 Simulation of the Screen

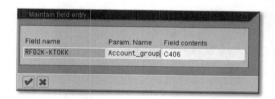

Figure 5.22 Parameterization of the Account Group Field

This dialog box consists of the **Parameter Name** and **Field Contents** fields. Define a parameter name, such as "account_group," and a default value for the field. This default value is taken from the recording; however, you can overwrite it if necessary. During the data migration, the fields are filled with default values whenever the respective data record doesn't provide corresponding field contents. If the field in question is not a required entry field, you might consider doing without a default value altogether, which would result in a blank field in the corresponding data record. As you will see, it is much easier to manage the migration if you use mnemonic names for the parameters as was the case in the previous example.

Parameterization of the Fields

When you click on **Enter** to close the dialog box, you return to the screen (see Figure 5.23) where you started.

As you see, the screen field is no longer ready for input after parameterization. Its contents are merely a default value; when values are passed during the test case execution, it will be overwritten and highlighted. Field contents for fields that are ready for input are simply fixed values that are copied identically to the corresponding fields of all the data records for migration. Consequently, you can determine which fields were assigned default values during the migration and which fields received variable contents.

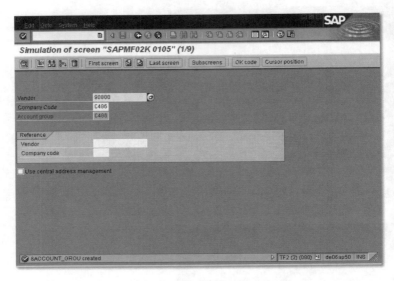

Figure 5.23 Simulation of the Screen after Parameterization

Parameterization as Iterative Process

Once you have parameterized the **Company Code** and **Vendor** fields, using the same method described for the **Account Group**, you have processed all the fields in the first screen and can switch to the next screen. To do so, click on the **Next Screen** button. The display will look like the screen shown in Figure 5.24.

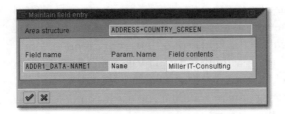

Figure 5.24 Parameterization of the Name1 Field

Once again, parameterize the fields as necessary. Repeat this iterative process until you have maintained all the screens and parameterized all the appropriate fields. Then, return to the initial screen of the function editor and save your changes.

Thus far, you have learned that by parameterizing the fields of a test case, you can execute a test run not only with fixed values, but also with variable field contents that you transfer dynamically at runtime for each field and data record. This is essential for the data migration. The following sections describe how these different field contents are ultimately passed on.

5.3.2 Processing External Variants

The preceding sections utilized a variant, without mentioning it explicitly. In this context, a variant is defined as a complete set of field contents that is passed on to the input fields of the transaction being tested during the execution of a test case. The SAP R/3 system creates a variant automatically each time a test case is recorded. This variant is used by default when no other variant is chosen explicitly. When you execute a test case, you can use a variant to determine which values you want to use for the current test run.

Variant

Variants are useful, for example, whenever you need to pass specific combinations of values on to the input fields of a test case frequently. You merely have to enter the name of the variant when you start the test case in order to process the corresponding combinations of values. We mention this type of variant only so you know it exists. Because its lack of flexibility makes it inadequate as a migration tool, it is not described in any detail here.

Purpose and Objective of Variants

Much more interesting and relevant is the connection between a variant and the parameterization of the input fields in the test case. Parameterization makes it possible to process a number of variants—that is, a number of different data records—by starting a single test case: the exact function you need for data migration. The next section describes how to create such variants.

Once you have saved your parameterization, the CATT has an option for exporting variants for (external) additional processing in a spreadsheet program, such as Microsoft Excel. Choose menu path **Goto · Variants · Export Proposal** to generate a text file that contains all the parameters of the test case, with its texts and default values according to the declaration in Section 5.3.1. The corresponding dialog box is shown in Figure 5.25.

Creating Variants

You can first enter the path that specifies the storage location of the proposal on your PC. SAP R/3 automatically proposes the default path configured in your SAP GUI settings. You can overwrite this value if necessary. The important thing here is the file format of the proposal. You save the

Text File

proposal as a text file with extension *.txt*. This means that the individual elements in the file must be separated by tabs to enable processing. You should give the file a name similar to the name of the test case. That way, you'll easily recognize which files you need to process with which test cases. Accordingly, *ZFK01.txt* would be a logical alternative in our example. Click on the **Transfer** button to save the file on your PC.

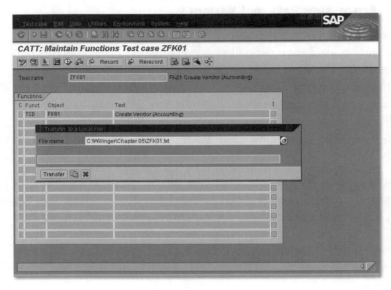

Figure 5.25 Exporting Variants as Proposals

Structure of the Text File

To better understand the structure of the file, we recommend that you examine its contents more closely in the text editor (see Figure 5.26).

Figure 5.26 Format of file ZFK01.txt

Columns

When you export the proposal, the SAP R/3 system generates a four-line text file that consists of the following columns:

▶ **[Variant ID]**
This is the technical ID of the variant. Because SAP R/3 generated the variant automatically and you didn't assign it an explicit name, the text file merely provides a placeholder for the ID. This has no significance on any of the following lines.

▶ **[Variant Text]**

The same applies to the short text of the variant.

▶ **Parameters**

The parameters represent the parameterized fields of the test case. The parameters listed in the test file must match the texts of the parameters in the test case.

The individual lines contain the following information: Lines

▶ The first line contains the column headers, as you defined them above.

▶ Below the column headers are the SAP R/3 field texts, which are the parameters. One parameter in the test case, for example, is "Vendor," just like the corresponding R/3 field text.

▶ Line 3 lists the default values of the parameters as you configured them during parameterization.

▶ Line 4 provides information on how to use the file.

To ensure a seamless data migration, we recommend that you leave the structure of this file unchanged. It forms the basis for processing external variants, which you carry out using a spreadsheet program. Due to the popularity of Microsoft Excel, this program is used for the demonstration. Processing External Variants with Excel

Start Microsoft Excel and open the text file *ZFK01.txt*. The dialog box shown in Figure 5.27 opens.

Files with type *.txt* are only displayed when you select **All Files (*.*)** for the file type. You can now select file *ZFK01.txt* and click on **Open**. The screen shown in Figure 5.28 opens. Opening the Text File

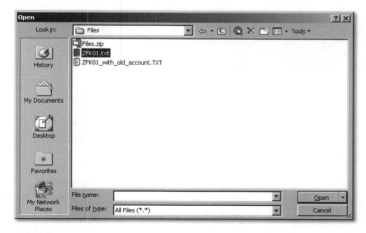

Figure 5.27 Opening File ZFK01.txt with Microsoft Excel

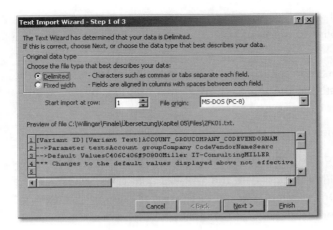

Figure 5.28 Text Import Wizard—First Dialog Box

Excel detects that the file you want to open is not an *.xls* file and activates the Text Import wizard. The wizard has already preset the appropriate parameters. Click on **Next** to continue. The screen in Figure 5.29 opens.

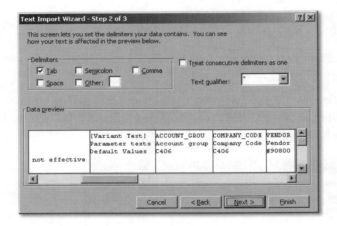

Figure 5.29 Text Import Wizard—Second Dialog Box

Once again, you can click on **Next** to use the default settings, because the elements of *.txt* files are always separated by tabs as described above. The dialog box shown in Figure 5.30 opens.

Column Formatting

You define here which data format the individual columns will have. All columns/fields that can begin with a leading zero—such as phone, fax, region, or ZIP code—should be set to **Text** format. This ensures that Excel will protect the leading zeros. You can leave the remaining columns set to

Default. Once you have formatted the columns, click on **Finish**. Excel opens the text file in a screen similar to Figure 5.31 below.

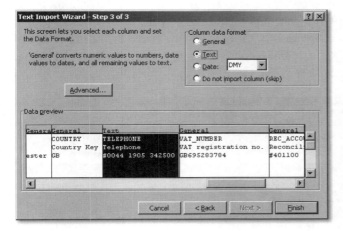

Figure 5.30 Text Import Wizard—Third Dialog Box

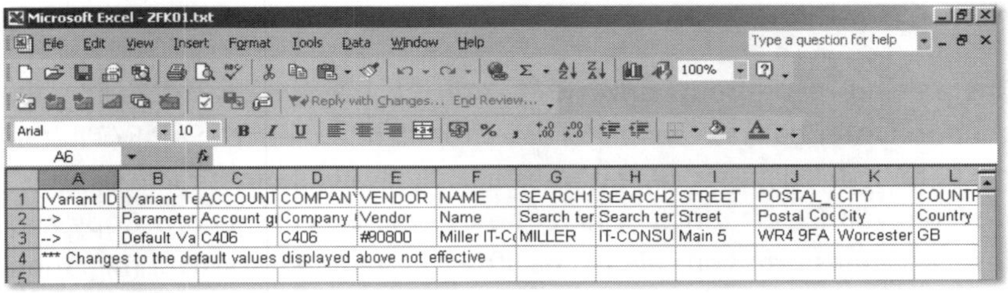

Figure 5.31 ZFK01.txt—Opened in Excel

You see the same data structure and contents from Figure 5.26. To make maintaining the variant user-friendly, you opened file *ZFK01.txt* with Excel. Once again, leave rows 1 to 4 unchanged, and maintain the variants starting with line 5. One row is reserved for each variant. Accordingly, the maximum number of variants is limited only by the maximum worksheet size in Excel.

To create a new variant—that is, a new data record—for a vendor, start in row 5 and follow the structure specified in rows 1 to 3. Specifically, this means entering the account group of the vendor in the appropriate column, and so on. As a reference, you can use the SAP R/3 field text **Account Group**, the name of the parameter "Account Group," or the default value from the recording, C406. Proceed accordingly for the rest of the fields in the data record. If no field contents are available, leave the

Processing External Variants

corresponding field in row 5 blank. The result is that the field in question will be set to the default value from the recording. If no default value is available from the recording, as you can see from row 3, the field contents will remain empty for this data record. Once you have defined the first variant, you can continue with the next variant in row 6. The procedure is identical. File *ZFK01.txt*, which consists of five variants, might look like the screen in Figure 5.32.

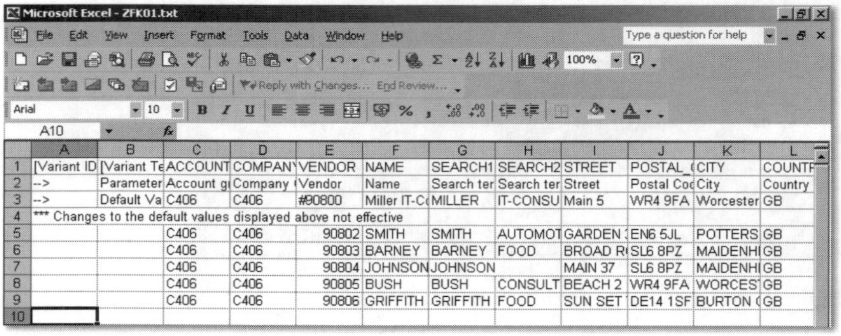

	A	B	C	D	E	F	G	H	I	J	K	L
1	[Variant ID	[Variant Te	ACCOUNT	COMPANY	VENDOR	NAME	SEARCH1	SEARCH2	STREET	POSTAL_(	CITY	COUNTR
2	-->	Parameter	Account gı	Company (	Vendor	Name	Search ter	Search ter	Street	Postal Coc	City	Country
3	-->	Default Va	C406	C406	#90800	Miller IT-C(	MILLER	IT-CONSU	Main 5	WR4 9FA	Worcester	GB
4	*** Changes to the default values displayed above not effective											
5			C406	C406	90802	SMITH	SMITH	AUTOMOT	GARDEN :	EN6 5JL	POTTERS	GB
6			C406	C406	90803	BARNEY	BARNEY	FOOD	BROAD R(	SL6 8PZ	MAIDENHI	GB
7			C406	C406	90804	JOHNSON	JOHNSON		MAIN 37	SL6 8PZ	MAIDENHI	GB
8			C406	C406	90805	BUSH	BUSH	CONSULT	BEACH 2	WR4 9FA	WORCES	GB
9			C406	C406	90806	GRIFFITH	GRIFFITH	FOOD	SUN SET	DE14 1SF	BURTON (	GB
10												

Figure 5.32 Maintaining External Variants with Excel

Data Migration through Maintaining External Variants

The previous figure summarizes this entire chapter. You can save all your vendor master data as variants in order to migrate them to SAP R/3 in the next step. The data for migration is usually available in a table-like file, preferably in Excel. You can therefore use the Excel functions **Copy** and **Insert** to transform your file to the structure required for data migration shown in Figure 5.32. Once all the data records for migration are present in *ZFK01.txt*, you must save your changes. The important thing here is that you save the file as a text file again, as this is the only format that the CATT supports. When you save the file, Excel will inform you that file *ZFK01.txt* already exists and ask you whether you want to overwrite it. Confirm all prompts with **Yes**. In order to import file *ZFK01.txt* to SAP R/3, you have to close it first. In the process, confirm all messages from Microsoft Excel with **Yes** or **OK**.

5.3.3 Uploading the Data to SAP R/3

Uploading to SAP R/3

Once you have completed the preparations described in Section 5.3.1 and Section 5.3.2, you can begin loading file *ZFK01.txt* into SAP R/3. To do so, call the initial screen of the CATT (SCAT), enter test case `ZFK01`, and choose **Execute**. The CATT start menu from Figure 5.33 opens.

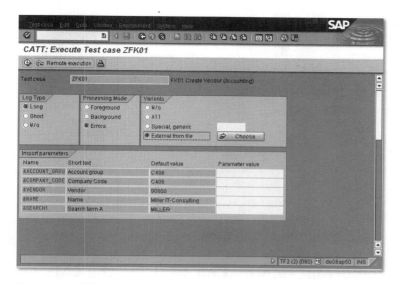

Figure 5.33 CATT—Execute Test Case ZFK01

We already introduced you to the settings for the log type and processing mode in a previous section. In this section, we address the **Variants** area, where the options for variant processing are displayed. Because you processed the variants in an external file, choose the fourth option, **External from File**, and click on **Choose**.

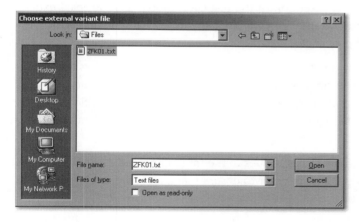

Figure 5.34 Selecting an External Variant

In the screen shown in Figure 5.34, enter the path of the data transfer file *ZFK01.txt* and click on **Open** to confirm.

The lower half of Figure 5.34 lists all the parameterized fields (import parameters) again, including their default values. When you press **Execute** again, the data is transferred in accordance with the defined settings. If processing mode **Display Errors** is active and the migration runs without errors, the log file mentioned above is shown, which is ideal for documenting the data migration.

Brief Appraisal

Where performance is concerned, this procedure is similar to the batch input technique—not only regarding the screens to be processed, but also with the consistency checks that are performed for the input values. A major advantage over the batch input technique, however, is that absolutely no ABAP coding is required, which makes this method accessible to less technically oriented individuals as well. Chapter 8 contains a comprehensive appraisal of all the data migration techniques.

5.4   Important Information on Using the CATT

5.4.1   General Recommendations

This section contains several recommendations that will help you to simplify your work with the CATT.

**Use Only Familiar
Transactions**

▶ Create test cases for only those transactions with which you are very familiar. This ensures that you know the system response during recording and execution of the test case; moreover, your past experience with the transaction will enable you to deal with any error messages that may occur.

**One Transaction
per Test Case**

▶ Process only one transaction per test case, even though it is technically possible to process several transactions. This approach lets you split the overall data migration into smaller, transaction-specific packages, which will help you to allocate responsibilities for the migration within your enterprise.

Using Parameters

▶ Use parameters to pass values to the transaction and avoid fixed values whenever possible in order to ensure that a test case can be applied as widely as possible.

▶ Consider the universal character of the test case when choosing its parameters and screen sequence.

**Modifying Test
Cases**

▶ Avoid creating new test cases when you can modify existing ones. For more information, see Section 5.4.2.

▶ Document every test case. To do so, choose menu path **Goto · Long Text** in edit mode for the test case.

Documentation

▶ If you want to use transactions from other applications, use its specific test cases and request their extension, if necessary.

▶ Set individual lines to inactive within the CATT function editor. If you want to deactivate a function temporarily, you don't necessarily have to delete it. Instead, you can set the I column for the corresponding function in the function editor to flag it as inactive.

Deactivating Functions

5.4.2 Modifying Test Cases

Often, you may have to deal with situations whereby someone else has already created a test case for a transaction that you now want to test yourself, or use for a data migration. On closer examination, however, it seems that the test case includes fields that you don't need for your own project, or that required fields are missing. In such cases, it doesn't make sense to create a new, redundant test case for the same transaction. Instead, you should modify the existing test case to address the changed situation, which may require coordination with the person responsible for the original test case.

Initial Situation

To illustrate this problem, consider the example for creating a vendor (Transaction FK01) introduced in Section 5.2. In this example, the situation demands that the **Old Account Number** field be maintained, in addition to the fields have already been filled or parameterized. This field contains the vendor number in the legacy accounting system, which will enable you to select and analyze reports based on this old number in SAP R/3 as well.

Example

To add additional information to an existing test case, you have to modify it. To do so, call the initial screen of the CATT (SCAT), enter test case ZFK01, and choose **Change**. This opens the function editor, which contains all the screens involved in recording the test case. Navigate to the detail view of the screen that contains the company code-specific information for account management (see Figure 5.35).

Procedure

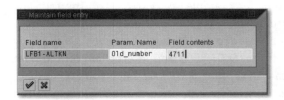

Figure 5.35 Parameterization of the Old Account Number Field

Parameterize a field as described in Section 5.3.1 and define an appropriate default value. Finally, save your changes, so you can use **Goto · Variants · Export Proposal** to export another four-line text file that you can use as the foundation for the data migration (see Figure 5.36).

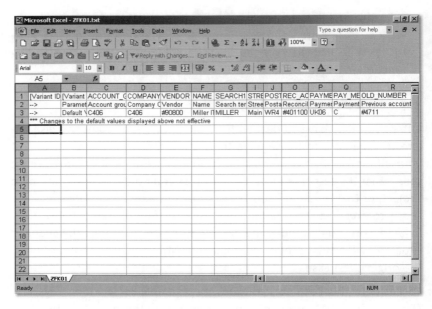

Figure 5.36 Old Account Number as Parameter in ZFK01.txt

The text file has now been supplemented with an additional parameter (an additional column) that is reserved for the old account number. You can now enter the data records for migration, as described in Section 5.3.2, and then start the upload to SAP R/3.

Modifying the Structure of the Text File

Situations are also possible in which you have nearly completed your preparations for data migration, as far as recording the test case and maintaining the external variants is concerned, but the user department then asks you to migrate additional fields to SAP R/3. In such situations, we recommend that you change the test case, as described above, and add and parameterize the additional fields accordingly. You then have to export the variant proposal and save it, for example, as *ZFK01_1.txt*. The four-line *ZFK01_1.txt* file is merely an auxiliary file, because only its structure—particularly the columns with the added parameters—is relevant. Now, copy these additional columns from *ZFK01_1.txt* and insert them on the right border of your actual data transfer file, *ZFK01.txt*. Once you are finished, the structure of *ZFK01.txt* must agree with that of *ZFK01_1.txt*. You can then delete file *ZFK01_1.txt* and begin maintaining the values of the new parameters in *ZFK01.txt*, starting with line 5. Alternatively, you can also copy the data records from *ZFK01.txt* to *ZFK01_1.txt* and use *ZFK01_1.txt* as the data transfer file.

5.4.3 Initializing Field Contents

When you execute a test case, you may get an error message indicating that a master record with the identical number already exists; however, you cannot create another master record with the same number. This error occurs because SAP R/3 does not automatically initialize (that is, reset to blank) the field that identifies the master record (such as the G/L account number) after it is created with the CATT.

Initial Situation

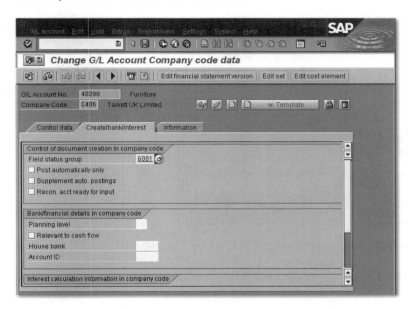

Figure 5.37 Create General Ledger (G/L) Account—Company Code Data

To learn how to resolve this problem, return to the example of creating G/L accounts in the company code (Transaction FSS0). Call the initial transaction of the CATT (SCAT) and record a test case called ZFSS0 for Transaction FSS0. To keep the example simple, maintain only the fields **G/L Account**, **Company Code,** and **Field Status**. Figure 5.37 shows an excerpt of the maintained values.

Example

After you have maintained the field status and saved your data—and ensured that the transaction recorder is still active—initialize the **G/L Account** field. To do so, you can use an old function taken from SAP R/2: Position the cursor in the **G/L Account** field, add an exclamation point (!)

Initialization

to the existing G/L account number, and click on **Enter** to confirm your entries. See the subsequent dialog box shown in Figure 5.38.

Figure 5.38 Initialization of the G/L Account Field

The transaction recorder records an entry for the initialization that you just performed. Click on the green arrow (**F3**) to go back and end the recording. You can now start parameterizing the fields. The last recorded screen, which contains the information for the initialization, is particularly important. Figure 5.39 shows the corresponding dialog box.

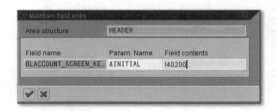

Figure 5.39 Parameterization of the Initialization

Define the corresponding parameter "Initial" for the **G/L Account** field and save an exclamation point (!) as the default value. Then, save your changes.

Structure of the Text File   Use menu path **Goto · Variants · Export Proposal** to export the text file for the data migration as usual. When you open the file with Microsoft Excel, you will see the screen in Figure 5.40.

	A	B	C	D	E	F	G	H	I
1	[Variant ID]	[Variant Text]	&ACCOUNT	&COMPANY_CODE	&FIELD_STATUS	&INITIAL			
2	-->	Parameter texts	G/L account no.	Company code	Field status group	G/L account no.			
3	-->	Default Values	40200	DE01	G001	!40200			
4	*** Changes to the default values displayed above not effective								
5									
6									

Figure 5.40 ZFSS0.txt—Opened in Excel

Assign the corresponding field contents to the G/L accounts for migration. Note that you must enter an exclamation point (!) in every line for parameter "Initial," as this initializes the **G/L Account** field when you upload the file to SAP R/3. Figure 5.41 shows the results of this maintenance.

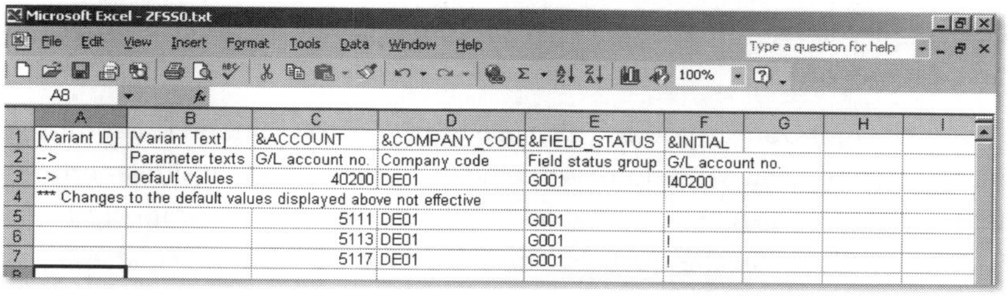

Figure 5.41 Maintaining External Variants with Excel

5.4.4 Table Maintenance with the CATT

You can also use the CATT to maintain customer tables, which once again underscores the cross-application character of this tool. If you want to use this option, the transaction to record is called **Extended Table Maintenance**; the corresponding transaction code is SM30. The procedure—recording the test case, parameterizing the fields, processing the external variants with Microsoft Excel, and uploading the file to SAP R/3—is analogous to the description in Section 5.3 and is therefore not repeated here.

General Approach

There is one special feature, however, which you don't encounter in any other application but table maintenance. This special situation occurs whenever you want to record a test case for a blank table, that is, one that does not have any entries yet. In this situation, this table receives its first entry when you record the test case. Because the screen sequence depends on the table entries, a different screen sequence is presented when you record the test case (the table does not have any entries yet) than when you execute it (the table already has an entry)—which will result in the error message **Batch input data not available for screen ...** (see Section 5.2.2). This applies regardless of whether customer tables or Customizing tables are involved.

Differing Screens

To avoid this problem, ensure that the tables have at least two entries before you begin recording the test case. This guarantees that the system presents identical screen sequences during both the recording and the execution of the test case and prevents the initial error message from being displayed.

Solution

You could encounter similar problems in Controlling when creating CO objects (cost centers, internal orders, and so on). If the controlling area is not set, a dialog box for entering the controlling area appears during processing of the first data record, but not for subsequent data records. The solution here is to set the controlling area manually before you begin processing. If you do, the dialog box won't appear during processing of the first data record.

Maintaining Customizing Tables

As already mentioned, you can also use the CATT to maintain Customizing tables. This approach is helpful whenever you have to enter similar entries that are already available in a table-like file and have to be imported into SAP R/3. If possible, the Customizing tables should have only *one level*, as shown in Figure 5.42.

New Entries: Overview of Added Entries

Co...	Clerk	Name of Accounting Clerk	Office user
DE01	01	Jamie Bazley	BAZLEYJ
DE01	02	Henry King	KINGH
DE01	03	David Jepson	JEPSOND

Figure 5.42 One-level Customizing Tables

Do Not Record Transport Requests

You should also take steps to prevent the creation of transport requests while recording a test case. Otherwise, the system will create an additional transport request for every imported data record. If you processed 100 data records, for example, 100 transport requests would have to be transported to the consolidation and production systems, which would be extremely time-intensive. In this case as well, it is better to create an entry in the corresponding Customizing table manually and then save it in a separate transport request. You can then refer to this transport request when you record the test case, which will prevent the creation of another test case during recording.

5.5   Case Example: Migrating Transaction Data

Migrating Open Credit Items

In addition to migrating master data from a legacy system to SAP R/3, you can also use the CATT to migrate transaction data. This once again underscores the flexibility of this tool. As mentioned previously, the procedure is completely independent of the type of data to be migrated and the underlying application. Finally, we want to outline another case example that examines the migration of open credit items in more detail (see Section 2.2.5). This is an issue that faces everyone who implements R/3 Financial Accounting.

SAP R/3 always provides one transaction code to create master data in the corresponding transaction. Conversely, a variety of transaction codes are available for transaction data, giving you more choices. You can create postings to vendor accounts, for example, in accounts payable accounting, in the general ledger, and even in accounts receivable accounting and asset accounting. You can also choose between different input templates—the "conventional" transactions versus the "Enjoy" transactions. We selected the conventional transaction, FB01, to migrate the transaction data, because it's the most neutral transaction for field default values.

Data Migration with FB01

Figure 5.43 Posting Documents with FB01

Once you confirm your entry, you run through all the screen templates (see Figures 5.44, 5.45, and 5.46) that are relevant for document entry.

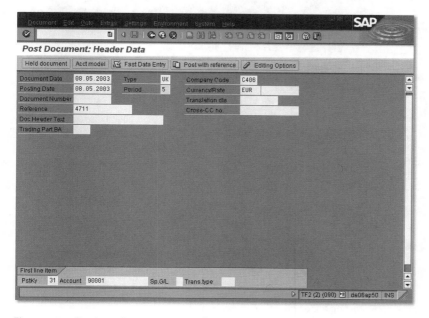

Figure 5.44 Posting a Document—Header Data

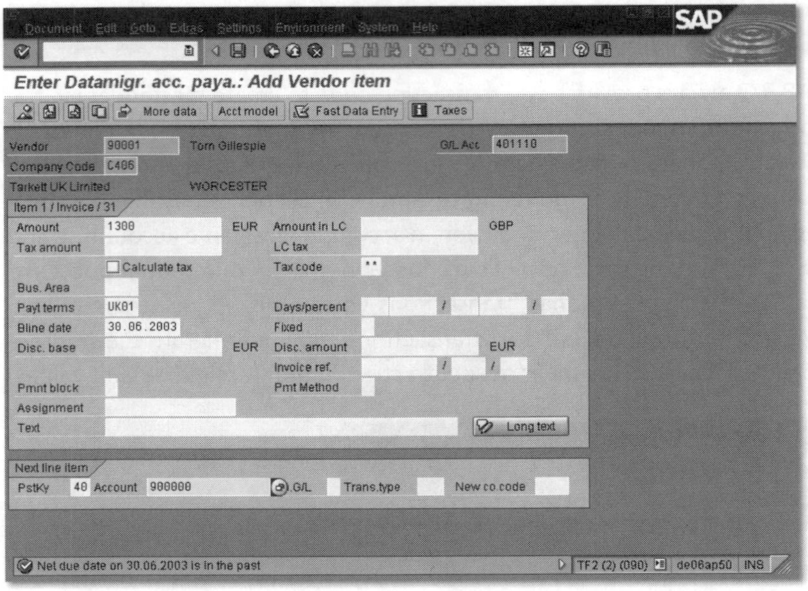

Figure 5.45 Posting a Document—Vendor Item

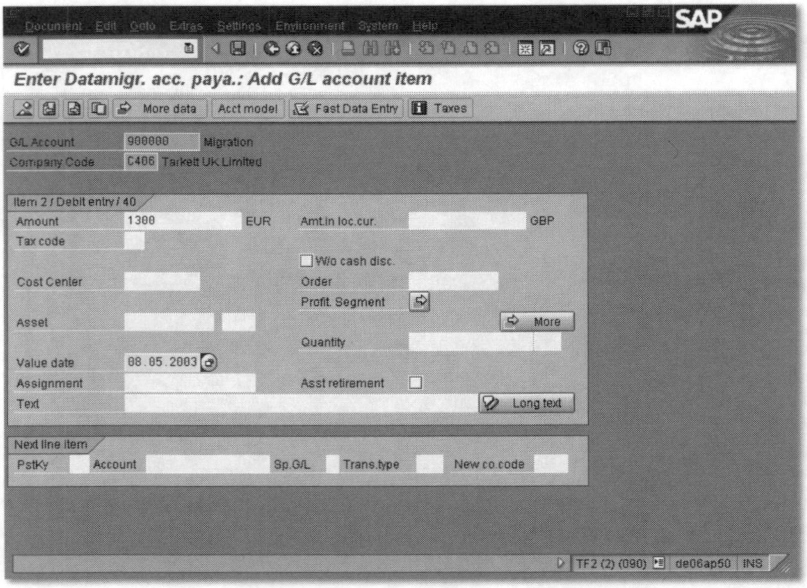

Figure 5.46 Posting a Document—G/L Account Item

Post the document that you just entered and end the recording. This allows you to save test case ZFB01.

The next thing you have to do is set the parameters for the fields that require variable contents for the data migration. To ensure maximum usability for the test case, we recommend that you assign parameters to as many fields as possible, as shown in Figures 5.47 to 5.49.

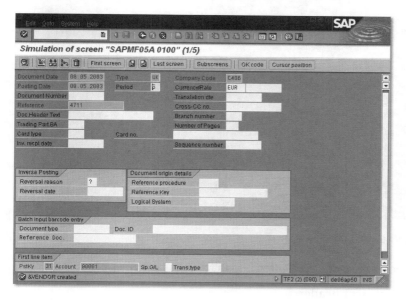

Figure 5.47 Parameterization of the Document Header

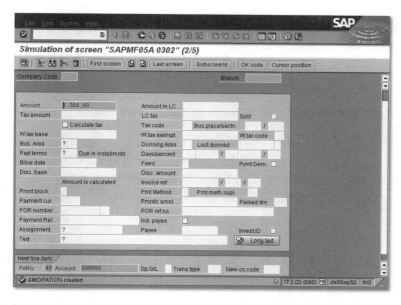

Figure 5.48 Parameterization of the Vendor Line Item

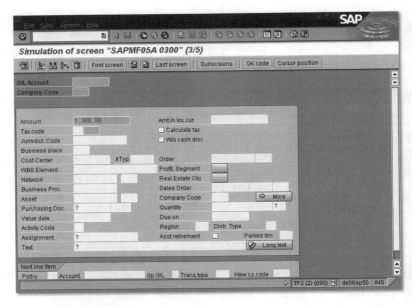

Figure 5.49 Parameterization of the G/L Line Item

As you can see in the figures, the following fields were parameterized:

▶ **Document header**
Document date, posting date, document type, company code, and reference

▶ **Document item 1**
Posting key, account, and amount

▶ **Document item 2**
Posting key, account, and amount

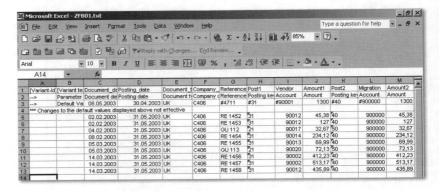

Figure 5.50 Maintaining External Variants with Excel

You can now choose menu path **Goto · Variants · Export Proposal** to download the automatically generated variant to your PC, as text file *ZFB01.txt*, and make it available for external variant processing. If you open *ZFB01.txt* with Microsoft Excel (see Figure 5.50), you can easily maintain the open credit items you want to migrate.

Processing External Variants

The greatest difficulty here is translating the vocabulary from the legacy system into the R/3 terminology. Only rarely will the postings in the legacy system be based on posting keys, which would enable a simple translation. In most cases, the postings in the legacy system will have an indicator that at least qualifies the posting in question as an invoice or credit memo. Of course, this indicator must be extracted from the legacy system together with the open items, to enable you to assign appropriate R/3 posting keys. If the posting key for posting to the vendor account is known, you can extract the posting key for the G/L account line (data transfer account; see Section 2.2.5). Furthermore, SAP R/3 does not support the entry of negative values. The posting key controls whether a value is to be interpreted as positive or negative. The data extract from the legacy system might set all vendor credit memos with a minus sign, however, which would have to be removed prior to the data migration. As these brief examples show, you will have to format the data with Microsoft Excel before you can transfer this structured data with *ZFB01.txt*. The versatile filter, copy, and replace options in Microsoft Excel make it an outstanding tool for this task.

Formatting the Data with Excel

Once you have entered your data in the *ZFB01.txt* file, you can execute test case ZFB01 with this file.

If this chapter has taught you to appreciate the CATT as an easy-to-use tool for data migration, it has served its purpose. If, however, your situation is more complex than the test cases illustrated here, thus rendering the CATT unsuitable to your needs, we suggest that you look at the next chapter. In Chapter 6, you will learn about a tool specifically designed for cases of greater complexity, namely, the Legacy System Migration Workbench or LSM Workbench.

Outlook

6   Legacy System Migration Workbench

In this chapter, you'll learn about a powerful, flexible tool that you can use to transfer data from non-SAP systems to an SAP R/3 system with minimal programming. This tool is useful whenever the structure of the legacy data differs widely from the structure in the SAP R/3 system, thus making data conversion necessary.

6.1   Overview of the LSM Workbench

The *Legacy System Migration Workbench* (also called the *LSM Workbench* and *LSMW*) has its roots in the R/2-R/3 Migration Workbench. The primary concepts and experience with R/2-R/3 migration influenced the development of the LSM Workbench.

The LSM Workbench is a powerful, SAP R/3 technology-based tool that supports both one-time and periodic data transfer from non-SAP systems (*legacy systems*) to SAP systems based on the SAP R/3 technology.[1]

The LSM Workbench features easy-to-use functions for *reading* data from files from non-SAP systems, *converting* this data to SAP formats, and *importing* the converted data into an SAP R/3 system, using the following standard SAP interfaces: batch input, direct input, BAPIs (Business Application Programming Interfaces), and IDocs (Intermediate Documents).

The LSM Workbench also has functions for recording SAP transactions (similar to those in the CATT). Consequently, you can record an entry or change a transaction and use the resulting recording as the basis for your data migration.

The LSM Workbench was based on the following principles:

▶ The LSM Workbench is not used to migrate individual tables or field contents; instead, it is used to migrate integral business data objects, such as customer masters, material masters, financial documents, and so on.

▶ The full functionality is contained within the SAP R/3 system. There should not be a collection of scattered, unrelated, difficult-to-maintain programs on different platforms.

History

Features

Basic Principles

---

1 When "SAP Systems based on R/3 technology" is mentioned, they refer to SAP R/3, SAP APO, SAP CRM, and so on.

▶ The quality and consistency of the data imported into the SAP R/3 system are more important than the speed of the data migration.

▶ No ready-made data conversion programs are provided. Instead, the necessary programs are generated from defined conversion rules.

▶ These conversion rules are reusable.

On this basis, a concept was developed that is illustrated in Figure 6.1.

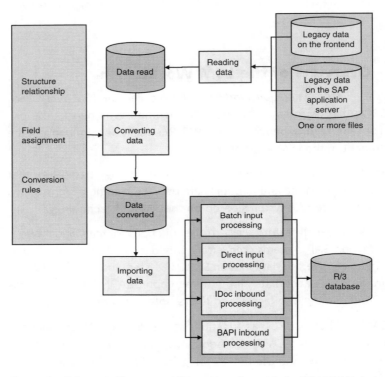

Figure 6.1 Schematic Illustration of Data Migration with the LSM Workbench

Core Functions   The LSM Workbench has the following core functions:

1. **Reading data**
   Reading data from the legacy system, which is stored in files on the frontend or the SAP application server

2. **Converting data**
   Converting the data to SAP R/3 format. The terms *converting data* and *translating data* are used synonymously.

3. **Importing data**
   Posting the data in the database of the SAP R/3 system

The main benefits of the LSM Workbench can be summarized as follows:

- ▶ It is part of the SAP R/3 system and is therefore platform-independent.
- ▶ It offers a wide range of technical data conversion options.
- ▶ It ensures data consistency via the use of standard SAP import techniques (standard interfaces).
- ▶ It generates ABAP programs from defined conversion rules.
- ▶ It offers clear user guidance.
- ▶ It supports reading the data from both the frontend and the SAP R/3 application server.
- ▶ It can record an SAP R/3 input or change transaction and use the resulting recording as the basis for data migration.
- ▶ It's available to SAP customers and partners free of charge.

If you're already familiar with the *Data Transfer Workbench* (*DX Workbench*, transaction code SXDA), you can also use the LSM Workbench in this context. The Data Transfer Workbench is described in detail in Section 10.2, especially in combination with the LSM Workbench.

The LSM Workbench can be used in any SAP system with a Basis Release 4.0 or later, but is only a standard component starting in SAP Basis Release 6.20. Therefore, the LSM Workbench is available in SAP R/3 Enterprise and in CRM 3.1 and 4.0. If your SAP system has an earlier Basis release, you will have to install the LSM Workbench separately. You can download the corresponding transport request free of charge from the SAP Service Marketplace (*https://service.sap.com/lsmw*). More information on the Data Transfer Workbench is also available at this site, in addition to the software itself.

6.2   Data Migration with the LSM Workbench

This section shows you, using a step-by-step approach and based on a specific example, how you can use the LSM Workbench to migrate data. Note that this is the most important section of the chapter.

In this example, the goal is to migrate customer master data from a legacy system to the R/3 system. This example assumes that you have already extracted the legacy data and saved it in two worksheets of an Excel file, *Customers.xls*:

- ▶ Worksheet *Customers_Headerrecord* contains a header record for every customer (see Figure 6.2).

▶ Worksheet *Customers_Contact* contains one or more records with contact person data for every customer (see Figure 6.3).

	CUSTOMER NUMBER	NAME	STREET	CITY	ZIPCODE	COUN TRY	LANG UAGE	TELEPHONE NUMBER
1								
2	1001	Alpha Hardware Market	Hauptstraße 123	Nuernberg	90455	GER	D	09256-4548-0
3	1002	Light Paradise	Ringstraße 54	Frankfurt	65936	GER	D	069-234345-0
4	1003	Weaver Industrial		High Wycombe	HP12 3TL	GBR	E	00-170866345
5	1004	Editorial Cataluña	Carrer de la Marina 34, Pl. 13	Barcelona	08005	ESP	S	34-91-556159
6	1005	France International	ZI Les Echarmeaux	Longjumeau	91230	FRA	F	0165489712

Figure 6.2 Example "Migrating Customer Master Data"—Header Records (Excerpt)

	CUSTOMER NUMBER	LASTNAME	FIRSTNAME	FORMOF ADDRESS	DEPARTMENT	POSITION	TELEPHONENUMBER CONTACT
1							
2	1001	Schmidt	Ralf	Herr	Purchasing	Head of Purchasing	09256-45485
3	1001	Huber	Luise	Frau	Purchasing	Purchaser	09256-45486
4	1002	Luchs	Harald	Herr	Organization	Head of Marketing	069-467653-145
5	1002	Wolf	Susanne	Frau	Purchasing	Head of Purchasing	069-467653-146
6	1003	Winchester	George	Mr	Executive Board	Head of Purchasing	170877755
7	1003	Smith	Judy	Ms	Finance	Head of Finance	170877756
8	1004	Lopez	Juan Carlos	Sr.	Management Board	Member of Executive Board	34-91-556153

Figure 6.3 Example "Migrating Customer Master Data"—Contact Person Records (Excerpt)

6.2.1 Getting Started with the LSM Workbench

Initial Transaction

To start working with the LSM Workbench, use Transaction LSMW. The first time you call the transaction, you'll see the LSM Workbench Welcome message shown in Figure 6.4.

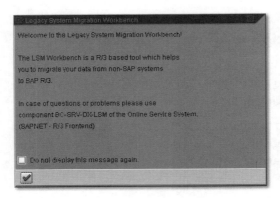

Figure 6.4 LSM Workbench—Welcome Message

When you confirm this dialog box, the initial screen opens (see Figure 6.5).

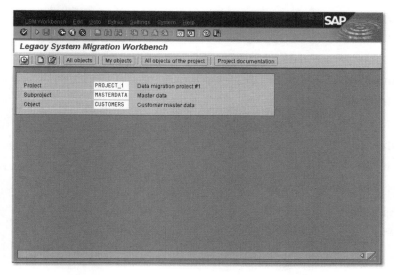

Figure 6.5 LSM Workbench—Initial Screen

As you can see in the initial screen, the data units to be migrated (also called *data migration objects*) are organized by *projects* and *subprojects* in the LSM Workbench. A project can contain any number of subprojects and a subproject can contain any number of data migration objects. You can apply this breakdown to your specific requirements.

Project, Subproject

There are no general guidelines for using these breakdown options. In this context, packing an extremely large data migration project into a single project makes as little sense as does creating hundreds of microprojects.

Our example will use the following breakdown:

Example

▶ **Project**
  ▷ ID: PROJECT_1
  ▷ Name: Data migration project #1
▶ **Subproject 1**
  ▷ ID: MASTERDATA
  ▷ Name: Master data
▶ **Subproject 2**
  ▷ ID: TRANSDATA
  ▷ Name: Transaction data

Alternatively, you could also use the following breakdown, independently of this example:

▶ **Project**
  ▶ ID: MASTERDATA
  ▶ Name: Master data

▶ **Subproject 1**
  ▶ ID: CUSTOMERS
  ▶ Name: Customer master data

▶ **Subproject 2**
  ▶ ID: VENDORS
  ▶ Name: Vendor master data

Object   A subproject can contain any number of *objects*. An object refers to a business unit of data (customer master, material master, financial documents, and so on), including all the definitions required for data migration (source, target, mapping, conversion rules, and so on).

Creating a Project/ Subproject/Object   Therefore, in this example, you must first create a project with ID PROJECT_1 and text "Data migration project #1." To do so, position the cursor in the **Project** field and click on **Create**. Enter the above data in the dialog box that opens (see Figure 6.6).

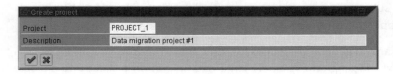

Figure 6.6   LSM Workbench—Create Project

Proceed in a similar fashion to create the subproject with ID MASTERDATA and text "Master data," as well as the subproject with ID CUSTOMERS and text "Customer master data."

You can choose any IDs for projects, subprojects, and objects up to the maximum permissible length of ten characters (SAP Basis Release 6.20 and later: 15 characters).

Useful Functions in the Initial Screen   Before you continue, you should first learn about a number of useful functions that are available in the initial screen of the LSM Workbench (see Figure 6.5):

- The **All objects** button displays an overview of all defined projects, subprojects, and objects.

- The **My objects** button displays an overview of all the objects you have created (under the current user ID).

- The **All objects of the project** button displays an overview of all sub-projects and objects of the selected project. Figure 6.7 shows this display for your project, PROJECT_1, with all subprojects and objects.

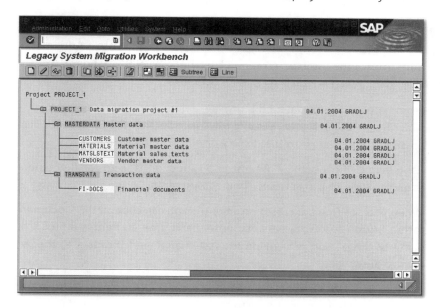

Figure 6.7 LSM Workbench—Overview of a Project

- The **Project documentation** button displays the full documentation—if any—that you have created for the individual dialog boxes and steps. You can print the project documentation, mail it, and save it in different file formats.

- The **Documentation** button enables you to enter your comments. After clicking on it, a popup appears in which you can write down your personal documentation.

- When you choose menu path **Extras Display LSMW Version**, information about the installed version of the LSM Workbench is displayed (see Figure 6.8). If you need to contact SAP Support, you must always provide this version number.

Version

Figure 6.8 LSM Workbench—Display Versions

Administration The **Administration** function goes one step further than **All Objects of the Project**. To start this function, choose menu path **Goto · Administration** from the initial screen. All the projects defined in the LSM Workbench are displayed in an overview.

From here, you can create, edit, display, delete, copy, or rename projects, subprojects, objects, and reusable rules (see Section 6.2.8). Double-click on an entry to branch to the display or edit screen for that entry.

As its name implies, the Administration function is used for the general administration of projects and their components.

When you position the cursor on an entry, you can click on the **Documentation** button to save a personal note. Each time an item is edited, the name of the person who made the last change and the date of the last change are saved.

Authorization Concept Because the LSM Workbench manipulates data in the R/3 system, access to these functions must be restricted. Fortunately, this is a simple task because the LSM Workbench is integrated in the R/3 authorization concept. You can use the four nested authorization profiles that are listed in Table 6.1 below.

These profiles aren't contained in the standard profiles of the R/3 system in SAP Basis Release 4.6C and earlier. When the LSM Workbench is installed in such systems, the profiles are created in client 000. Then, you must distribute them to the other clients.

Profile	Name	Authorizations
B_LSMW_SHO=W	Display	Display projects and their steps without switching to edit mode
B_LSMW_EXEC	Execute	Authorizations of B_LSMW_SHOW; plus: read, convert, and import data

Table 6.1 Authorization Profiles of the LSM Workbench

Profile	Name	Authorizations
B_LSMW_CHG	Change	Authorizations of B_LSMW_EXEC; plus: create and change objects
B_LSMW_ALL	Administrate	Authorization for all functions of the LSM Workbench

Table 6.1 Authorization Profiles of the LSM Workbench (continued)

6.2.2 User Guidance: The Main Steps of Data Migration

Now that you have created or selected your project, subproject, and object, click on **Enter** or **Continue** to display the user guidance for the LSM Workbench (see Figure 6.9).

From this screen, the LSM Workbench guides you through the individual steps of the data migration in the required order: You navigate from here to the individual steps and then return when you have completed the data migration. In the process, the radio button in the left margin moves to the next required step; however, you should see this as a "non-binding recommendation." If necessary, you can return at any time to any step that you have already completed. Navigation

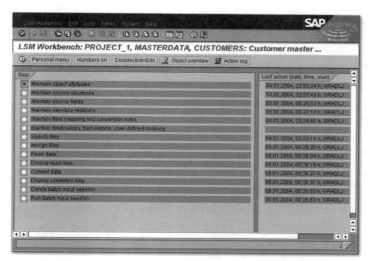

Figure 6.9 LSM Workbench—User Guidance

The following functions are available in this screen:

▶ **Execute**
Executes the step where the radio button is currently set. Alternatively, you can also double-click on an item to execute it.

▶ **Personal menu**

Lets you select your own set of steps from the ones displayed. This is advisable, for example, when you have already completed certain steps and no longer want them to appear in the list. You can also display steps that you've chosen to hide at any time. When you click on the **Main steps** button, all the processing steps that are mandatory for a data conversion are automatically activated (see Figure 6.10).

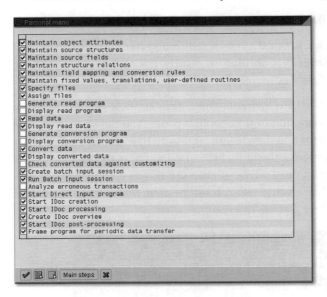

Figure 6.10 LSM Workbench—Personal Menu

▶ **Numbers on or Numbers off**

Enables you to choose whether or not you want to number the selected steps sequentially.

▶ **Double click=Display or Double click=Edit**

Use this button to define the function of a double-click: Either display mode or edit mode. If you select **Double click=Edit**, you will not have to switch from display mode to edit mode in every step.

▶ **Object overview**

Displays all the information for the select object at a glance (see Section 6.2.18).

▶ **Action log**

Displays a detailed overview (date, time, user name) of all the steps performed so far. You can use menu path **Extras · Reset Action Log** to reset the action log. This action is recorded with a reference to the user and the date.

Now, let's begin with the first step.

6.2.3 Maintaining Object Attributes

In the **Maintain object attributes** step, you define which data will be migrated and how it will be imported into the R/3 system. In the LSM Workbench terminology, this means that you select the object type and the import technique (see Figure 6.11).

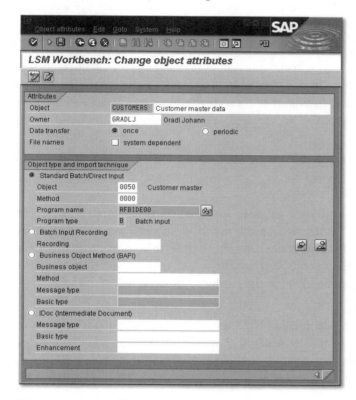

Figure 6.11 LSM Workbench—Change Object Attributes

All the settings in the **Attributes** section are already preset. In the **Object Type and Import Technique** sections, choose **Batch Input** as the import technique and use the **F4** input help to select object **Customer Master** (ID 50). When you make your selection, you see that program RFBIDE00 is used, and that it is a standard batch input program.

Object Type and Import Technique

When batch input and direct input are used, you can click on the **Display** button (eyeglasses icon) to display the documentation for the program and learn about its functions in detail.

Program Documentation

As previously mentioned, the LSM Workbench also supports other import techniques, or standard SAP interfaces. Therefore, it may make sense to use the following import techniques for various data objects:

► Customers and vendors: Batch input

► Material master: Direct input

► Purchase orders: IDoc

When choosing an import technique, you should consider the following aspects:

► **Availability**
Not all data import techniques are available for every data object. You can press the **Display Available Interfaces**[2] in the **Maintain object attributes** step to display all the available interfaces available for a data object and adopt an appropriate value (see Figure 6.12).

► **Ease of use**
The batch input technique features easy-to-use functions for postprocessing erroneous data.

► **Runtimes**
When very large data volumes are involved, direct input is preferred over batch input, because the batch input technique may result in intolerably long runtimes. A general rule to approximate the time required is 3,000-5,000 transactions per hour, albeit this value can vary widely depending on the hardware used.

► **Complexity**
If the legacy system data is structured so simply that it can be saved in a single table, the recording technique may be preferable. The mapping for this technique (see Section 6.2.7) is usually not a problem, because only a manageable number of fields have to be filled in SAP R/3.

► **Flexibility**
Use the recording technique only if the corresponding SAP transaction always uses the same screen sequence, regardless of the content of the data record. If your legacy data is structured such that a header record can have a variable number of item records, the recording technique is not applicable.

---

2 Available from LSMW Version 1.7.2; not shown in Figure 6.11.

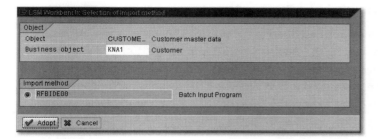

Figure 6.12 LSM Workbench—Display Available Interfaces for a Business Object

Please note that if you apply import technique BAPI or IDoc, the program checks during the save operation whether a *partner agreement* is already available for the preset partner (see Section 6.7) and the selected message type. If not, the system attempts to create it.

In addition to the main settings for object type and import technique, you can also maintain a number of other useful attributes in this step (see Figure 6.11), for example, enter a text for an object or change an existing text.

Other Object Attributes

By entering data into the **Owner** field, you add the project to the list of all projects you created. You can display it afterwards in the initial screen under **My Objects**.

Owner

You can use this field for a "mini-workflow" as described below:

"Mini-Workflow"

▶ User 1 executes steps 1, 2, and 3 and changes the owner to user 2.

▶ User 2 executes steps 4, 5, and 6 and changes the owner to user 3, and so on.

Accordingly, you can see who is performing a step (or has to perform it) at any time.

You can also define whether the data transfer will be one-time or periodic; one-time data transfer is the normal case. In the event of periodic data transfer, you cannot read files from the frontend. In this case, the list of steps contains the additional step **Main program for periodic data transfer** (see Section 6.5).

Periodic Data Transfer

You can also choose whether you want the file names to be *system-dependent*. If you do, you can enter separate file names for each SAP R/3 system later on. This is especially useful when you have to migrate data into several SAP R/3 systems.

System-Dependent File Names

After you've defined that you want to migrate customer data using the batch input technique, you can begin to define the legacy data.

6.2.4 Maintaining Source Structures

Knowledge of the Legacy Data Structure is Needed

In the procedures described in the previous chapters, you were responsible for converting the data to SAP R/3 format. The SAP R/3 system didn't require any information on the format of the data exported from the legacy system. Because the LSM Workbench is responsible for converting the data here, it must know the structure of the data in the legacy system.

Two Record Types

The legacy data for an application object usually consists of one or more *record types*. Typical record types are the header record and the item record. These record types are called *source structures* in the LSM Workbench. Two record types are involved in the example: The header record for each customer (see Figure 6.2) and the contact record for each contact person (see Figure 6.3), which, formally speaking, is an item record, because each customer can have any number of contact persons.

In the **Maintain source structures** step of data migration, you must define the source structures of the object, with name, text, and hierarchical relationships. Therefore, in the navigation screen (see Figure 6.9), choose **Maintain source structures**, click on the **Create** button, and create a source structure with ID and text "Customer—header record." Then, position the cursor on the source structure that you just created and click on **Create** again. The system asks whether the second source structure will be of *equal rank* or *subordinate*. Choose **Subordinate** and enter the ID CONTACT and the text "Customer—contact person record." The result is shown in Figure 6.13.

Equal Ranking or Subordinate?

When should you choose "equal ranking" or "subordinate"? Typically, record type 2 is "subordinate" to record type 1 when exactly one record with record type 1 exists for each record with record type 2. In the example, this means that each contact person record has exactly one corresponding header record, however, the reverse does not apply. Each header record can have one contact partner record, or several, or no contact partner records.

Other Functions

In addition, this step contains functions that can create new source structures, and change, move, and delete existing structures. Pushbuttons are provided for each of these functions.

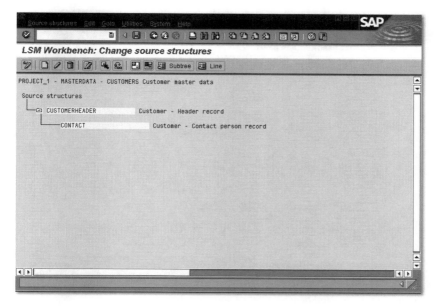

Figure 6.13 LSM Workbench—Change Source Structures

6.2.5 Maintaining the Source Fields

Typically, a source structure consists of several fields. These fields are called *source fields* in the LSM Workbench.

In this step—**Maintaining source fields**—you create the source fields for the source structures you created in the previous step and set the necessary attributes (see Figure 6.9).

Defining Source Fields and Attributes

In the example, you have to define the fields **CUSTOMERNUMBER**, **NAME**, **STREET**, **CITY**, and so on for source structure CUSTOMER-HEADER. This means you model the structure of your legacy data (see Figures 6.2 and 6.3) in the LSM Workbench.

A source field in the LSM Workbench is described by its field name, text, field length, and field type. You can enter this information individually, field by field.

Attributes of a Source Field

If you wanted to use this method, you must position the cursor on header structure CUSTOMERHEADER, click on the **Create Field** button, and enter the required attributes for the **CUSTOMERNUMBER** field. Then, position the cursor on source field **CUSTOMERNUMBER**, click on the **Create Field** button again, and enter the required attributes for the **NAME** field, and so on, until you reach the same results shown in Figure 6.14.

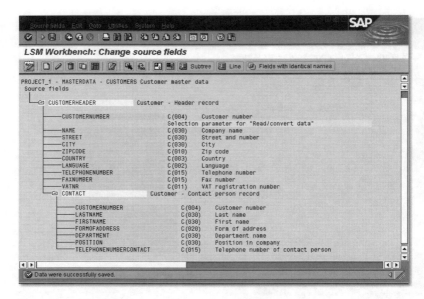

Figure 6.14 LSM Workbench—Change Source Fields

The individual options for defining and maintaining the source fields are described in the following sections.

Creating Individual Source Fields

As we already mentioned, position the cursor on a source structure or existing source field and click on **Create Field**. The dialog box shown in Figure 6.15 opens.

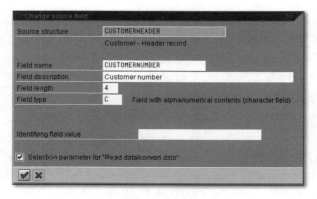

Figure 6.15 LSM Workbench—Create Source Fields

You can define the field length as required. You can use the **F4** input help to select the field type (see Figure 6.16).

If you define a field as a date field (field types DDMY, DMDY, or DYMD) or amount field (field types AMT1, AMT2, AMT3, or AMT4), you can choose later when you read the data (see Section 6.2.13) whether you want to convert date values to the internal date format (YYYYMMDD — four-digit date, followed by two-digit month, followed by two-digit day) and amount fields to the calculation format (1234.56 — no thousand separators, decimal point).

Date Fields, Amount Fields

If a file contains legacy data for multiple source structures, the LSM Workbench will need additional information on how to identify a record. To do so, you must enter a value in the **Identifying field value** field that can be used to determine which source structure belongs to that record. You can specify identifying field contents for only one field in each source structure.

Identifying Field Values

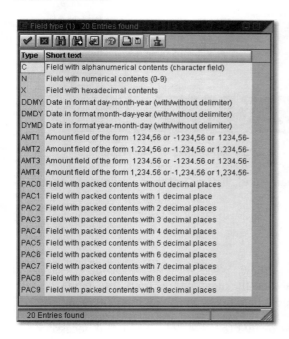

Figure 6.16 LSM Workbench — Possible Types of Source Fields

You can set a flag for the fields of structures in the top hierarchy level — the fields of source structure CUSTOMERHEADER in the example — in the **Selection parameter for "Read data/Convert data."** If you set this flag, the corresponding field is made available as a selection parameter during steps **Read data** and **Convert data**. The flag is normally used to limit the scope of data during tests (see Figure 6.15).

Selection Parameters

Maintaining Source Fields in Table Form

Instead of maintaining each source field individually, you can also maintain all the fields of a source structure at once. To do so, position the cursor on a source structure or existing source field in Figure 6.14 and click on **Table Maintenance**. A screen like the one shown in Figure 6.17 opens.

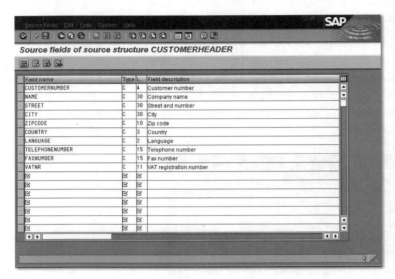

Figure 6.17 LSM Workbench—Maintain Source Fields in Table Form

Default Values When you enter a field name and click on **Enter**, the following values are proposed:

▶ Field type: C

▶ Field length: 10

▶ Field text: If there is a domain (see Section 6.8.4) in the SAP R/3 system whose name matches the field name, then, the name of this domain is proposed as the field text; otherwise, the field name is used.

Of course, you can always overwrite these default values if necessary.

Copying Source Fields from Other Sources

In order to reduce the manual maintenance effort required, the LSM Workbench also supports options for copying descriptions of source fields from other sources. To copy source fields from other sources, position the cursor on a source structure or existing source field in Figure 6.14 and click on **Copy Source Fields**. You are prompted to select a source in the dialog box shown in Figure 6.18.

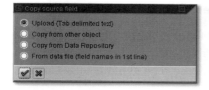

Figure 6.18 LSM Workbench—Copy Source Fields

The following sources are available:

▶ **Upload (Tab delimited text)**

In this case, the system expects the texts of the source fields in a text file whose columns are separated by tabs, like the one shown in Figure 6.19.

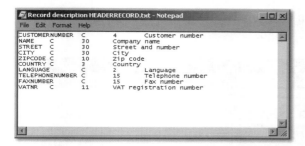

Figure 6.19 LSM Workbench—Copy Source Fields from Text File (Tab Delimited Text)

▶ **Copy from other object**

You can also copy source fields from the source structure of another object in the LSM Workbench. If you choose this variant, in the next step, you're prompted to select the corresponding object (specifically: project, subproject, object).

▶ **Copy from Data Repository**

You can copy the source fields from a structure of the ABAP Dictionary in the SAP R/3 system. If you choose this variant, in the next step, you're prompted to select the required structure in the ABAP Dictionary.

▶ **From data file (field names in 1st line)**

You can copy the source fields from a file that contains the corresponding legacy data. This file must be available on the PC in **Text (Tab-Delimited) (*.txt)** format and contain the field names in the first line. In the process, field type C is assigned as the field type and the field name is the field text, while the field length is set to the length of the longest field contents.

6.2.6 Maintaining Structure Relations

As we discussed in Section 6.2.4, data for an object in the legacy system consists of one or more record types, which are called *source structures* in the LSM Workbench. Consequently, the record types of the target format, R/3 format, are called *target structures*.

Relationships Between Source and Target Structures

In the data migration step **Maintain structure relations**, you define the relationships between source and target structures. Here, you determine the possible target structures when you select the object type and the import technique (see Figure 6.11).

In this case, this means your selection **Customers/Standard batch input** implicitly specified the format the data must have in order to enable processing by batch input program `RFBIDE00`. You can see the result when you call step **Maintain structure relations** (see Figure 6.20) in the navigation screen (see Figure 6.9).

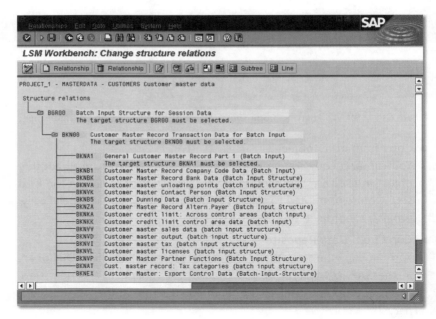

Figure 6.20 LSM Workbench—Change Structure Relations—Initial State

Required Target Structures

Typically, there are target structures that have to be selected (*required structures*). In this case, the following note is displayed: "The target structure _____ must be selected." (See Figure 6.21.)

To define structure relations, position the cursor on a target structure and click on the **Relationship** button. A dialog box opens, displaying the existing source structures for selection. If you want to change a relationship, first delete the existing relationship. A pushbutton is also provided for this purpose.

In addition, you can use **Check** to check the structural relationships for errors. The status bar then displays an error message or the message: "The structural relationships do not contain any errors."

Checking the Structure Relations

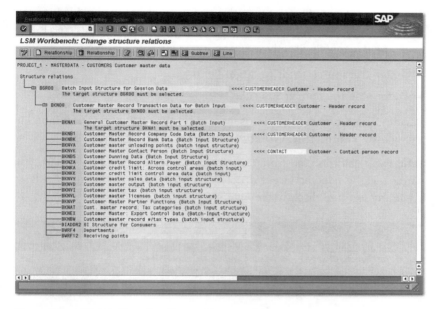

Figure 6.21 LSM Workbench—Change Structure Relations

In the example, you will assign header structure CUSTOMERHEADER to each of the target structures BGR00, BKN00, BKNA1, and BKNB1, and source structure CONTACT to target structure BKNVK. The result is shown in Figure 6.21.

Choose Your Target Structures Well

Conversely, your definitions mean that the customers you will create in the R/3 system will *not* contain a lot of information, namely, all the information contained the structures that you did not select—bank data, unloading points, dunning data, alternative payer, and so on.

In conclusion, we should add that many batch input and direct input programs use a control record named BGR00 or BI000. We highly recommend that you always assign the top-level source structure (header structure) to this control record.

Control Records

6.2.7 Maintaining Field Mapping and Conversion Rules

Step Requiring the Most Effort

You have now come to the data migration step that usually requires the most effort. Please note that thus far, you have only modeled the structure of the legacy data in the LSM Workbench and described the relationships between the legacy system and the R/3 system at the structural level. You will now continue at the level of the individual fields.

Two Steps in One

Therefore, the specific activity in this step is to assign source fields to the target fields, and define how to convert the field contents. This step is also called *field mapping*. Strictly speaking, two steps are involved:

▶ Assign the source fields to target fields

▶ Determine the conversion rules

Because these two steps are closely related, they have been combined in a single step in the LSM Workbench.

All Target Fields at a Glance

When you call this step from the navigation screen (see Figure 6.9), you can see all the selected target structures, and their corresponding fields, in a hierarchical tree display (see Figure 6.22).

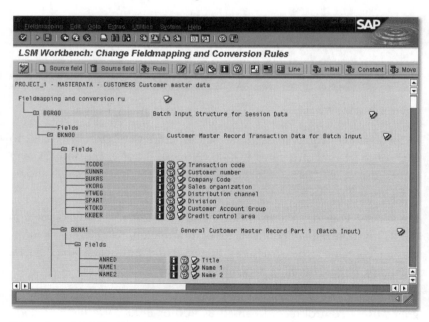

Figure 6.22 LSM Workbench—Field Mapping—Initial State

Because all the available target fields are now displayed, you can begin mapping the source fields to target fields, initially "on paper." This preparatory step is usually the user departments' responsibility, with the possible assistance of SAP consultants, as the necessary application skills are available there.

In the example, you arrive at the following results:

No.	Target field	Source field	Conversion rule
1	BKN00-TCODE	—	Constant XD01
2	BKN00-KUNNR	CUSTOMERHEADER-CUSTOMERNUMBER	Prefix 9
3	BKN00-BUKRS	—	Fixed value FV_BUKRS
4	BKN00-KTOKD	—	Constant 0001
5	BKNA1-NAME1	CUSTOMERHEADER-NAME	Transfer (MOVE)
6	BKNA1-SORTL	CUSTOMERHEADER-NAME	Transfer (MOVE)
7	BKNA1-STRAS	CUSTOMERHEADER-STREET	Transfer (MOVE)
8	BKNA1-ORT01	CUSTOMERHEADER-CITY	Transfer (MOVE)
9	BKNA1-PSTLZ	CUSTOMERHEADER-ZIPCODE	Transfer (MOVE)
10	BKNA1-LAND1	CUSTOMERHEADER-COUNTRY	Translation
11	BKNA1-SPRAS	CUSTOMERHEADER-LANGUAGE	Translation
12	BKNA1-TELF1	CUSTOMERHEADER-TELEPHONENUMBER	Transfer (MOVE)
13	BKNA1-TELFX	CUSTOMERHEADER-FAXNUMBER	Transfer (MOVE)
14	BKNA1-STCEG	CUSTOMERHEADER-VATNR	Transfer (MOVE)
15	BKNB1-AKONT	—	Constant 140000
16	BKNVK-NAME1	CONTACT-LASTNAME	Transfer (MOVE)
17	BKNVK-TELF1	CONTACT-TELEPHONENUMBER-CONTACT	Transfer (MOVE)
18	BKNVK-ABTNR	CONTACT-DEPARTMENT	Translation
19	BKNVK-NAMEV	CONTACT-FIRSTNAME	Transfer (MOVE)

Table 6.2 "Mapping on Paper"—Mapping and Conversion Rules for Customer Master Data

No.	Target field	Source field	Conversion rule
20	BKNVK-ANRED	CONTACT-FORMOFADDRESS	Transfer (MOVE)
21	BKNVK-PAFKT	CONTACT-POSITION	Translation

Table 6.2 "Mapping on Paper"—Mapping and Conversion Rules for Customer Master Data (continued)

Fields of Control Structure BGR00

Attentive readers will surely not have overlooked the fact that Table 6.2 does not contain a single field from control structure BGR00. This is because the LSM Workbench considers all the fields of this structure to be "technical fields" and presets them automatically. As a rule, no changes are required for these fields.

Once you have completed your "mapping on paper," the major part of your work is finished. Now, you only have to define this information in the LSM Workbench. The procedure is shown in the following table. The sequence number in the first column refers to the sequence number in Table 6.2.

No.	Activity
1	Position the cursor on field BKN00-TCODE in Figure 6.22. Click on **Rule**. Select the **Constant** rule in the dialog box shown in Figure 6.23. Enter "XD01" in the next dialog box and confirm your entries.
2	Position the cursor on field BKN00-KUNNR in Figure 6.22. Click on **Assign Target Field**. Double-click to select CUSTOMERHEADER-CUSTOMERNUMBER from the list of possible source fields. Click on **Rule**. Select the **Prefix** rule in the dialog box shown in Figure 6.23. Enter "9" in the next dialog box and confirm your entries.
3	Position the cursor on field BKN00-BUKRS in Figure 6.22. Click on **Rule**. Select the **Fixed Value (Reusable)**[3] rule in the dialog box shown in Figure 6.23. The LSM Workbench proposes BUKRS for the name. Adopt this proposal. You can enter the specific value in the next dialog box. Use this option and enter "0001".
4	Analogous to 1

Table 6.3 Implementing the "Mapping on Paper" in the LSM Workbench

---

3 These "reusable rules" are described in detail in Section 6.2.8.

No.	Activity
5	Position the cursor on field BKNA1-NAME1 in Figure 6.22. Click on **Assign Target Field**. Double-click to select CUSTOMERHEADER-NAME from the list of possible source fields. Because the LSM Workbench automatically selects rule **Transfer (MOVE)**, you don't have to configure any other settings.
6	Analogous to 5 In this case, however, the source field is longer than the target field. This means the content of the source field will be cut off during the migration.
7	Analogous to 5
8	Analogous to 5
9	Analogous to 5
10	Position the cursor on field BKNA1-LAND1 in Figure 6.22. Click on **Assign Target Field**. Double-click to select CUSTOMERHEADER-COUNTRY from the list of possible source fields. Click on **Rule**. Select the **Translation (Reusable)** rule in the dialog box shown in Figure 6.23. The LSM Workbench proposes LAND1 for the name. Adopt this proposal.
11	Analogous to 10
12	Analogous to 5
13	Analogous to 5
14	Analogous to 5
15	Analogous to 1
16	Analogous to 5
17	Analogous to 5
18	Analogous to 10
19	Analogous to 5
29	Analogous to 5
21	Analogous to 10

Table 6.3 Implementing the "Mapping on Paper" in the LSM Workbench (continued)

When you follow the directions in Table 6.3, you will notice that the LSM Workbench translates your instructions into ABAP coding. It also lets you change or supplement this ABAP coding as needed, however, this isn't required in the example.

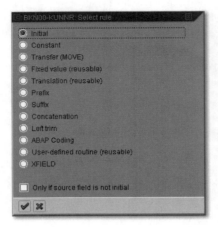

Figure 6.23   LSM Workbench—Predefined Conversion Rules

Summary   You have now processed all the instructions from Table 6.3. The result of your efforts is shown in Figures 6.24 and 6.25. Therefore, you have a complete picture of the data migration process. We should point out that the initial fields are hidden in the diagrams. This was performed using the **Display Variant** button, which you read about in detail in Section 6.8.1.

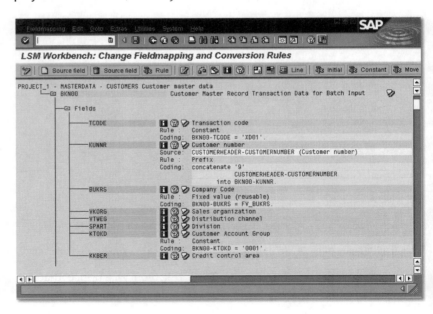

Figure 6.24   LSM Workbench—Field Mapping (Excerpt 1)

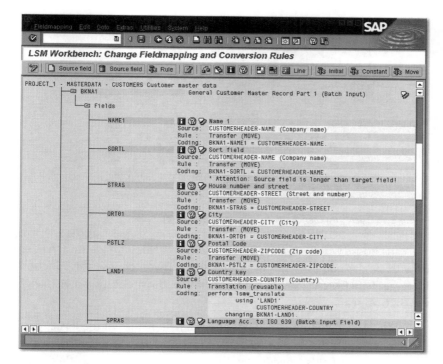

Figure 6.25 LSM Workbench—Field Mapping (Excerpt 2)

At the same time, you can see whether your efforts have proved successful. To do so, click on **Check Syntax** (see Figure 6.25). This enables you to exit the LSM Workbench in order to generate the data conversion program and ensure that it has the correct syntax. When you have done everything correctly, the success message appears in the status bar: "The data conversion program was generated." If you use predefined rules exclusively and don't add any user-defined coding, syntax errors are unlikely.

Syntax Check

You now know the most important functions of the **Maintain field mapping and conversion rules** step. Other useful functions are also available, the most important of which are introduced below.

Other Useful Functions

Auto-fieldmapping is an extremely useful function. If you choose **Extras • Auto-Fieldmapping** in Figure 6.22, the LSM Workbench proposes assignments for all your source and target fields.

Auto-Field-mapping

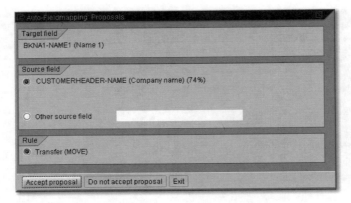

Figure 6.26 LSM Workbench—Auto-Fieldmapping: Proposals

You can choose whether you want to search for fields with identical names or with similar names (with hit probability[4]). If you choose this function for target field BKNA1-NAME1 in the example, the proposal shown in Figure 6.26 appears.

If you are working with many fields and the field names of the legacy system (specifically: the source fields) are identical with (or similar to) the SAP R/3 system fields (specifically: the target structures), auto-fieldmapping can help you to accelerate your work. Furthermore, you don't have to call the function individually for each field; instead, you can tab through all the fields using the cursor, or even navigate through all the fields of all target structures, with or without a confirmation after every step.

Technical Fields   Some target fields are preset by the system. These fields are called *technical fields* and are marked with rule type **Default setting**. The conversion rules for the fields are not displayed in the field-mapping at first; however, you can display them (see Figure 6.25) by pressing the **Display Variant** push-button (see Section 6.8.1). Changing the default setting may seriously affect the flow of the data conversion. If you inadvertently change the default settings, you can restore them by selecting **Extras · Restore default**.

Information for Each Target Field   The following information is displayed for each target field (see Figure 6.25):

▶ R/3 field text

▶ Any assigned source fields

---
4   The hit probability is the measure of similarity between two words. The more similar the words are, the higher the hit probability. Accordingly, the hit probability for two identical words will be 100%.

- Rule type (fixed value, translation, and so on)
- Coding

In addition, the following functions are available for each source and target field:

Functions in Each Source and Target Field

- **Field Documentation**
  Short documentation is displayed for the target field on which the cursor is positioned. This documentation may contain links to additional information.
- **Possible Values**
  A list of all possible values for this target field is displayed. Whether this list is available depends on the definition of the target field in the Data Dictionary.
- **Documentation**
  You can maintain the documentation for a field or other object, and explain the conversion rule in more detail, if necessary.
- **Source Fields Not Assigned**
  When working with many fields, you can lose track of which source fields you have already assigned and which source fields you have not assigned. **Choose Extras · Source Fields Not Assigned** (see Figure 6.25) to display the source fields that have not yet been assigned.
- **Remove the Assignment of a Source Field**
  To remove a source field assigned, position the cursor on a target field in the tree structure and select **Remove Source Field**. If only one source field has been assigned, this field is removed. If several source fields have been assigned, a list of all assigned source fields is displayed. You can then select the corresponding source field by double-clicking on it.

Several of the predefined conversion rules for the step **Maintain field mapping and conversion rules** (see Figure 6.23) are described in detail below.

Predefined Conversion Rules

Initial

This deletes the coding assigned to a target field, and all the source fields that are assigned to the target field. Lastly, the target field is set to an initial value, which can differ depending on the selected import technique:

Resetting a Field

- **Standard batch input/standard direct input**
  The target field is set to the value of the character for "No data," called the "nodata character," which is usually defined in the control record (BGR00, BI000) and set to the default value "/".

▶ **Batch input recording**
The target field is filled with "/" as the nodata character.

▶ **BAPI, Idoc**
The ABAP CLEAR command is applied to the target field, filling character fields with blanks and numeric fields with zeros.

Constant

The target field is assigned a fixed value.

Transfer (MOVE)

Assignment   You transfer data from the source field to the target field with ABAP statement MOVE. The statement has the following function, depending on the field type (see Figure 6.16):

Field type	Type of transfer
C (character)	1:1 transfer
N (numeric)	1:1 transfer, including any leading zeros
Packed field	Pack in target field using the ABAP statement WRITE ... TO ...
Date field	A dialog box opens, prompting you to transfer the date field: Internal format (YYYYMMDD) User format (such as 01/30/2003)
Amount field	If batch input or direct input is used, the amount value is formatted according to the settings in the user master. If BAPIs or IDocs are used, the amount value remains in the internal format.

Table 6.4 Type of Data Transfer Based on Field Type

Moreover, the conversion rules that apply to the ABAP MOVE command also reach the application. For more details, refer to the corresponding documentation in the SAP R/3 system.

Fixed Value (Reusable)

The target field is assigned a "fixed value object," that is, a variable whose name begins with "FV_". This variable is set to a specific value in the step **Maintain fixed values, translations, and user-defined routines**. Fixed values are reusable, therefore, you can use them in multiple objects in a project, which is in direct contrast to constants. You only have to define the specific value once.

In the example, you used a fixed value for the **Company Code** field. Assume that you want to migrate data for different company codes in sequence. You can use the corresponding fixed value in different objects, however, you have to set the specific value only once, which is the primary advantage that fixed values have over constants. Therefore, a fixed value can be considered as a constant that is valid project-wide.

Constants Valid Project-Wide

Translation (Reusable)

The target field is assigned coding, which converts the field contents of the source field based on a translation table. You can enter values of this translation table in the step **Maintain fixed values, translations, and user-defined routines** (see Figure 6.9). This procedure is described in detail in Section 6.2.8.

Prefix

You can specify any prefix to precede the contents of the source field.

Suffix

You can specify any suffix to follow the contents of the source field.

Concatenation

You can join two or more source fields and transfer the merged values to the target field.

Joining Two Source Fields

Transfer Left Trim

The field contents are transferred left justified.

ABAP Coding

When you choose this option (or double-click on a target field), the ABAP editor starts. You can now edit generated ABAP coding or write and save your own coding. Most of the functions in the standard SAP editor are available here—such as **Syntax Check**, **Pretty Printer**, and so on.

Click on the **Insert button** to add the following to your coding:

► **Source fields**: All available source fields are displayed for selection.
► **Global variables**: See Section 6.8.2.
► **Global functions**: See Section 6.8.3.

User-Defined Routine (Reusable)

User-Defined Subroutine The system creates the frame of a form routine (ABAP subroutine) with the name prefix "UR_". This routine is reusable, which means you can also use it in other objects of the project. This represents the difference to ABAP coding, which you can define for a target field.

Names for Reusable Rules For all kinds of reusable rules, the LSM Workbench proposes one to three possible names. One name is recommended by the system. We recommend using the proposed name. For detailed information on naming conventions, see Section 6.8.4.

When creating user-defined routines, observe the following:

▶ You must assign the correct number of source fields first (according to the number of input parameters in the routine).

▶ You must assign the source fields in the proper sequence (that is, in the sequence of the parameters).

X-FIELD

X-Field in IDoc Processing This is a special function for processing IDocs. In some cases, a *checkbox structure* exists in addition to the data transfer structure (where the values to be transferred appear). This checkbox structure has the same field names as the data transfer structure, but all the fields in the structure have a length of 1 and are set to X or blank. These checkboxes determined whether the corresponding field is copied from the data transfer structure.

The following coding is generated automatically for an X-field:

```
IF NOT <field in the data transfer structure> IS INITIAL.
      <field in X-structure> = 'X'.
ELSE.
      <field in X-structure> = '  '.
ENDIF.
```

Filling X-Structures You can use menu path **Extras · Fill X-Structures** (see Figure 6.22) to insert this coding for entire target structures.

Only If Source Field Is Not Initial

The dialog box with the predefined rules (see Figure 6.23) contains a checkbox: **Only if Source Field Is Not Initial**. If you set this flag, the selected rule will be applied only if the source field in question contains a non-initial value.

6.2.8 Maintaining Fixed Values, Translations, and User-Defined Routines

You will now learn how to edit the reusable rules of a project.

You used the following reusable rules in the example: Fixed value FV_ **Reusable Rules**
BUKRS for the **Company Code** field and translations for the fields **Country**, **Language**, **Department**, and **Position**.

When you call the step **Maintain fixed values, translations and user-defined routines** (see Figure 6.9), the screen template shown in Figure 6.27 opens.

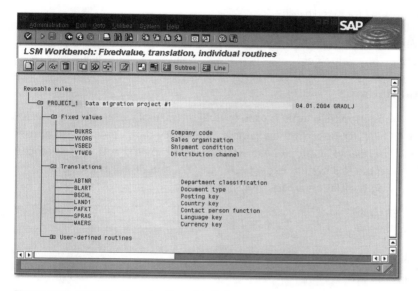

Figure 6.27   LSM Workbench—Reusable Rules

Alternatively, you can also double-click on a rule in step **Maintain Field Mapping and Conversion Rules** (see Figure 6.9) to maintain that rule.

Fixed Value

Here you can specify the length, type, flag for lowercase/uppercase, and value, in addition to the description of the fixed value.

In the example, you already assigned the value 0001 for fixed value FV_ BUKRS in the previous step. If you have not done so yet, you can catch up now. To do so, position the cursor on entry "BUKRS" and click on **Process entry** or, alternatively, double-click on the entry. The dialog box shown in Figure 6.28 opens.

Figure 6.28 LSM Workbench—Fixed Value

Input Help We should also mention that the **F4** key is a very useful tool for getting help on any value field.

Translation

The translation technique is used several times in our example, such as for the COUNTRY field. In the example, the legacy data contains the entries GER (Germany), GBR, (Great Britain), ESP (Spain), and FRA (France). Because the R/3 system expects DE, GB, ES, and FR for these values, the following translation is required:

- ▶ GER → DE
- ▶ GBR → GB
- ▶ ESP → ES
- ▶ FRA → FR

This is exactly what the translation rule does. Several steps are required to define a translation rule (see Figures 6.29 to 6.31):

- ▶ **Source field, target field**
  You can enter information on the source field and target field here. If you want to create a new translation, you must save your entries first before you can go to the next tab page.

- ▶ **Control**
  You can define the translation type here. You can specify which of the two translation tables will be searched for a value first (Variant) and which alternative (First Alternative, Second Alternative) will be selected if no suitable entry is found (see Figure 6.30). In the example, the default settings are sufficient: If the search in the 1:1 translation table fails, the target field remains initial.

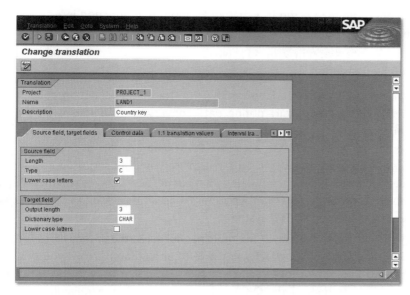

Figure 6.29 LSM Workbench—Translation: Source Field, Target Field

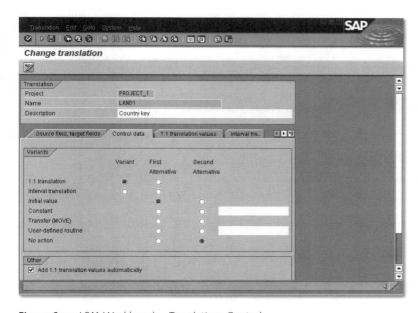

Figure 6.30 LSM Workbench—Translation: Control

▶ **1:1 translation values**

Here you specify the value table to be used during translation. You can also upload the values from a PC file in **Text (Tab-Delimited) (*.txt)** format. To do so, click on **Upload**.

Another big help is the fact that an **F4** input help function is available for the **New value** column.

Please note that only values for which the OK flag was set are included during translation.

An especially useful function is that the translation function collects the values automatically during data conversion. This means all the various values in the source fields are collected when you perform the conversion data step (see Section 6.2.15). The benefits of this feature cannot be overemphasized. In most cases, you'll be surprised at how many entries have accumulated in your legacy data over time. To ensure a proper conversion, you must map all these values to values accepted by the SAP R/3 system.

In the example, the conversion table has collected the entries ESP, FRA, GBR, and GER for COUNTRY in the left-hand column. Now, you only have to enter the proper values in the right column, with the aid of input help, and check the **OK** fields. The result is shown in Figure 6.31.

You have to set the checkbox **Add 1:1 translation values automatically** (see Figure 6.30) in order to activate the automatic value collector.

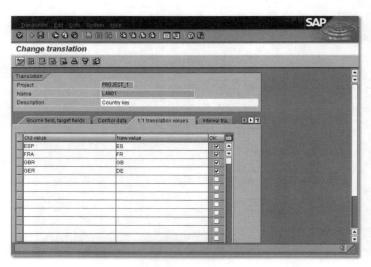

Figure 6.31 LSM Workbench—Translation—1:1 Translation Values

▶ **Interval Translation Values**

Here you specify the value table to be used during translation by intervals. An upload option and **F4** input help are also available. Furthermore, only values that were checked in the **OK** field are included here.

This translation feature is only rarely used. One possible application case is when you want to merge different groups of accounts from a number interval (old value) to new respective accounts (new value) when cleaning up a chart of accounts.

User-Defined Routine

As previously mentioned, you can add any coding to any target field. If your specific situation requires you to use such ABAP coding at various junctures within a project, you might want to use a user-defined routine.

Assume that the phone numbers in your legacy data contain illegal characters that you must remove. Because phone numbers are used in different places in the SAP R/3 system and can also be part of external correspondence, we highly recommend that you clean up these illegal characters.

Example: Processing Phone Numbers

In the overview of reusable rules (see Figure 6.27), position the cursor on label **User-defined routines** and click on **Create**. In the dialog box that opens (see Figure 6.32), enter the name and description and click on **Enter** to confirm.

Creating a User-Defined Routine

Figure 6.32 LSM Workbench—User-Defined Routine—Name and Description

Another dialog box opens (see Figure 6.33) in which you are prompted to enter the number of input and output parameters. In the example, you must pass one phone number to the routine and get a "cleaned up" phone number back. Enter a "1" in both fields and click on **Enter** to confirm.

Maintaining Input and Output Parameters

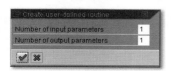

Figure 6.33 LSM Workbench—User-Defined Routine—Number of Parameters

You now see the ABAP editor, where the LSM Workbench has already provided a frame that you can now fill with your own ABAP coding. All the familiar functions in the ABAP editor (Pretty Printer, syntax check, and so on) are available here.

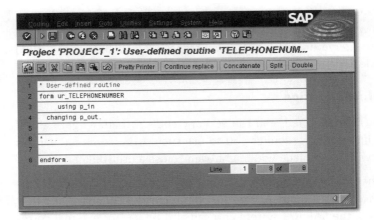

Figure 6.34 LSM Workbench—User-Defined Routine—Frame for ABAP Coding

The result is shown in Figure 6.35. You can now use this routine as part of the field mapping anywhere within the project.

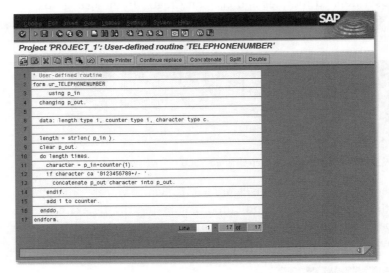

Figure 6.35 LSM Workbench—User-Defined Routine—Finished ABAP Coding

6.2.9 Addendum: Files

Before you continue with the steps that involve files in the LSM Workbench, read about the attributes that you can use to describe these files, as well as the types of files supported in the LSM Workbench.

File Structures Data can be saved in files in different ways. For a program to process these files correctly, the following file information has to be available:

▶ **End-of-record indicator or fixed record length** Record Delimiter
There are different ways to determine where one record ends and the next record begins within a file. The LSM Workbench supports the following three options:

▷ **End-of-record indicator:** Most common delimiter. It is used whenever the file is created with a text editor or exported from a spreadsheet program. Files with end-of-record indicators are also called *text files*.

▷ **Fixed record length:** Each record has the same length in bytes. This is frequently the case when the data has been exported from a mainframe application.

▷ **Hexadecimal length field (4 bytes) at start of record:** This delimiter is used for records in R/2-R/3 data migration.

▶ **Table or sequential file** Structure of the File Contents
There are two basic options for the contents of a file:

▷ The file contents can have a *table-like character*. This occurs when all the records in the file have the same structure, that is, all the records in the file belong to the same source structure.

▷ If the file contains *records for different source structures*, you need to determine which records belong together. The only logical way to do this is via looking at the sequence. In this case, the file is called *sequential*.

▶ **Separator** Field Delimiter
Use the following options to determine when one field ends and the next field begins:

▷ **Separator:** A defined separator is inserted between two fields. Typical separators are tabs (tab-delimited), commas (comma separated file), and semicolons. In practice, the use of commas or semicolons as separators often causes problems, because these characters can appear in text fields, which produces undesired results.

▷ **No separator:** The LSM Workbench uses the defined source structure as a template; this information determines the field delimiters for the fields.

▶ **Field names at the start of the file**
The field names may appear at the start of the file. When table-like files are involved, this information can be used to assign the file content to the source fields. Consequently, the sequence of the source fields within the source structure doesn't necessarily have to map to the

sequence of the columns in the file; however, the system does expect to find separators between the individual fields.

▶ **Character set (code page)**
If your legacy system runs in a different operating-system environment than does your SAP R/3 system, the data in the legacy system may be encoded in a character set that the SAP R/3 system cannot interpret. In this case, the code page must be converted, which the LSM Workbench does automatically. To enable this automatic conversion, you must specify the character set used to encode the data in the legacy system. Easy-to-use input help is also available.

When you work with files on the frontend, we recommend that you use the **Text (Tab-Delimited) (*.txt)** format. There are three advantages to using this type of file:

▶ You can generate these files in all widely-used spreadsheet programs (such as Microsoft Excel).

▶ Uploading the text files into the R/3 system is much faster than uploading files in the original format of the spreadsheet program (such as *.xls).

▶ The tab character doesn't usually appear in the data. In contrast, field values may contain commas and semicolons. Therefore, when you choose semicolons as your separator and your data contains a semicolon, this semicolon will be interpreted incorrectly as a separator—with the likely consequence that the data record in question cannot be processed properly.

6.2.10 Specifying Files

You have now come to the step where you describe the files that will be used in all the subsequent steps and specify them in the system.

Specifically, the following files are involved:

▶ The files on the PC and/or SAP application server that contain your legacy data

▶ Two internal work files from the LSM Workbench:

▶ The file for the read data

▶ The file for the converted data

In our example, the legacy data is available in two worksheets of an Excel file. Before you can specify them in the LSM Workbench, you must save each worksheet in **Text (Tab-Delimited) (*.txt)** format. Enter the names *Customers_Headerrecord.txt* and *Customers_Contact.txt* (see Figure 6.36).

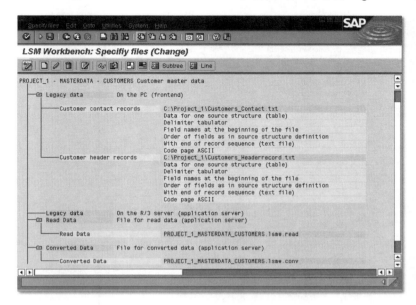

Figure 6.36 LSM Workbench—Specify Files

Legacy Data on the Frontend (PC)

In this example, you assume that all the legacy data is available on your PC. Therefore, proceed as follows:

▶ In the navigation screen (see Figure 6.9), choose the step **Specify Files**.

▶ In Edit mode, position the cursor on line **Legacy data—On the PC (frontend)** (see Figure 6.36).

▶ Choose **Add entry** to display the dialog box shown in Figure 6.37.

▶ You now enter the file path, the file name, the file description, and the other attributes as appropriate. Input help is available to assist you when selecting the file path.

Legacy Data on the SAP Application Server

The procedure is similar if you want to use files saved on the application server:

▶ In edit mode, position the cursor on line **Legacy data—On the R/3 server (application server)** (see Figure 6.36).

▶ Choose **Add entry** to display the dialog box shown in Figure 6.38.

► Again, enter the file path, the file name, the file description, and the other attributes as appropriate.

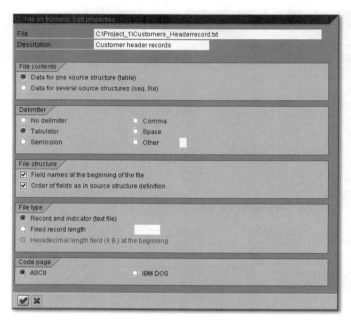

Figure 6.37 LSM Workbench — Specify the File on the Frontend

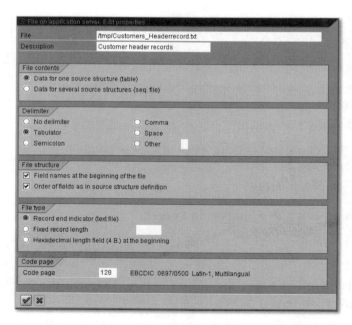

Figure 6.38 LSM Workbench — Specify Files on the SAP Application Server

As far as the files with the legacy data are concerned, the LSM Workbench requires you to follow certain rules that, although they're not relevant for the example, may be important in your specific data migration situation. The most important rules are listed below:

Additional Rules for Files

▶ The SAP system registers with the operating system as user ID `<sid>adm` (`<sid>` stands for the three-character name of the SAP R/3 system). Therefore, ensure that you have read/write authorization for the selected directory.

Required Authorizations for the SAP System

▶ If a file contains data for multiple source structures, the field sequence in the file must match the sequence of the source fields defined in the LSM Workbench.

▶ If a file contains data for a single source structure, either the field sequence has to correspond to the source structure definition, or the field names have to be specified at the beginning of the file, which you can use to assign the columns in the file to the source fields.

Field Sequence or Field Names

▶ If a file contains end-of-line indicators (text file), packed fields are not allowed.

▶ If a file contains separators, packed fields are not allowed.

▶ You can also use files on the frontend and the SAP application server within an object.

Combination of Frontend and Application Server Allowed

▶ In the following step (**Assign files**), a file containing data for several source structures can be assigned to several source structures. Conversely, a file containing data for a single source structure can only be assigned to a single source structure.

▶ If several files are used in an object, the corresponding source structures must contain fields of the same name. In the example, this is field CUSTOMERNUMBER. The respective records are assigned using the fields of the same name. You can highlight the fields that can be used for this assignment when maintaining the source fields (see Figure 6.14). Click on the **Fields with identical names** button.

File of Read Data, File of Converted Data

The LSM Workbench provides complete proposals for these two working files, which you can usually adopt as they are, that is, unchanged.

Complete Proposals

The *SAP home directory* of the SAP application server, or the last directory that you used in the LSM Workbench, is selected as the file path.

Transaction AL11 displays an overview of all SAP directories. The physical path of the SAP home directory is located under DIR_HOME.

The file name consists of the IDs for project, subproject, and object (separated by underscores), plus the file extension *lsmw.read* (for the file with the read data) or *lsmw.conv* (for the file with the converted data). The files in the example have the following names (see Figure 6.39):

▶ *PROJECT_1_MASTERDATA_CUSTOMERS.lsmw.read* for the file with the read data

▶ *PROJECT_1_MASTERDATA_CUSTOMERS.lsmw.conv* for the file with the converted data[5]

Logical Path,
Logical File Name

The **Logical Path** and **Logical File Name** fields are only displayed when required by batch input/direct input programs called later. **F4** input help is available for both fields. Under no circumstances, should you use logical paths or file names that other applications can also use.

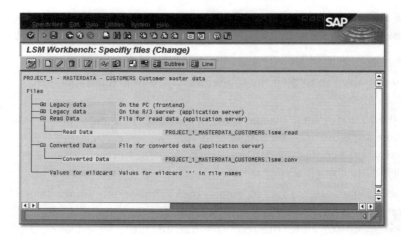

Figure 6.39 LSM Workbench—Specifying Files for the Read and Converted Data

6.2.11 Using Wildcards in File Names

Example

The use of wildcards is described based on an example. Assume that the legacy data is stored in the following four files:

▶ File 1: *C:\Project_1\Customers_Headerrecord_1.txt*

▶ File 2: *C:\Project_1\Customers_Contact_1.txt*

---

5 An undocumented feature is the **F4** input help for files on the application server. To activate this feature, you have to use Transaction SE16 (Data Browser) to make an entry in the SAP R/3 database table /SAPDMC/LSGCUST.

▶ File 3: *C:\Project_1\Customers_Headerrecord_2.txt*

▶ File 4: *C:\Project_1\Customers_Contact_2.txt*

Two files each (*1.txt* and *2.txt*) form a "set"—that is, file 2 contains the item data for the header records in file 1, while file 4 contains the item data for the header records in file 3.

When reading the data, you should process files 1 and 2 before files 3 and 4. You can achieve this with the appropriate settings in the **Specify files** step, shown in Figure 6.40.

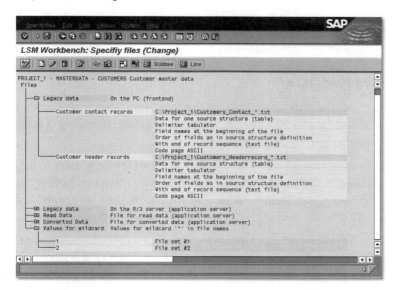

Figure 6.40 LSM Workbench—Use of Wildcards in File Names

Note that you can also use wildcards in the names of the files of read data and converted data.

Wildcards in All File Names

6.2.12 Assigning Files

In this step, you take the files you defined in the previous step and assign them to the source structures (see Figure 6.41).

In the example, you call the step **Assign files** from within the navigation screen (see Figure 6.9), position the cursor on the header structure, and click on **Assign file**. From the list of defined files, select the file that contains the header records. Proceed accordingly with source structure CONTACT.

Note that if you change file names or properties subsequently, the file assignment is kept.

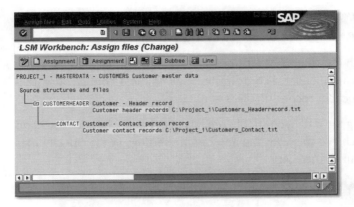

Figure 6.41 LSM Workbench—Assign Files

6.2.13 Reading Data

When you read the data, the files with the data from your legacy system are transformed to a technically homogeneous format. In the next step, the data is converted to SAP format.

Program Generated If Necessary

From the navigation screen (see Figure 6.9), call the step **Read data** to display the screen shown in Figure 6.42. The system first checks whether the data read program is still up-to-date. If it isn't current, it is regenerated automatically.

Selection Parameters

If you want to process all data belonging to an object, click on **Execute**. The process is started. If you want to migrate only a part of the data, you can limit the amount of data to be transferred in the **General selection parameters section**. Select the data in the **Transaction number** fields. We don't recommend using this option for your production migration, however, as you run the risk of skipping important data during the data migration.

If you marked one or more source fields (see Section 6.2.5) as selection parameters when defining the source fields, these fields are also offered as selection parameters. There are also two checkboxes:

▶ **Amount fields**: Amount fields are converted to calculation format (with decimal point).

▶ **Date values**: Date values are converted to the internal SAP format (YYYYMMDD).

Wildcards

If you use a wildcard in the file names for the legacy data, and at least one value has been defined for the wildcard, a selection parameter for the wildcard is offered as well. If you don't enter any values here, all defined wildcard values are processed.

Figure 6.42 LSM Workbench—Read Data—Selection Screen

In the example, adopt the proposed values and choose **Execute**.

When the transaction is complete, a brief summary log appears (see Figure 6.43), indicating whether all the records were processed correctly.

Log

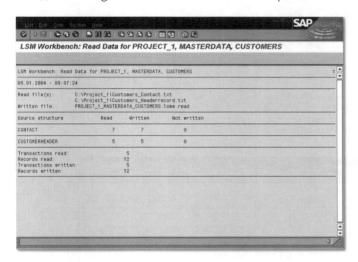

Figure 6.43 LSM Workbench—Read Data—Log

6.2.14 Displaying Read Data

After you have read the data, you will want to view the results. You can display all or a part of the read data in table form. To help you better distinguish the results, the individual record types (source structure) are assigned different colors (see Figure 6.44).

Color Codes

Click on **Change display** to toggle between a one line and multiline view. When you click on **Display color legend,** the colors for the individual hierarchy levels are displayed.

When you click on a specific line, all the information is highlighted. When you click on the **Field contents** button, you can achieve this same result, that is, you can display the details of the line (see Figure 6.45).

Recognizing Errors   Now, you can see any errors that occurred during the conversion of character sets or the processing of separators. Before you continue on to the next step, you should correct any such errors.

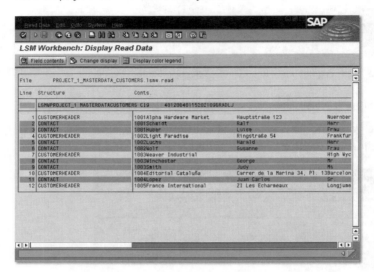

Figure 6.44 LSM Workbench—Display Read Data

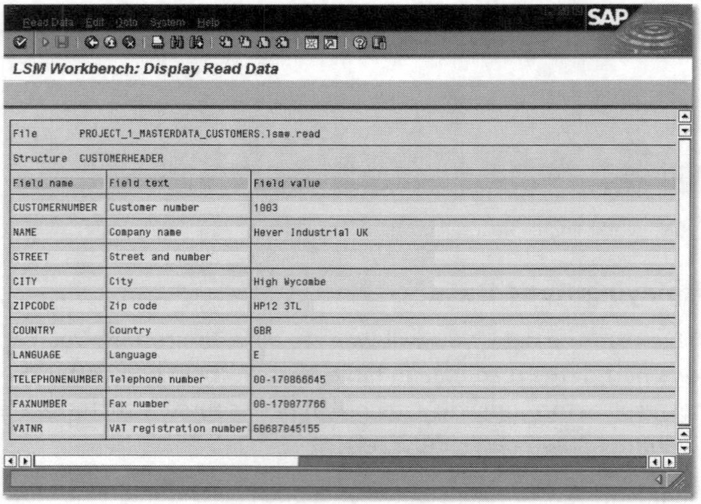

Figure 6.45 LSM Workbench—Display Read Data—Details

6.2.15 Converting Data

Once you have transformed the data from your legacy system to a technically homogeneous format with the read transaction, the data will now be converted to an SAP R/3 format, based on the field mappings and conversion rules you have defined.

Conversion According to Mappings and Conversion Rules

From the navigation screen (see Figure 6.9), call the **Convert data** step to display the screen shown in Figure 6.46. Once again, the system checks whether the data conversion program is still up-to-date. If not, it is regenerated automatically.

If you want to restrict the data selection, click on **Execute** to start the process. Otherwise, enter a range in the **Transaction number** fields.

If you marked one or several source fields as selection parameters when defining the source fields, these fields are also offered as selection parameters.

Selection Parameters

If you use a wildcard in the file names for the legacy data and have defined at least one value for the wildcard, a selection parameter for the wildcard is also provided. If you don't enter a wildcard or value here, all defined wildcard values are processed.

Wildcards

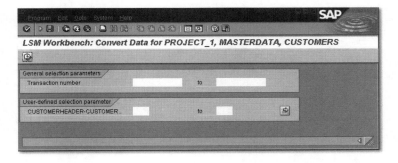

Figure 6.46 LSM Workbench—Convert Data—Selection Screen

If you selected BAPI or IDoc as the import technique under **Maintain object attributes** (see Section 6.2.1), additional selection parameters appear in the selection screen for the data conversion program (see Figure 6.47).

Additional Function for BAPI/IDoc

If you select **Create file**, a file is created during data conversion. If you select **Create IDocs directly**, IDocs are collected during data conversion and submitted for IDoc creation in packages. You can determine the package size with parameter **Number of IDocs per package**. The default value is 50.

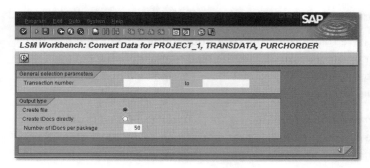

Figure 6.47 LSM Workbench—Data Conversion Program—Selection Screen—Additional Selection Parameters for BAPI/IDoc

Log   In the example, you would click on **Execute** and then see a log like the one in Figure 6.48.

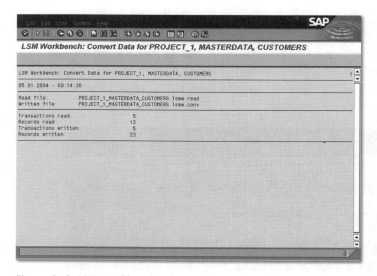

Figure 6.48 LSM Workbench—Convert Data—Log

6.2.16 Displaying Converted Data

Different Number of Records

Once you have triggered the data conversion, you can check the results. In this step, you have the same options as those described in the **Displaying Read Data** step (see Section 6.2.14). You should note, however, that the number of records here generally differs from the number of records in the legacy data, due to the different structures between legacy data and SAP format. However, the number of data units (here: five customers) should be identical.

In the example, a single BGR00 record is created, and for each customer a BKN00 record, a BKNA1 record, and a BKNB1 record. One BKNVK record is created for each contact person record (23 records).

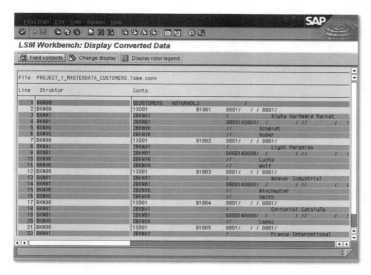

Figure 6.49 LSM Workbench—Display Converted Data

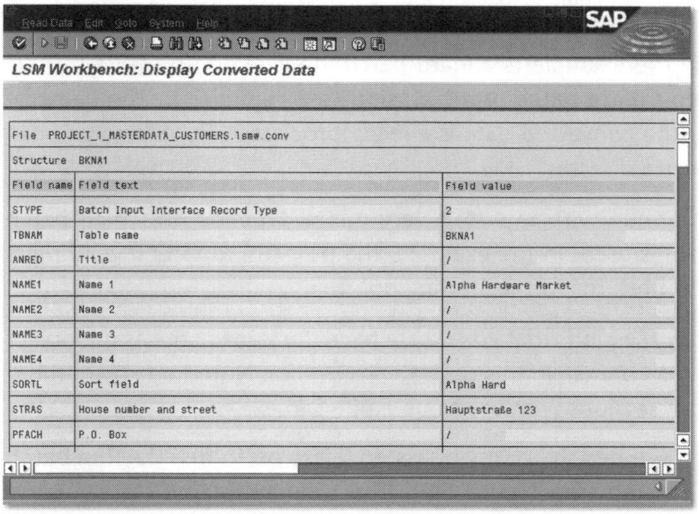

Figure 6.50 LSM Workbench—Display Converted Data—Details

Once again, you can double-click on a line to display the details for that line (see Figure 6.50).

Figure 6.50 shows several fields with value /. The batch input program that is called next interprets this value as "Not specified"—in contrast to the entry "".

6.2.17 Importing Data

Dependent on the Import Technique The activities displayed in the **Import data** step depend on the import technique that you selected in the **Maintain object attributes** step (see Section 6.2.1):

Import technique	Data import step
Standard batch input or recording	Generate batch input session
	Process batch input session
Standard direct input	Start direct input session
BAPI or IDoc	Start IDoc creation
	Start IDoc processing
	Create IDoc overview
	Start IDoc postprocessing

Table 6.5 Data Import Steps Dependent on The Import Technique

Importing Data with Batch Input Therefore, in the example (standard batch input), you first have to perform the step **Create batch input session** (see Figure 6.9). The name of the file with the converted data is already proposed. Therefore, you can click on **Execute** directly.

How you continue with this step very much depends on which batch input program is used. In the example, the program reports several messages and then returns to the starting point.

The batch input sessions that you create have the same name as the object in the LSM Workbench, in this case, CUSTOMERS. Note that any number of batch input sessions with the same name can exist.

Final Step: Processing the Batch Input Session You're almost finished. Now, the only step left to perform is the **Run batch input session** step (see Figure 6.9). The program starts SAP standard Transaction SM35. However, only the batch input sessions for the selected object are displayed. Note that if you used the name of the object in other projects or subprojects as well, batch input sessions from these objects may also be displayed.

Because we already discussed how to process batch input sessions in Chapter 4, we will not repeat that same information here.

If you selected the direct input import technique (see Table 6.5), you can either call the standard direct input program for the object, or choose between the direct input program and direct input transaction, depending on the object type, in the **Start Direct Input Session** step.

When you select BAPI or IDoc as the import technique, the import takes place in three main steps:

▶ **Start IDoc creation**
First, the file of the converted data is read. The "information packages" contained are stored in the SAP database in IDoc format; however, they're not stored in the database of the corresponding application. The system assigns a number to every IDoc and then deletes the file of the converted data.

▶ **Start IDoc processing**
The IDocs created in the first step are submitted to the corresponding application program. This application program checks the data and, is appropriate, posts it in the application's database.

▶ **Create IDoc overview**
A status overview appears, in which you can drill down to the individual IDoc level.

Note that if you choose the **Create IDocs directly** option during data conversion, the **Create IDocs** step is skipped (see Figure 6.47).

Whether the second step (**Start IDoc processing**) is initiated automatically depends on the settings in ALE-EDI Customizing. One essential setting is made in the partner agreement (for a partner and a message type, see Section 6.2.3). This agreement specifies whether the IDocs are to be processed immediately or via a background program.

Please also note the following:

▶ Partner agreements automatically created by the LSM Workbench are set to **Initiation by background program**. You can change this setting manually at any time.

▶ When inbound IDocs are processed, *work items* are created in the standard system. Work items are elements of the SAP workflow that are usually not required during data migration. To learn how you can prevent the creation of work items—and the consequences of doing so—see SAP Note number 149368.

Your example, which introduced you to the most important functions in the LSM Workbench, is now complete.

6.2.18 Object Overview

Before you exit the example completely, however, you should learn about one more function, which creates an overview of all the definitions you entered for the CUSTOMERS object.

Return to the navigation screen (see Figure 6.9) and click on the **Object overview** button. The result is shown in Figures 6.51 to 6.53.

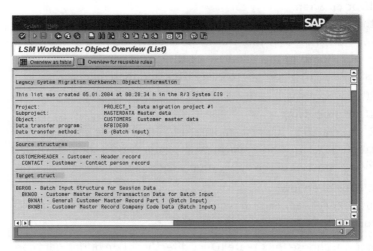

Figure 6.51 Object Overview in List Form—General Data, Source Structures, Target Structures

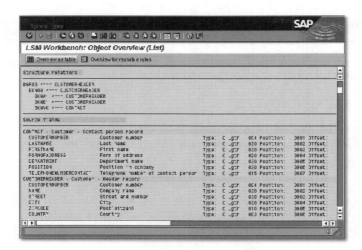

Figure 6.52 Object Overview in List Form—Structure Relations, Source Fields

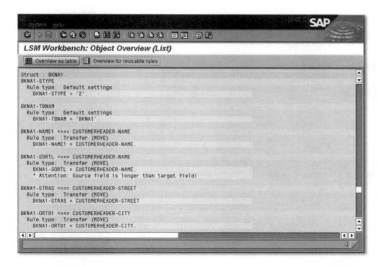

Figure 6.53 Object Overview in List Form—Conversion Rules (Excerpt)

In addition to the list-based overview, you can also display the overview in table form (**Overview as table** button). You can use this overview as a template for your "mapping on paper" (see Section 6.2.7).

In addition, you can also list all the reusable rules that are actually used in the object (**Overview for reusable rules** button). This function is especially useful because the contents of the conversion table are also displayed for conversions.

6.3   Recordings

In the previous section, you learned about the main functions of the LSM Workbench based on the example "Migrate customer master data using standard batch input." In this section, you will work on another example to learn how the LSM Workbench is integrated with the recording function of the SAP R/3 system. You already learned about the transaction recorder in Chapter 4. In the second example, we will not go into as much detail as we did with the first example. Instead, we will focus on those areas in the example where the procedure differs.

We have called our example "Create G/L Account." You may ask why you shouldn't use the standard batch input program, RFBISA00, to migrate the G/L accounts. This is entirely possible. Because the legacy data here has only a few fields, however, you should be convinced, by the end of this section, that the recording function is the faster alternative.

Example: Creating a G/L Account

Assumptions

Assume that your task is to create G/L accounts in the SAP R/3 system based on the legacy data shown in Figure 6.54.

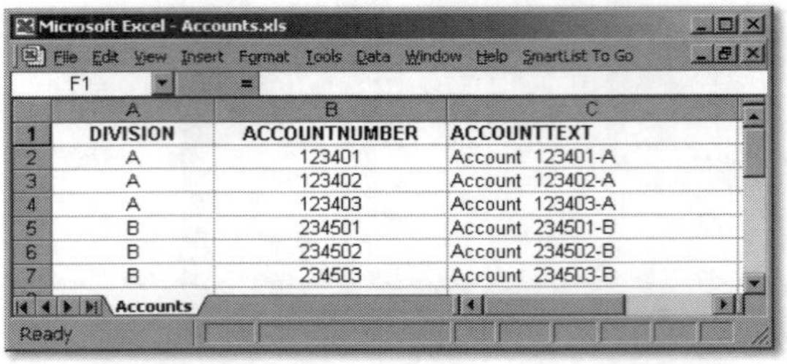
Microsoft Excel - Accounts.xls

	A	B	C
1	DIVISION	ACCOUNTNUMBER	ACCOUNTTEXT
2	A	123401	Account 123401-A
3	A	123402	Account 123402-A
4	A	123403	Account 123403-A
5	B	234501	Account 234501-B
6	B	234502	Account 234502-B
7	B	234503	Account 234503-B

Figure 6.54 Example "Migration of G/L Account Master Data" (Excerpt)

Furthermore, it is assumed that you're familiar with the corresponding transaction, Transaction FS01, and therefore know which data you must enter and where:

Field from Transaction FS01	Input
Account number	**Account number** field from legacy data
Company code	Derive through translation of **controlling area** field from the legacy data A → 0001 B → 1000
Short text	**Account text** field from legacy data
Balance sheet account	X
Account group	SAKO
Group account number[6]	110100
Balances in local currency	X
Field status group	G001

Table 6.6 Create G/L Account—"Mapping on Paper"

Your preparations are now complete and you can start working with the LSM Workbench.

6.3.1 Creating and Editing Recordings

No Simulation

From the initial screen (see Figure 6.5), choose **Goto · Recordings**. An overview screen is displayed that lists all the recordings for the current project (Figure 6.55). Note that a recording always belongs to a project.

6 The group account number was set to a constant here in order to keep the example as simple as possible.

Also, remember that when you create a recording, the corresponding transaction is actually executed, and not merely simulated. Therefore, you'll use an account that isn't listed among the legacy data to create the recording.

Unfortunately, you cannot use recordings that were created directly in Transaction SM35, because the LSM Workbench requires additional information that isn't contained in SM35 recordings.

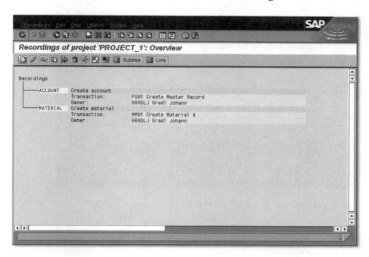

Figure 6.55 LSM Workbench—Recordings

In the overview screen of the recordings, click on the **Create recording** button. In the dialog box that opens (see Figure 6.56), enter the ID ACCOUNT and the description "Create account."

Figure 6.56 LSM Workbench—Create Recording

When you click on **Continue**, you are prompted to enter the Transaction code, FS01 (see Figure 6.57).

Figure 6.57 LSM Workbench—Enter Transaction Code for Recording

Enter the transaction code and confirm your entry. Transaction FS01 now appears, which you process with account 123499 (see Figures 6.58 through 6.60).

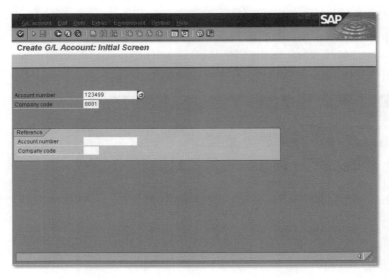

Figure 6.58 LSM Workbench—Recording—Transaction FS01 (Screen 1)

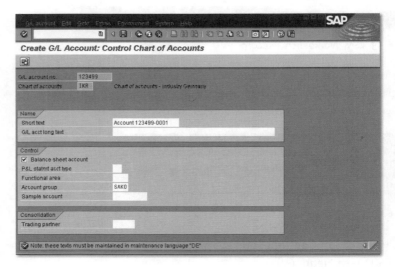

Figure 6.59 LSM Workbench—Recording—Transaction FS01 (Screen 2)

When you save the new account, the recording ends and the LSM Workbench assumes control again.

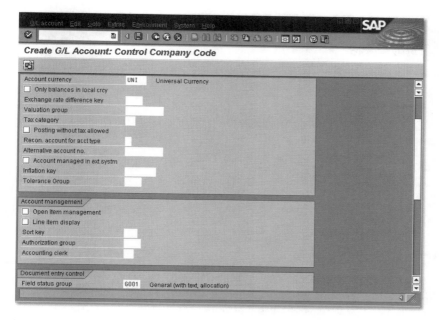

Figure 6.60 LSM Workbench—Recording—Transaction FS01 (Screen 3)

A screen opens in which the recording is displayed with its technical components (see Figure 6.61). The display corresponds to the structure that you learned about in Chapter 4. The tree structure is arranged by transaction (FS01), screen (SAPMF02H 0402 and so on), and field (RF02H-SAKNR and so on). The highlighted fields in the middle column[7] contain the values that you used when you created the recording or that were proposed by the SAP R/3 system. The right column is blank, which indicates that postprocessing is required.

Tree Display of Recording—Three Columns

As you learned in Section 6.2, the LSM Workbench requires a target structure to map the legacy data during the course of data migration. A structure requires field names. You must assign these field names now. To do so, position the cursor on the first input field in the list—screen field RF02H-SAKNR with value 123499—and double-click. A dialog box opens (see Figure 6.62), prompting you to enter a name and a description for the field. This information will appear later in the target structure. Enter ACCOUNTNUMBER as the name and "Account number" as the description and click on **Continue**.

Defining the Field Names of the Target Structure

---

7 When you test this in the system, you will see the three columns clearly in different colors. The right column is highlighted insufficiently in a black-and-white screen shot.

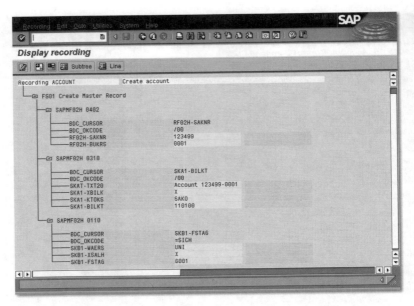

Figure 6.61 LSM Workbench—Result of Recording with Transaction FS01

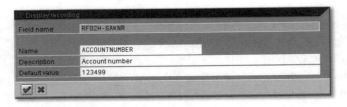

Figure 6.62 LSM Workbench—Recording—Assign Field Names

Naming the Fields to Be Supplied

Proceed accordingly with all the input fields that you want to supply with field values from the legacy data. Leave the names and descriptions for the other fields blank. If the name and description of a field are blank, the LSM Workbench automatically uses the defined default value (see Section 5.3.1).

Therefore, you need enter only the names and descriptions for three fields: ACCOUNTNUMBER, COMPANYCODE, and ACCOUNTTEXT (see Figure 6.63).

For technical reasons, you must assign a name and a description to at least one field.

Save the results and return to the overview screen with all the recordings in the project (see Figure 6.55).

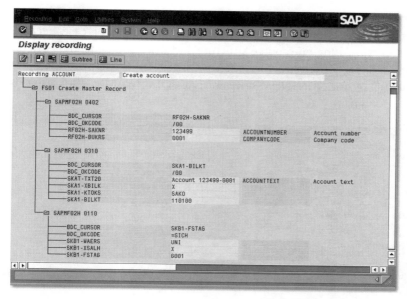

Figure 6.63 LSM Workbench—Result of Recording with Transaction FS01—with Field Names and Descriptions

Before you continue, you might want to learn about a useful shortcut for the last step. The screen in Figure 6.61, where you just postprocessed the recording, also contains the buttons **Default** and **All default**. If you use these buttons, the LSM Workbench automatically assigns the names and descriptions derived from the underlying screen fields, either to the field with the current cursor position or to all fields. The advantage of this function is its speed; the disadvantage is that the field names involved are not always mnemonic.[8]

Shortcut "Default"

6.3.2 Using a Recording

You can now use the recording as usual in the LSM Workbench. In project PROJECT_1 and subproject MASTERDATA, create an object with ID ACCOUNTS and the text "Account master data." In step **Maintain object attributes**, under **Object Type and Import Technique**, select **Batch Input Recording** and, using the input help, the recording named ACCOUNT (see Figure 6.64).[9]

---

8 In addition, two fields can be assigned the same name. Consequently, only one field with this name is available in the field mapping.

9 The LSM Workbench also allows you to chain several recordings; that is, to run two or more transactions in sequence for the same data record. This feature is rarely used, however.

Defining the Source Structure and Source Fields

Define the source structure and source fields, using the procedure described in Section 6.2. This is not especially difficult in this case, because you are only using one source structure and three source fields.[10] Therefore, define a source structure called ACCOUNTRECORD with the fields DIVISION, ACCOUNTNUMBER, and ACCOUNTNAME. The result is shown in Figure 6.65.

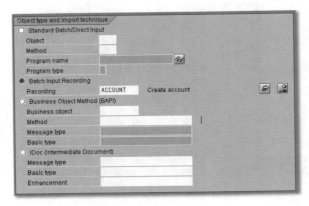

Figure 6.64 LSM Workbench—Recording—Maintain Object Attributes

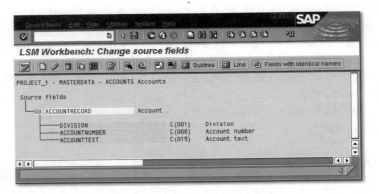

Figure 6.65 LSM Workbench—Recording—Source Field

Structure Relations

The structure relations are nearly trivial, because you are only dealing with one source structure and one target structure. When you start the step **Maintain structure relations**, you see that the LSM Workbench is intelligent enough to define the sole possible allocation automatically.

Field Mapping and Conversion Rules

It is now time to maintain the field mapping and conversion rules. Once again, this usually complicated step is quite simple in this case, as you

---

10 In general, you can define only one source structure when you use the recording technique.

need to supply only three target fields with data. You already defined the strategy in Table 6.5. The result is displayed in Figure 6.66.

Once again, all the fields in the recording are automatically set to the default values defined in the recording.

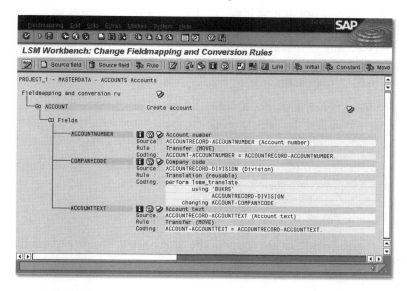

Figure 6.66 LSM Workbench—Recording—Field Mapping

You can perform the last steps quickly:

Additional Steps

▶ Specify the file with the legacy data (not the Excel file, but instead the copy in **Text (Tab-Delimited) (*.txt)** format) and assign it.

▶ Read the data and display it on screen for verification.

▶ Convert the data and display it on screen for verification.

▶ Generate and process a batch input session.

As this example illustrates, the recording technique in the LSM Workbench can help you to attain your goals quickly, provided it is applicable to your situation.

Applicability of the Recording Technique

What requirements must be met to enable use of the recording technique?

▶ The legacy data must be displayable in a single table, such that one line in the table corresponds to one transaction. Think of the first example in Section 6.2. In this example, each customer had a variable number of contact persons, therefore, the recording technique is not applicable here.

> ► The transaction must run through the same screen sequence for each data record.

6.4 Long Texts

Multiline Texts Now, you will learn about long texts, a subject that is frequently neglected but one that can cause a lot of aggravation when not handled properly. Long texts are multiline texts. Usually, long texts for an object have to be migrated separately, because the SAP R/3 system has a central repository for long texts in the database.

Object Type 0001 The LSM Workbench provides an object type with ID 0001 to migrate long texts. To make this object available, you must run the program /SAPDMC/SAP_LSMW_SXDA_TEXTS in the system in question.

Before you can begin to migrate the long texts, however, you must first learn how long texts are stored in the SAP R/3 system.

6.4.1 Long Texts in the SAP R/3 System

Long texts are stored in a text pool in the SAP system. The key of a long text is composed of four parts:

Key field	Meaning	Example	Length	Check table
OBJECT	Application object	MVKE = Material sales texts	10	TTXOB, TTXOT
ID	Text ID	0001	4	TTXID, TTXIT
NAME	Actual text key	Material number (18-place) + sales organization (4-place) + distribution channel (2-place)	70	(none)
SPRAS	Language	EN	1-2	T002

Table 6.7 Components of a Long Text Key

Text Key: No Standard Rules There is no uniform rule for the structure of the actual text key NAME. To determine the values for OBJECT and ID for a specific text type and the structure of NAME, proceed as follows:

> ► Display the requested text type (material sales text, for example) and open the editor.

> ► You can now choose **Goto · Header** to display the required information.

6.4.2 Target Structures and Field Mapping

You will now learn how you can use object type 0001 to migrate long texts. This object has the following two target structures:

Two Target Structures

▶ /SAPDMC/LTXTH: Long text header

  ▶ STYPE: Record type (technical field, value = 1)

  ▶ OBJECT: Application object

  ▶ NAME: Text name

  ▶ ID: Text ID

  ▶ SPRAS: Language

▶ /SAPDMC/LTXTL: Long text text line

  ▶ STYPE: Record type (technical field, value = 2)

  ▶ TEXTFORMAT: Format field (two places)

  ▶ TEXTLINE: Text line

The TEXTFORMAT field contains text formatting information. To map the field 1:1, enter character * in all fields.

An object in the LSM Workbench could then resemble the screens in Figures 6.67 to 6.70, which use the material sales texts as an example.

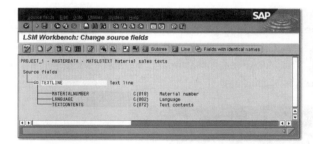

Figure 6.67 LSM Workbench—Long Texts—Source Fields

Figure 6.68 LSM Workbench—Long Texts—Structure Relations

Target field	Activity
/SAPDMC/LTXTH-OBJECT	Assign constant MVKE
/SAPDMC/LTXTH-NAME	Assign source field TEXTLINE-MATERIALNUMBER
	Double-click on /SAPDMC/LTXTH-NAME
	Enter ABAP coding:
	/SAPDMC/LTXTH-NAME = TEXTLINE-MATERI-ALNUMBER.
	/SAPDMC/LTXTH-NAME+18 = '0001'.
	/SAPDMC/LTXTH-NAME+22 = '01'.
/SAPDMC/LTXTH-ID	Assign constant 0001
/SAPDMC/LTXTH-SPRAS	Assign source field TEXTLINE-LANGUAGE
/SAPDMC/LTXTL-TEXTFORMAT	Assign constant *
/SAPDMC/LTXTL-TEXTLINE	Assign source field TEXTLINE-TEXTCONTENTS

Table 6.8 Overview of the Activities Performed on the Target Fields

If you use the default settings, you'll get an unwanted side effect, namely, a text header will be created for every text line, making each text line a separate text. To avoid this problem, you will have to reach into the "bag of tricks" in the LSM Workbench (see Section 6.8.3):

▶ Click on the **Display Variant** button and set the **Processing Times** checkbox.

▶ Various labels appear, including __END_OF_RECORD__ at the end of every target structure. Click this label at the end of target structure /SAPDMC/LTXTH. The ABAP editor appears, where you enter on_change_transfer_record.

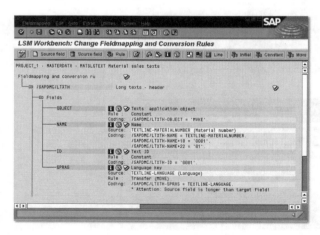

Figure 6.69 LSM Workbench—Long Texts—Field Mapping (Part 1)

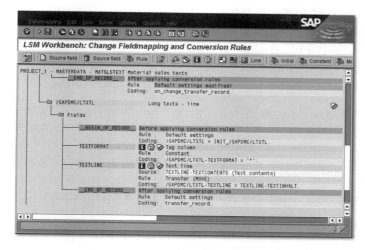

Figure 6.70 LSM Workbench—Long Texts—Field Mapping (Part 2)

Specifically, perform the following steps:

Long Text Step by Step

► **Define an object**

In project PROJECT_1 and subproject MASTERDATA, create an object with ID MATSLSTXT and the text »Material sales texts.«

► **Maintain object attributes**

In screen section **Object Type and Import Technique**, choose **Standard Batch/Direct Input**, **Object** 0001, and **Method** 0001.

► **Maintain source structures**

Define a source structure with the ID TEXTLINE and the text »Text line.«

► **Maintain source fields**

Three fields are required: MATERIALNUMBER (length 18), LANGUAGE (length 2), and TEXTCONTENTS (length 72). All fields have type C.

► **Maintain structure relations**

Assign the only source structure, TEXTLINE, to the two target structures /SAPDMC/LTXTH and /SAPDMC/LTXTL.

► **Maintain field mapping and conversion rules**

Perform the following activities:

This statement means that the text header will be transferred only when it has changed, which is exactly what you want. This is the exact opposite of what occurred with the previous record.

Refer to Section 6.8 for more detailed information.

6.4.3 Importing Long Texts

You use the direct input technique to import the texts in to the SAP R/3 system. You can call the relevant direct input program, `/SAPDMC/SAP_LSMW_IMPORT_TEXTS`, from the LSM Workbench with **Start Direct Input Session**.

After you've imported the long texts, the corresponding application may not always be able to read them, even though they've been saved properly in the database. This is because some applications have a field in the master data that indicates whether a long text exists. The direct input programs don't fill this field, because these programs apply to all applications, and at runtime, they cannot determine to which application a text belongs.

There are two possible solutions:

▶ Use a user-defined report to set the field and run it after you import the long texts.

▶ Set the field when you define the conversion rules for the corresponding object (see Section 6.2.7).

6.5 Periodic Data Transfer

The LSM Workbench also supports periodic data transfers. In this case, we use the term *source system* instead of legacy system, because the system is not being replaced. The following requirements must be met to enable periodic data transfer:

▶ The corresponding object in the LSM Workbench must be completely defined and tested.

▶ The application in the source system periodically makes one or more files available on the SAP application server.

▶ The object in the LSM Workbench doesn't access files on the frontend, because files on the frontend cannot be read during background processing.

When all these requirements are met, you can set the **Periodic** button in step **Maintain object attributes** (see Figure 6.11). The navigation screen (see Figure 6.9) displays step **Main Program for Periodic Data Transfer**. This program performs the steps **Read Data**, **Convert Data**, and **Import Data** in the listed order.

You can schedule program /SAPDMC/SAP_LSMW_INTERFACE as needed. The numerous selection parameters for the program are illustrated in Figures 6.71 to 6.73.

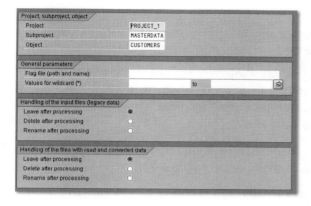

Figure 6.71 Main Program for Periodic Data Transfer—Selection Parameters (Part 1)

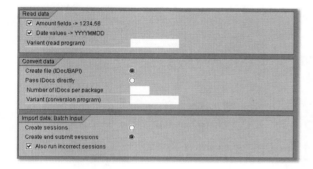

Figure 6.72 Main Program for Periodic Data Transfer—Selection Parameters (Part 2)

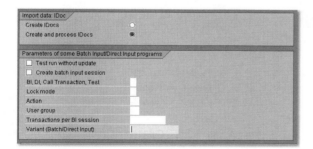

Figure 6.73 Main Program for Periodic Data Transfer—Selection Parameters (Part 3)

Flag File   Specification of a *flag file* is optional. A flag file serves to create a "hand-shake" with the source system, which provides the input files:

- ▶ The main program for periodic data transfer is only executed if the specified flag file exists.
- ▶ After finishing data transfer, the main program for periodic data transfer deletes the flag file.
- ▶ The supplying application should behave in a complementary way. It checks whether the flag file exists before it creates new files.[11] If the flag file does exist, the program terminates. Otherwise, the files are generated, and the flag file is created.

The interaction between the source system and the SAP R/3 system — with regard to the flag file — is illustrated in Figure 6.74.

Variants   You can specify variants for the read program, the conversion program, and (in the batch/direct input case) the batch input or direct input program. These variants must be defined beforehand. If you don't specify a variant, the default settings of main program /SAPDMC/SAP_LSMW_ INTERFACE are used.

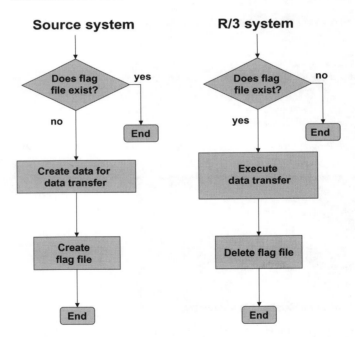

Figure 6.74 LSM Workbench — Periodic Data Transfer — Flag File Handling

---

11 The flag file can be blank. The system checks only whether the flag file exists.

Some of the batch input and direct input programs provided by SAP use additional parameters, and some of these parameters are also used in other programs.

Additional Parameters

Program	Parameter					
	Test run without update	Generate batch input session	BI, DI, Call Transaction, Test	Lock mode	Action	User group
RAALTD01 RAALTD11 (assets)	X					
RCCLBI01 RCCLBI02 RCCLBI03 (classes) RCCTBI01 (attributes)		X				
RCSBI010 RCSBI020 RCSBI030 RCSBI040 (BOMs)		X				
RCVBI010 (document info records		X				
RFBIBL00 (financial documents)			X			
RHALTD00 (personnel planning data)			X			
RLBEST00 (balances) RLPLAT00 (storage bins)		X				

Table 6.9 Parameters of the Batch Input and Direct Input Programs

Program	Parameter					
	Test run without update	Generate batch input session	BI, DI, Call Transaction, Test	Lock mode	Action	User group
RMDATIND (material masters)				X		
RPUSTDOO (personnel master data)					X	X

Table 6.9 Parameters of the Batch Input and Direct Input Programs (continued)

6.6 Transporting Projects

The LSM Workbench supports data transport for a project through both the SAP transport system and download/upload between two SAP R/3 systems. In the process, the programs generated by the LSM Workbench are not actually transported; instead, new versions of the programs are generated in the target system.

6.6.1 Creating a Change Request

When you create a change request, this function creates an SAP change request that contains all the relevant information about an LSM Workbench project.

You can export and import this SAP change request with the usual tools in the SAP Correction and Transport System. This function is located in the initial screen (see Figure 6.5) under **Extras · Create Change Request**.

SAP Correction and Transport System

When you transport project data in this way, you can trace the transports any time in the SAP Correction and Transport System.

Please also note the following:

▶ When you import a change request, the complete project is deleted from the target system first and then created again.

▶ When you export the transport request, the current version is exported (not the version that existed when you created the transport request).

▶ Because the entire project is exported, ensure that the project is "clean" when you export it.

6.6.2 Exporting Projects

In the initial screen (see Figure 6.5), choose **Extras · Export Project**. This first screen displays the structure tree of the selected project (see Figure 6.75). You can click on the **Select / Deselect** button to select whether you want to export the entire project or only parts of it. Then, select **Export** (**F8**). A text file is created.

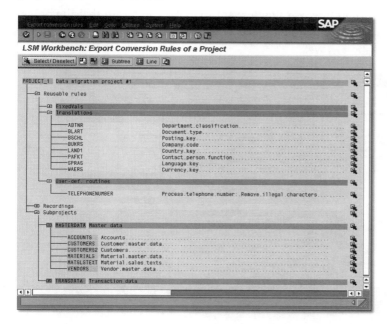

Figure 6.75 LSM Workbench—Export Project

The selected elements are exported together with their documentation.

6.6.3 Importing Projects

You can then take the exported project and import it into a different SAP R/3 system.

Choose **Extras · Import Project** in the initial screen of the other SAP R/3 system. The system prompts you to enter the name of the text file. The file is imported and its contents are analyzed. After the analysis, a list of the subprojects and objects found is displayed.

Now, select the objects to be imported. Project data that already exists is check marked and will be overwritten by the import. To prevent an existing project in the target system from being overwritten, use the function **Import under different name**.

Existing Elements Are Overwritten

6.7 Preparations for Using IDoc Inbound Processing

IDocs (*Intermediate Documents*) were developed to exchange messages between different systems (for example, two SAP R/3 Systems, an SAP R/3 system and an SAP R/2 system, or an SAP R/3 System and a non-SAP system). Comprehensive coverage of this topic would far exceed the scope of this book. Therefore, we simply want to make you aware that the procedure involves a standard interface, which makes the technique suitable for data migration as well.

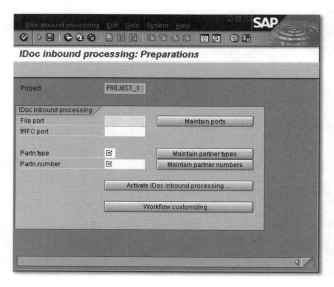

Figure 6.76 LSM Workbench—Settings for IDoc Inbound Processing

As mentioned previously, the LSM Workbench supports this import technique. To use it, however, several settings and preparations are required. These settings are grouped in the initial screen of the LSM Workbench (see Figure 6.5) under **Settings · IDoc Inbound Proc.** (see Figure 6.76). You must maintain these settings for each client and project.

Perform the following steps:

File Port
- ▶ The first requirement is a *file port* for the file transfer. If necessary, create a port with the required file type with **Maintain ports**. To do this, position the cursor on **File** and click on **Create** (you must be in Edit mode). The following settings are recommended:
    - ▶ Port: LSMW
    - ▶ Name: "Legacy System Migration Workbench"

- ▶ Version: 3
- ▶ Output file: Enter any directory path and file name (such as *filelsmw*)

▶ As an addition, you can specify a *tRFC port*. This port is needed if you do not want to create a file during data conversion, but instead submit the data directly to IDoc inbound processing in packages. The following settings are recommended:

tRFC Port

- ▶ Port: assigned by the system
- ▶ Version: 3
- ▶ RFC destination: Name of the SAP System
- ▶ Name of port: "Legacy System Migration Workbench"

▶ Define a partner type or choose an existing one. The following settings are recommended:

Partner Type

- ▶ Partner type: US

This partner type is available in the standard system in Release 4.5A and later. The partner type is not available in the standard system in Release 4.0B and earlier, and must be added. The following settings are recommended:

- ▶ Partner type: Create US
- ▶ Report name: /SAPDMC/SAP_LSMW_PARTNERTYPES
- ▶ Form routine: READ_USER
- ▶ Short text: any

▶ Define a partner number or choose an existing one. The following settings are recommended:

Partner Number

- ▶ Partner number: LSMW
- ▶ Partner type: US
- ▶ Partner status: A
- ▶ Type: US
- ▶ Language: EN or DE
- ▶ Processed by: Your user ID

▶ Activate IDoc inbound processing. Confirm the prompt with **Yes**. You have to do this once in each system.

▶ Verify the workflow Customizing. You also have to do this once in each system.

Workflow Customizing

The following entries of the workflow runtime system should be marked with a green checkmark (see Figure 6.77):

▶ **Workflow administrator maintained**

▶ **Workflow RFC destination configured completely**

▶ **Generic decision task classified completely**

▶ **Sending to objects and HR objects activated**

To do this, you can start automatic Customizing. After this, set item **Monitoring job for work items with errors** to **not scheduled** (to do so, change item **Monitoring of work items with temporary errors** from checked to not checked). If you don't do this, the SAP system will repeatedly try to post incorrect IDocs created during data migration.

Check the function by clicking on the **Test RFC destination** button. The following message should be displayed:

'Ping' executed successfully. The RFC destination for the SAP Business Workflow is fully configured.

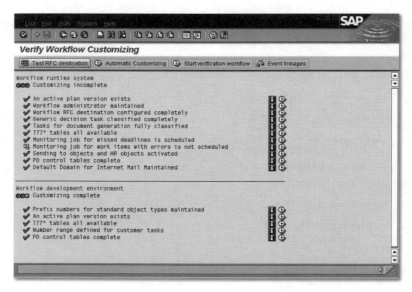

Figure 6.77 Workflow Customizing

6.8 Advanced LSM Workbench Features

This section deals with several topics that you will find to be relevant only if you want or must work with the LSM Workbench intensively.

6.8.1 Display Variant and Processing Times

Click on the **Display variant** button in step **Maintain field mapping and conversion rules** (see Figure 6.22). The dialog box **Determine display variant** opens (see Figure 6.78). This function is useful mainly for experienced users who want to modify their field mappings. You can specify which information is displayed.

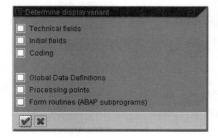

Figure 6.78 LSM Workbench—Determine Display Variant

Technical fields are target fields for which the LSM Workbench proposes a conversion rule (such as a constant). Typically, no changes are required.

Technical Fields

Initial fields are fields that have not been assigned a source field or conversion rule. This selection can help you summarize the display, but you should not use it until you have already identified the target fields that are necessary for your migration.

Initial Fields

When you check **Coding**, any existing ABAP coding is displayed, whether generated implicitly by the LSM Workbench or user-defined.

Coding

If **Global Data Definitions** is set, label __GLOBAL_DATA__ is displayed. There, you can define variables, structures, tables, and so on to use in the field mapping of your own coding. Consequently, all the data definitions are consolidated at a central point, which helps to improve manageability.

Global Data Definitions

Processing times enable you to insert your own coding at specific processing times. The following processing times are available:

Processing Times

Processing time	Default setting
__BEGIN_OF_PROCESSING__	Before the beginning of data processing
__BEGIN_OF_TRANSACTION__	Before the beginning of transaction data processing

Table 6.10 Processing Times

Processing time	Default setting
__BEGIN_OF_RECORD__	Before applying the conversion rules for a source structure
__END_OF_RECORD__	After applying the conversion rules for a source structure Default setting: `Transfer_record`.
__END_OF_TRANSACTION__	After finishing transaction processing `Transfer_transaction`.
__END_OF_PROCESSING__	After finishing transaction processing

Table 6.10 Processing Times (continued)

Form Routines

You can also display the label __FORM_ROUTINES__ for *form routines* (ABAP subroutines). This enables you to define ABAP subroutines in your own coding in the field mapping, as well as use include programs with form routines.

6.8.2 Global Variables

The LSM Workbench uses a number of global variables internally. You can use these variables in your own ABAP coding within the LSM Workbench. Choose **Maintain field mapping and conversion rules** in the list of steps (see Figure 6.22). Double-click on a target field to display the coding and choose **Insert · Global Variable**.

You can use the following variables in your ABAP coding.

Global variable	Name
g_project	Current project
g_subproj	Current subproject
g_object	Current object
g_record	Current target structure
g_cnt_records_read	Number of records read
g_cnt_records_skipped	Number of records skipped
g_cnt_records_transferred	Number of records transferred to output file
g_cnt_transactions_read	Number of records read
g_cnt_transactions_skipped	Number of transactions skipped

Table 6.11 Global Variables in the LSM Workbench

Global variable	Name
`g_cnt_transactions_trans-ferred`	Number of transactions transferred to output file
`g_cnt_transactions_group`	Number of transactions contained in the current batch input session
`g_userid`	User ID
`g_groupname`	Name of the current batch input session
`g_groupnr`	Sequence number of the current batch input session

Table 6.11 Global Variables in the LSM Workbench (continued)

6.8.3 Global Functions

The LSM Workbench provides a series of functions that you can use anywhere within ABAP coding. These functions permit you to influence the flow of the data conversion program considerably. Therefore, use them with extreme caution.

Choose **Maintain field mapping and conversion rules** from the list of steps (see Figure 6.22) and double-click on a target field to display its coding and choose **Insert · Global Functions**.

You can use the following functions:

Global function	Description
`transfer_record.`	Transfers current record (for the current target structure) to the output buffer.
`transfer_this_record '...'.`	Transfers a record of another target structure to the output buffer. The name of the target structure has to be specified as an argument in single quotes.
`at_first_transfer_record.`	Transfers the current record to the output buffer, if it is the first transaction.
`on_change_transfer_record.`	Transfers the current record to the output buffer, if it has changed when compared to the last record.
`transfer_transaction.`	Writes the current transaction to the output file. This transfers all the records in the output buffer to the output file.

Table 6.12 Global Functions in the LSM Workbench

Global function	Description
`skip_record.`	The current record is not transferred to the output buffer.
`skip_transaction.`	The current transaction is not written to the output file.

Table 6.12 Global Functions in the LSM Workbench (continued)

6.8.4 Reusable Rules—Naming Conventions

As you have learned, *reusable rules* are rules that can be used project-wide, that is, in all the objects of a project. Reusable rules are fixed values, translations, and user-defined routines.

Up to Three Name Proposals

If you assign a reusable rule to a target field, the system proposes up to three different names. To understand the naming conventions, see the definition of data objects in the SAP R/3 system.

Data Objects in the SAP System

Data object definition in the SAP system is performed on three levels:

▶ **Domain**
At the lowest level, technical attributes are defined, such as field type, field length, value table, and fixed values.

▶ **Data element**
At the second level, you define "semantic" characteristics, such as language-dependent texts and documentation, based on a domain and its characteristics.

▶ **Field**
At the top level, you define attributes of the field, such as foreign key dependencies, help searches, and so on, in the context of a structure or table.

Therefore, you can discern that there are usually several data elements that refer to any given domain at one time. Typically, a data element has multiple fields that refer to a specific element that is being highlighted.

Recommendation: Use the Proposal

We generally recommend that you accept the names proposed by the system. Exceptions apply only when the domain is extremely general in nature, such as `CHAR1` or `XFELD`. If you used the name of the domain in this case, the reusable rule might not be usable for another field, since this field may have a completely different meaning.

This naming procedure keeps the number of conversion rules small and maintains the consistency in data conversion.

Example:

No.	Field	Data element	Domain	Name
1	BUKRS	BUKRS	BUKRS	Company code
2	CO_CODE	CO_CODE	BUKRS	Company code

Both fields are named "Company code." The field names are different, but the domain is the same. Therefore, both fields should have the same fixed value, the same translation, or the same user-defined routine.

6.9 Tips and Tricks

This section describes several techniques that may come in handy when you need to use them, which is, hopefully, not too often. If you encounter similar situations (as those discussed here) in your migration project, however, the described solutions can save you a considerable amount of work.

6.9.1 Determining the Transaction Code at Runtime

Assume that you want to transfer a set of data records, some of which already exist in the system. If a given data record already exists, you may want to call the change transaction instead of the entry transaction. The following solution is explained based on the example of the customer master.

You first have to determine which case is involved. In the example with the customer master, this involves checking whether Table KNA1 already contains an entry with the customer number in question.

Create or Change

Perform the following steps:

▶ Insert the following under __GLOBAL_DATA__ (see Section 6.8.2):

```
TABLES: KNA1.
```

▶ Insert the following ABAP coding in field BKN00-TCODE:

```
SELECT count(*) FROM kna1 WHERE kunnr =
<old_customernumber>.
IF sy-dbcnt = 0.
  bkn00-tcode = 'XD01'.
ELSE.
  bkn00-tcode = 'XD02'.
ENDIF.
```

Consequently, Transaction XD01 is called for new records (which must be created) and Transaction XD02 is called for existing records (which must be changed).

6.9.2 Skipping a Record

You may want to exclude certain data records in your legacy system from the migration to SAP R/3. You can filter these values beforehand, when you export the data from the legacy system. The LSM Workbench provides a simple feature for performing this task. In this case, you want to skip a record, that is, you do not want to convert it or transfer it to the output file.

The solution is simple. You formulate the corresponding condition in ABAP and implement it in the following ABAP statements:

```
IF <condition>.
  skip_record.
ENDIF.
```

You can insert these ABAP statements in the coding of any field in the involved target structure.

Please note that only one record (such as one contact person for a customer) is skipped, and not the entire data object (such as the customer).

6.9.3 Skipping All Records of a Transaction

If you want to skip all the records of a data object (that is, a transaction) dependent on a specific condition, insert the following ABAP statements anywhere within the field mapping:

```
IF <condition>.
  skip_transaction.
ENDIF.
```

6.9.4 Duplicating a Record

Example   Assume that you want, or must, create two or more target records from a single source record. For example, the customer master consists of a record that contains the fields FIRSTNAME, LASTNAME, and TELEPHONE for two contact persons (see Figure 6.79). In contrast, BKNVK record has to be filled for each contact person in the SAP R/3 system.

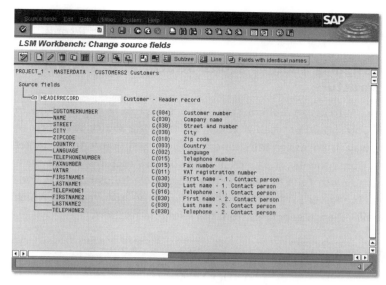

Figure 6.79 LSM Workbench—All Fields in a Source Structure

To solve this problem, you can define the rules shown in Figure 6.80 for target structure BKNVK.

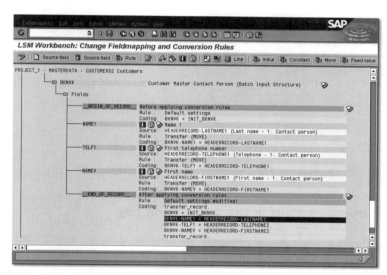

Figure 6.80 LSM Workbench—Duplicate a Record

The decisive point in the coding is at processing time __End_of_Record_ _. The first `transfer_record` statement transfers the BKNVK record with the data of the first contact person. The BKNVK record is then initialized, filled with the data of the second contact person, and written with the second `transfer_record` statement. This creates two BKNVK records.

6.9.5 Assigning Multiple Source Structures to a Target Structure

You may want to assign multiple source structures to a target structure. In this case, you should proceed as follows. Create the source structures in the usual way. Then, assign the subordinate source structure to the target structure. Consequently, the fields of both source structures will be available for the fields of the target structure. Figure 6.81 illustrates this constellation. The lower part of the diagram shows the ABAP coding, which the LSM Workbench generates from the structure relations.

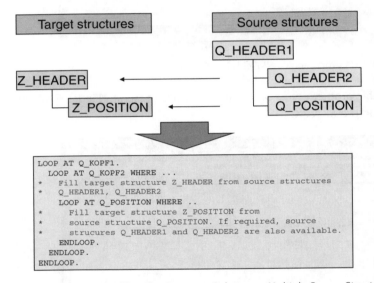

Figure 6.81 LSM Workbench—Structure Relations—Multiple Source Structures for One Target Structure

6.9.6 Error Messages in the Conversion Log

You will usually want to be informed about errors that occur during conversion. To do so, you can output your own error messages to the conversion log. Two options are available:

▶ Use the ABAP `WRITE` statement in the coding, for example, `WRITE:` `'Error during conversion of field ....'`.

▶ In the field mapping, go to the ABAP editor and choose **Insert · Message**. You can also output existing messages in the SAP R/3 system, for example:

```
WA_ERRORTAB-ID = '/SAPDMC/LSMW'.
WA_ERRORTAB-MSGNO = 012.
WA_ERRORTAB-PAR1 = 'A'.
WA_ERRORTAB-PAR2 = 'B'.
WA_ERRORTAB-PAR3 = 'C'.
WA_ERRORTAB-PAR4 = 'D'.
INSERT WA_ERRORTAB INTO TABLE G_ERROR_TAB.
```

The corresponding error message then appears in the conversion log.

6.10 Summary

We have now described all the functions in the LSM Workbench. You now know that the LSM Workbench is a tool that offers comprehensive support for your data migration requirements. And while you may not know every single detail about this tool, as you continue to work with the LSM Workbench, you will learn just how invaluable a tool it is. For more information and the latest news, visit the SAP Service Marketplace at *https://service.sap.com/lsmw*.

7 Techniques for Avoiding Programming

This chapter introduces several simple yet effective techniques to avoid programming during data migration projects, thus saving you time and money.

7.1 Problem Area: Data Conversion

When programming is required in a data migration project, it is usually needed for the following two activities:

▶ **Exporting the legacy data from the legacy system**
If the legacy system does not provide any functions for exporting the data, you will have to develop appropriate programs yourself or hire someone to do so. This step is usually not critical from a cost perspective, because the legacy system experts generally work at your company, which means costly external support is not needed.

Exporting Data

▶ **Converting the legacy data to the SAP data format**
The situation is much different here. This activity requires knowledge of both the structure of the SAP R/3 data format and of ABAP, SAP's programming language, because the data conversion (data transformation) takes place in the SAP R/3 system. These two skills are not always available in sufficient quantities during an SAP R/3 implementation.

Converting Data

Consequently, this chapter will concentrate on the problems associated with converting the data.

7.2 Techniques for Converting Data

The techniques for avoiding programming described here will show you how to use the CATT and Legacy System Migration Workbench (LSM Workbench) to migrate your legacy data to the SAP R/3 system with a minimum of programming—hopefully none at all.

How is this possible? You learned in Chapter 6 that a wide variety of conversion functions is available in the LSM Workbench at the touch of a button—without any programming. The predefined rules—assignment, translation, fixed value, prefix, constant, and so on—usually cover around 80% of all required conversion tasks. Therefore, this chapter is dedicated to the remaining 20%. To eliminate most of this remaining 20%, you will

80% Automation in the LSM Workbench

learn how to use programming-free techniques in Microsoft Excel and/or Microsoft Access to format your legacy data, thus enabling you to perform the entire conversion without programming—using the LSM Workbench, for example.

Modifying Structures and Field Contents

There are two basic problem areas or situations that the standard conversion functions in the LSM Workbench cannot deal with (or at least not do so gracefully). The following areas are affected:

▶ Modifying structures

▶ Modifying field contents

We will describe these problem areas in detail in next sections.

7.2.1 Modifying Structures

You have to modify structures when the fields are distributed to tables differently in the legacy system and the SAP R/3 system.

Flat Structures in the Legacy System Are No Problem

If the structure from the legacy system is "flatter" than the structure in the SAP R/3 system—that is, if certain data is stored in a single table in the legacy system, but distributed among several tables in the SAP R/3 system— the solution is simple. The LSM Workbench enables you to assign several structures from the SAP R/3 system (target structures) to the same structure in the legacy system (source structure). This was illustrated in the example involving customers in Chapter 6. The corresponding structure relations are shown again in Figure 7.1.

The opposite case, where the structures in the legacy system are "deeper" than those in the SAP R/3 system, is more complex. Based on the example of the customers, for example, this is the case when the data in the customer header is distributed between two structures in the legacy system. This situation is illustrated in Figure 7.2. As described in Chapter 6, you can assign only a single source structure to a target structure.[1] How can you solve this problem? Microsoft Access offers a simple solution.

Join with MS Access

The basic idea is to group the two structures HEADER1 and HEADER2 together to form a single structure. In database terminology, this is called a *join*.

---

1 One trick was described in Section 6.9.5; however, it cannot always be applied.

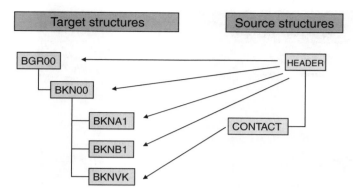

Figure 7.1 Source Structures Flatter Than Target Structures—Example "Customers"

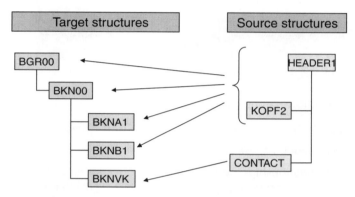

Figure 7.2 Source Structures Deeper Than Target Structures—Example "Customers"

Assume, for example, that the fields in the HEADER structure from the customer example are distributed between structures HEADER1 and HEADER2 as follows:

▶ **HEADER1**
CUSTOMERNUMBER, NAME, STREET, CITY, ZIPCODE, COUNTRY

▶ **HEADER2**
CUSTOMERNUMBER, LANGUAGE, PHONENUMBER, FAXNUMBER, VATRN (VAT registration number)

With Microsoft Access, you can use the drag-and-drop technique—without any programming—to effortlessly create a structure that contains all fields of both structures.

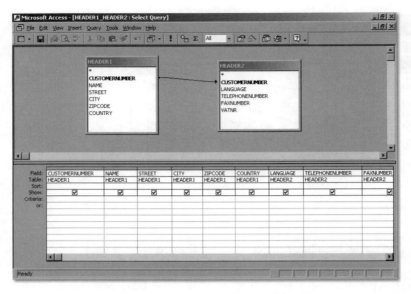

Figure 7.3 Microsoft Access—Join of HEADER1 and HEADER2

To do so, use the following procedure:

▶ Import tables HEADER1 and HEADER2 into Microsoft Access.[2]

▶ Define a *select query* for these two tables.

▶ Define the key relationships by dragging the corresponding fields— that is, drag the CUSTOMER_NUMBER field from HEADER1 to the CUSTOMER_NUMBER field of HEADER2.

▶ Use the drag-and-drop technique to select all the table fields from HEADER1 and HEADER2 for the results table.

▶ Save the query under the name HEADER1_HEADER2.

▶ Run the query.

▶ Export the results in format **Text (Tab-Delimited) (*.txt)**.

▶ Process this file with the LSM Workbench.

The select query described above is shown (in draft view) in Figure 7.3.

The structure relations are now simplified as shown in Figure 7.4. Therefore, you can take the case that the LSM Workbench could not solve initially (see Figure 7.2) and transform it to a situation whose structure rela-

---

2 Access can read worksheets from Excel files directly, without requiring them to be saved in format **Text (Tab-Delimited) (*.txt)**. You can also establish a link between Access and an Excel file. Access retrieves the information directly from the original file in this case.

tions correspond to those shown in Figure 7.1, which the LSM Workbench can now process.

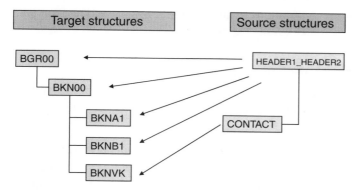

Figure 7.4 Simplified Structure Relations After Join of HEADER1 and HEADER2

This simple yet effective join technique can be applied in multiple areas, as the more abstract example shown in Figure 7.5 illustrates.

Generalization of the Technique

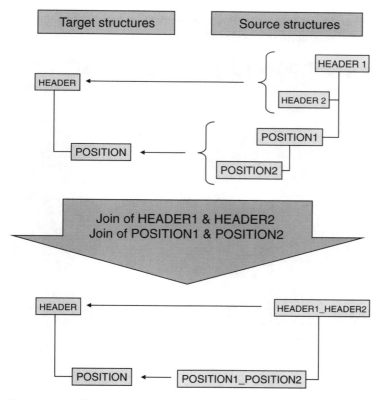

Figure 7.5 Join Technique—Abstract Example

7.2.2 Modifying Field Contents

This section shows you how you can use Microsoft Excel to perform frequently required modifications to field contents, again avoiding programming.

Date Formats

Date values appear in practically every data object. The SAP R/3 system expects these values in a specific format, depending on the selected import technique:

Batch Input
▶ Under the batch input technique, the system generally expects date values to have the same format as the one defined in the settings for the R/3 user ID—such as MM/DD/YYYY. Reminder: When you choose menu path **System · User Profile · Own Data** in the R/3 initial screen, and then click on the **Defaults** tab, you see the screen shown in Figure 7.6. You can specify here how you want date values to be displayed (among other things).

BAPI and IDoc
▶ The BAPI and IDoc import techniques generally require date values to be in the internal format YYYYMMDD.

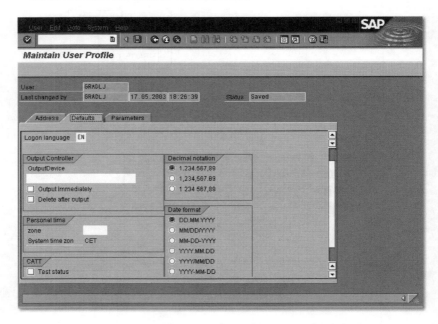

Figure 7.6 SAP R/3 System—Maintaining the User Defaults

How can you convert date values from MM/DD/YYYY to YYYYMMDD, for example? Proceed as follows:

▶ Select the appropriate table column in Microsoft Excel, right-click to open the context menu, and choose **Format Cells ...**

▶ Choose the **Number** tab.

▶ Click the category **Custom** and enter the value "YYYYMMDD" in the **Type** field, as shown in Figure 7.7.

▶ When you now save the file in format **Text (Tab-Delimited) (*.txt)**, the date values will be output in the format YYYYMMDD.

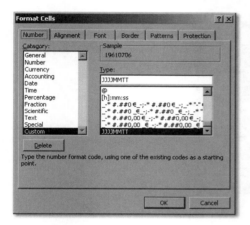

Figure 7.7 Selecting Date Format YYYYMMDD

Please note that the LSM Workbench described in Chapter 6 provides comprehensive support for converting date values: When you declare a field from the legacy system as a date value (see Section 6.4.3) and assign it to a date field in the SAP R/3 system later on, the LSM Workbench calculates the correct format automatically.

Support by the LSM Workbench

Number Formats

Like date values, number values appear in practically every data object. The SAP R/3 system also expects a specific format here, depending on the selected import technique:

▶ The batch input import technique generally expects number values to have the format configured in the settings for the SAP R/3 user ID—analogous to date values—for example, 123.456,78 with a comma as the thousand separator and period as the decimal point (see Figure 7.6).

Batch Input

▶ The BAPI and IDoc import techniques typically expect number values in the internal format 123456.78—that is, without thousand separators and with a period as the decimal point.

How do you convert a number format, for example, from 123,456.78 to 123456.78? Once again, the procedure is simple:

▶ Select the appropriate table column in Microsoft Excel, right-click to open the context menu, and choose **Format Cells ...** The dialog box shown in Figure 7.8 appears.

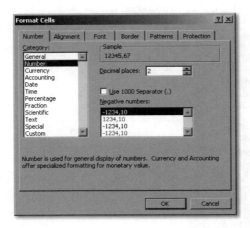

Figure 7.8 Selecting the Number Format—Without Thousand Separator

▶ Choose the **Number** tab.

▶ Click on the **Number** category and deactivate the checkbox **User 1000 Separator (.)**.

▶ When you now save the file in format **Text (Tab-Delimited) (*.txt)**, the number values will be output in the format 123456.78.

If your locale uses the decimal comma, you now have to convert the decimal comma to a decimal point. To do so, while Excel is open, select the **Regional Options** from the Windows system settings and make the appropriate changes there (see Figure 7.9). The data in Excel is updated instantly.

Once again, note that the LSM Workbench described in Chapter 6 provides support for converting number formats: When you declare a field from the legacy system as an amount field (see Section 6.2.5) and assign it to an amount field in the SAP R/3 system later on, the LSM Workbench calculates the correct format automatically.

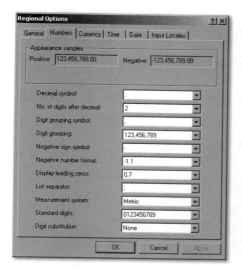

Figure 7.9 Regional Options—Selecting the Decimal Point

Modifying Currency Formats

Based on a currency field as an example, you will now learn how you can split data from a single field in the legacy system into two or more fields.

Assume the legacy system contains both an amount and a currency unit in a single field—for example, 123456,78 EUR. You have to provide the amount and currency unit separately in the SAP R/3 system. To do so, proceed as follows:

Splitting Field Contents

▶ Select the appropriate table column(s) in Microsoft Excel and choose **Data · Text in Columns ...** The first step of the Convert wizard appears (see Figure 7.10).

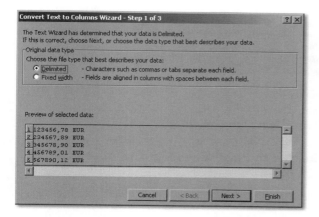

Figure 7.10 Convert Wizard—Step 1

▶ Choose the **Delimited** option and press **Next**. Step 2 of the Convert wizard now opens (see Figure 7.11).

▶ Select the option **Space** as the delimiter. You can check the results immediately in the preview.

▶ Press **Next** to continue to Step 3 (see Figure 7.12). You can now adopt the default settings and press **Finish** to end the transaction.

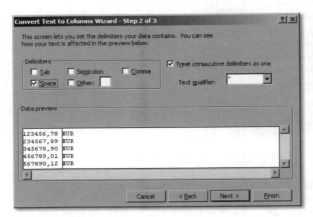

Figure 7.11 Convert Wizard—Step 2

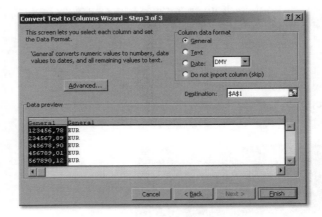

Figure 7.12 Convert Wizard—Step 3

▶ Save the file in format **Text (Tab-Delimited) (*.txt)**.

Converting Numbers with Plus/Minus Signs to Absolute Amounts

Eliminating Plus/Minus Signs
In this example, assume that your legacy system exports an amount field, which you have to import into the SAP R/3 system without plus/minus

signs, because the SAP R/3 saves these signs in the posting key. Therefore, you need the absolute amount of the field. How can you eliminate the plus/minus sign?

▶ Select the appropriate table column in Microsoft Excel, right-click to open the context menu, and choose **Format Cells ...** (see Figure 7.13).

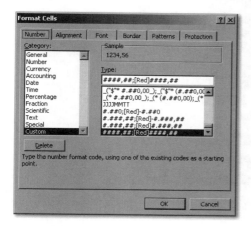

Figure 7.13 Selecting the Number Format—Negative Numbers in Red, but Without Plus/Minus Signs

▶ Choose the **Number** tab.

▶ Click on category **Custom** and select type **####.##;[Red]####.##**. This means negative numbers are displayed in red, but without plus/minus signs.

▶ When you now save the file in format **Text (Tab-Delimited) (*.txt)**, the number values will be output in the format 123456,78—without the plus/minus signs.

Leading Zeros in Bank Sort Codes

In some countries, such as Spain, banks have sort codes that can begin with zeros. If the customizing in your SAP R/3 system is configured such that sort codes must have a specific length, you will have to provide these leading zeros. Otherwise, the SAP R/3 system will reject the input with an error message.

If you open a file in Excel that has a column with bank sort codes, the leading zeros are removed because Excel interprets these values as numbers. **Saving Leading Zeros**

To suppress this Excel feature, proceed as follows:

▶ Open the text file with Excel. The first step of the Text Import Wizard opens.

▶ Choose the **Delimited** option as shown in Figure 7.14 and proceed with the second step.

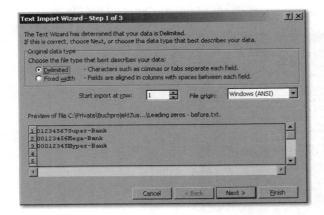

Figure 7.14 Text Import Wizard—Step 1

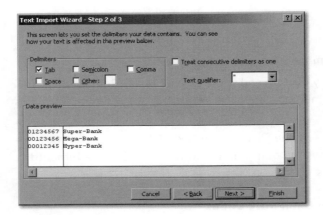

Figure 7.15 Text Import Wizard—Step 2

▶ Select **Tab** as the delimiter (see Figure 7.15). You can check the results immediately in the preview.

▶ In the third step, select the column with the sort codes, and activate the column data format **Text** (see Figure 7.16). The leading zeros will now be retained. Press **Finish** to exit the transaction.

▶ Save the file as usual in format **Text (Tab-Delimited) (*.txt)**.

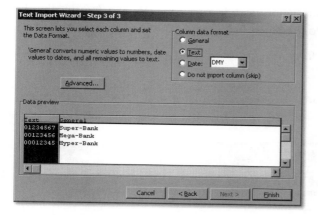

Figure 7.16 Text Import Wizard—Step 3

Joint Code Conversion of Two Fields

Chapter 6 described how you can use a table to convert a field from the legacy system to a field of the SAP R/3 system at the touch of a button. In some cases, however, the value of a specific field from the SAP R/3 system can be determined only by analyzing two (or more) fields in the legacy system at the same time.

Assume, for example, that you want to renumber your accounts in the course of replacing your legacy system. You want to determine a new account number dependent on the legacy account number and company code. Therefore, the challenge is to use a table like the one below to convert the data:

Renumbering Accounts

Source fields3		Target field
OldAccount	Company code	NewAccount
4000	1000	400001
5000	1000	500001
4000	2000	400002
5000	2000	500002, and so on

How can you take care of the translation in this case? To solve this problem, you can merge the two source fields in a single field, transforming the situation to a 1:1 translation, which you already dealt with above. Therefore, your solution strategy is:

Merging Two Source Fields in a Single Field

▶ Concatenate the two source fields to form a single source field.

▶ Perform a 1:1 translation from the new source field (created by the concatenation) to the target field.

You can easily perform the first step, the concatenation, in Microsoft Excel:

▶ Add a new column to your account file and name it **OldAccount_ CompanyCode**.

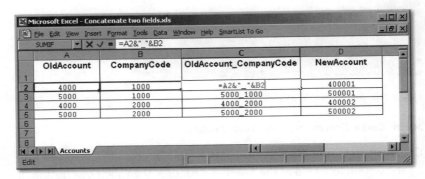

Figure 7.17 Concatenating Two Fields

▶ Enter the following formula in cell C2:

=A2&"_"&B2 .

This example assumes that the **OldAccount** field is located in column A and the **CompanyCode** field is located in column B (see Figure 7.17).

▶ Copy this formula to all the other rows. This concatenates the field contents of **OldAccount** and **CompanyCode** and separates them with an underscore (_) to improve readability.

▶ When you now save the file in format **Text (Tab-Delimited) (*.txt)**, you have merged the two fields **OldAccount** and **CompanyCode** to form a single field and can start the 1:1 conversion.

You could perform the translation in the LSM Workbench as shown in Figure 7.18.

Upload Function in the LSM Workbench
If you delete columns A and B from the Excel file and merely save columns C and D in format **Text (Tab-Delimited) (*.txt)**, you can use the upload function of the translation in the LSM Workbench. This saves you from having to enter the values manually.

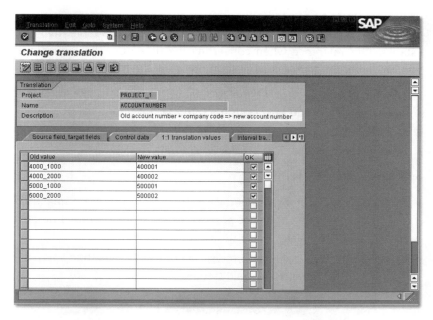

Figure 7.18 LSM Workbench—Translation of Concatenated Fields to the New Account Number

7.2.3 Accessing Data in the R/3 System

During the data conversion, you may have to access data in the SAP R/3 system.

Assume that customer numbers in your legacy system have evolved over time and that you want to reorganize them as part of your migration to SAP R/3. Accordingly, you decide to have the SAP R/3 system assign new customer numbers during the data migration. Therefore, you will choose *internal number assignment*. To avoid losing the reference between the old and new customer numbers, you will save the old customer number in a special table field in the SAP R/3 system that you define for this specific purpose.

Customer Numbers Evolved over Time

If you also want to migrate open debit items, however, which usually support only the old customer number, you will have to replace the old customer number with the new number in these open items, because the old number is used only for information purposes in the SAP R/3 system and does not represent an account that can be posted to.

The reference between the old and new customer numbers is available only in the SAP R/3 system, however—specifically in R/3 table KNB1. To establish this reference when converting the data from the documents, you can either program a custom solution or use the following procedure:

▶ Download the excerpt of the R/3 table that creates the reference between the old and new customer numbers to your local PC.

▶ Use Microsoft Access to replace the old customer number with the new customer number in the document data.

Specifically, proceed as follows:

▶ Migrate your customer master data to the SAP R/3 system using internal number assignment. In the process, store the old customer number in field KNB1-ALTKN.

▶ Start Transaction SE16 (Data Browser) in the SAP R/3 system and enter "KNB1" in the **Table Name** field (see Figure 7.19).

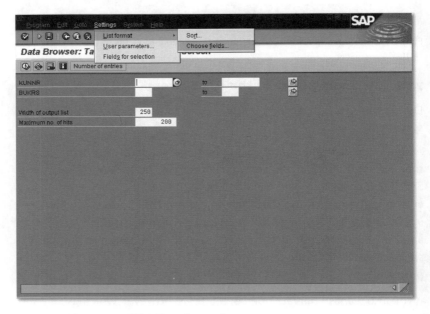

Figure 7.19 Transaction SE16 (Data Browser)

▶ Use fields KUNNR and BUKRS to select all the relevant data records.

▶ Enter a sufficiently large number in field **Maximum no. of hits**.

▶ Choose menu path **Settings · List Format · Field Selection ...** and select the fields MANDT, KUNNR, and ALTKN in the subsequent dialog box (see Figure 7.20). Press **Transfer** to confirm your selection.

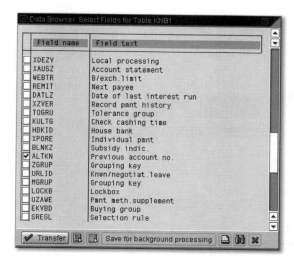

Figure 7.20 Transaction SE16 (Data Browser) — Field Selection

▶ When you press **Execute** (**F8**), the screen shown in Figure 7.21 opens.

▶ Now choose menu path **System** **List · Save · Local File**.

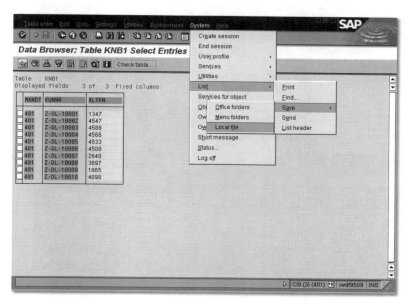

Figure 7.21 Transaction SE16 (Data Browser) — Saving the File

▶ In the dialog box that opens, choose **Spreadsheet** format.

▶ Enter a file name with extension *.xls* and press **Download**.

▶ When the data has been downloaded to your local PC, open the file in Excel. You will have to make several corrections—delete blank rows and columns, for example—so your file looks similar to the one in Figure 7.22.

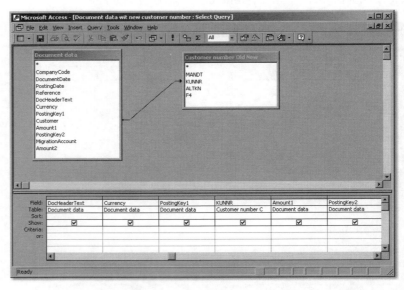

	A	B	C
1	MANDT	KUNNR	ALTKN
2	100	1000000040	3697
3	100	1000000041	1865
4	100	1000000042	1347
5	100	1000000043	4547
6	100	1000000044	4588
7	100	1000000045	4566
8	100	1000000046	4533
9	100	1000000047	4500
10	100	1000000048	2640
11	100	1000000049	3697
12	100	1000000050	1865
13	100	1000000051	4098
14	100	1000000052	1347

Figure 7.22 Table with Old and New Customer Numbers

Figure 7.23 Select Query in Microsoft Access for Replacing the Old Customer Number with the New One

You can now use Microsoft Access and this table to replace the old customer number, ALTKN with the new SAP R/3 customer number, KUNNR, in the document data.

To do so, define a select query in which you use the old customer number to establish a relationship between the table containing the document data and the table containing the relationship between the old and new customer numbers. Then select the new customer number as well (see Figure 7.23).

Replacing the Old Customer Number with the New One

Alternatively, you can upload the generated table (see Figure 7.22) without the **Client** column to a translation table in the LSM Workbench and use it there.

7.3 Summary

Make sure that all use of these techniques is documented in detail, as this is the only way to ensure that no essential steps have been left out during the migration of your production data.

Documentation Required

In addition, note that the techniques described here cannot be integrated directly in automated processes, such as periodic data migration.

Problems with Automatic Process Flows

Nonetheless, you are now aware of a number of situations that seem to require programming at first glance, but where the clever use of Microsoft Office applications can help you avoid more cost-intensive programming.

8 Assessment of Data Migration Techniques

Now that you have been introduced to the individual data migration techniques, you can critically assess them. In this chapter, you will learn about the advantages and disadvantages of each procedure, and the main criteria necessary to select a procedure for a specific situation.

8.1 Advantages and Disadvantages of the Procedures

8.1.1 Batch Input

Under the batch input procedure, comprehensive checks are performed when importing the data—processing the batch input session to the SAP R/3 system. These checks correspond to the checks performed during dialog processing. This minimizes the risk of incorrectly entered data, however, the additional checks pose a load on system performance. Depending on the system hardware and configuration, the batch input interface transfers between 10 and 40 data records per minute to the database server of the SAP R/3 systems.

Safe, but Slow

Incorrect transactions that the SAP R/3 system could not process during the batch input session remain in the batch input session (error session), while successfully executed transactions are removed from the batch input session. Consequently, during error handling—the repeated, visible processing of the batch input session—you see only the incorrect transactions that require manual postprocessing. You can either process the full error session right away or split it up for later processing, possibly by several different individuals.

Easy-to-Use Error Correction

The delivery scope of the SAP R/3 system contains standard batch input programs for a wide variety of applications, which you can use for your data migration—possibly in combination with the LSM Workbench (see Section 6.2). As a result, you can not only take advantage of the batch input technique features described above, but also benefit from the clear user guidance in the LSM Workbench.

Standard Batch Input Programs

Standard batch input programs are usually capable of generating the suitable screen sequence for a given set of input data, enabling it to be processed without errors.

As described in Section 4.4, two basic options for processing the supplied data are available when executing a batch input program:[1]

▶ **Processing with call transaction**

The call transaction technique nearly always processes the data more quickly than with batch input sessions. In contrast to the batch input sessions, however, the call transaction procedure does not support any automatic, interactive correction or log functions.

This technique also enables synchronous processing of the data. The user can choose between synchronous and asynchronous database updates in the selection screen when executing the program. The latter option is preferable for achieving a consistent system load.

▶ **Combined processing with batch input and call transaction**

The general benefits of the batch input procedure, such as data security and error correction options, have already been mentioned. If you want to combine these benefits with improved performance during the data transfer, you should consider the combined use of the batch input and call transaction procedures. To do so, you have to use the call transaction procedure to execute the data migration program, and also name an error session where all the incorrect transactions that the call transaction procedure cannot process will be placed. Manual post-processing of the error session can begin as soon as the initial program is complete. This procedure enables you to achieve two seemingly irreconcilable objectives: speed and data security.

If you need to migrate data for which no standard batch input programs are available, however (see Section 4.3), custom programming is unavoidable given the conventional approach. Even though the SAP R/3 system generates these programs almost automatically, based on an underlying recording, you will still have to enhance the coding, which requires at least rudimentary ABAP skills. You must equip the program with additional functionality, for example, to enable it to read more than just one data record—that is, a full data transfer file—into the SAP R/3 system and process it there (see Section 4.4).

A program generated from a recording models the process flow of that recording precisely; however, SAP transactions can react differently to different input data. This means the sequence of the screen templates is not always identical; it is frequently dependent on the specific input data.

A generated batch input program supports only the screen sequence from the recording, however. Therefore, you will have to define alternate

---

1 Some standard batch input programs also support this option.

screen sequences in the program logic that will be processed dependent on specific conditions, in order to react to the possibility of changing screen templates. This, in turn, means that you will have to create different recordings for the same transaction to generate the appropriate source code to deal with every eventuality, which can become an extremely complex task.

You can avoid custom programming altogether by exporting your recording and using it as the foundation for mail merge processing. Specifically, this means you have to transform all the data records for migration into the recording format, in order to import them back into the SAP R/3 system, generate a batch input session from them, and process that session (see Section 4.5).

Combined with Word Mail Merge Processing

You cannot assume that recording a transaction will always result in a data migration tool for producing the required batch input sessions. Accordingly, you should always reject recordings in which the number of line items per data record can vary. This is the case, for example, in the migration of purchase orders: In the extremes, purchase orders can consist of only one purchase order item or of several hundred.

Problem Case

Even though programming tricks can help you deal with such situations, this is not the objective of this book. Instead, we highly recommend that you use the LSM Workbench for such cases, as it enables you to solve such problems quickly, elegantly, and—the decisive factor—without programming.

The transfer of customer master data—including contact persons—described in Section 6.2 can also be attributed to this area.

8.1.2 CATT

The preparation involved in data migration using the CATT is extremely simple. You merely have to know which transaction you want to use to migrate the data. If you know this transaction, you can record a sample data record with all the relevant information for the data migration (variant), which you then parameterize to determine the format of the data to be migrated. You can export the variant to your PC to process it further there—that is, arrange all the data records for migration according to the format of the variant—and then import it back to the SAP R/3 system (see Section 5.3).

Simple Generation of Test Cases

If you need to perform a data migration that all the described procedures support, your preparation time will be the shortest if you use the CATT for data migration. Preparation time is defined as the time required to create

Shortest Preparation Time

an environment (batch input, CATT, LSM Workbench) where the data migration can take place.

No Programming Required Because the CATT does not require programming for data migration, it is also suitable for less technically oriented individuals.

Throughput Because the same input checks are performed when you execute a test case as in dialog or batch input processing, the speed with which the data can be imported is almost identical in both procedures.

Special Features of a Recording Like a batch input recording, the CATT transaction recorder records the exact sequence of processed transactions and their corresponding screen sequences. Once again, this means that the procedure is not flexible enough to react to differing screen sequences that can result from different data constellations.

Limited Error Correction Functions Unlike the batch input procedure, the CATT is not capable of collecting incorrect transactions from the data migration and presenting them for subsequent manual processing. When a test case is executed in the background and there is no opportunity for interaction, all error-free transactions are posted as expected. Incorrect transactions are skipped and, at most, highlighted in the log. Should you neglect to analyze the log subsequently, some data records that have to be migrated may be left out, permanently falsifying the results of the migration.

If you consider the original reason for creating the CATT, however—the automatic generation of test data to test business processes in the SAP R/3 system—there is no reason to expect sophisticated error correction functions like the ones that are available in batch input processing.

Display Errors Only If you use the CATT for data migration—as described in the previous section—you can avoid this problem by running all the test cases in **Display Errors** mode, which enables you to correct problems interactively as soon as errors in the dataset are detected. Once the error is corrected, the system automatically switches to background processing and continues in this mode until another error occurs. This switching between dialog and background processing continues until the session is complete.

Problems with Large Data Volumes If you assume that approximately 3,000 data records can be processed each hour (this assumption itself is highly dependent on the deployed hardware), it is apparent that this procedure can be extremely time-consuming when large data volumes are involved. Moreover, a constant user presence is required to correct any detected errors. If you can presume that the data is of high quality, however, with only a few errors or none at all, this issue is not as critical.

8.1.3 LSM Workbench

The undisputed strength of the LSM Workbench is its intuitive user guidance, which directs the user through the complex data migration process. The user is led through a logical sequence of work steps, while the thread is flexible enough to allow for variances that have proven useful in practice.

Clear User Guidance

The clear outline, with its organizational units "Project" and "Subproject," is very useful for keeping organized. The more complex your data migration project is, the more you will appreciate the outline. The project structure also supports the consistent distribution of the components relevant for the data migration—from the development system through the consolidation system to the production system.

Clear Organization

If you use different import techniques within a migration project (standard batch input, batch input recording, direct input, BAPI, IDoc), the LSM Workbench ensures that the procedure is still largely uniform from the user perspective, because all the work steps can be called from a single user interface.

All Import Techniques Under One Roof

The greatest strength of the LSM Workbench probably lies in its data conversion functions. Therefore, using the LSM Workbench is recommended whenever the structure and format of the data vary widely between the legacy system and the SAP R/3 system.

The LSM Workbench offers a high degree of flexibility at many different levels. Because it supports all the major import techniques, the range of data objects that can be migrated is very large. The combination of predefined conversion rules, which can be implemented at the touch of a button, and the option to implement your own ABAP coding at any juncture makes the possibilities nearly infinite.

Flexibility

However, a high degree of flexibility will inevitably lead to a certain amount of complexity. Although the LSM Workbench succeeds in hiding this complexity in a great many places, you should not underestimate the initial effort involved in learning how to use it. One indicator of this is the fact that Chapter 6 is by far the longest chapter in this book.

8.2 Reasons for Favoring a Certain Procedure

Once you have familiarized yourself with the strengths and weaknesses of each procedure, the next step is to select an adequate procedure for your specific migration task. Generally, you should always use the procedure that just provides the minimum number of functions that you need for

Assumptions

your specific situation. This means that the complexity of the procedure increases exponentially with the complexity of the migration task, with custom programming being the last resort.

8.2.1 Complexity of the Migration Task

Minor Complexity
If the migration task is not very complex—that is, it involves a uniform dataset with standardized transactions and screen sequences—you can use a recording. This can involve a batch input recording that you can combine with Word mail merge processing or the LSM Workbench. Alternatively, you could use the transaction recorder to create a recording with the CATT.

Increased Complexity
If the dataset is not homogeneous, as expressed in changing screen sequences, it is difficult to model such situations in recordings. Instead, you need a procedure that can process different screen sequences without requiring manual intervention. The solution here is a combination of the LSM Workbench and a standard batch input program. If the standard batch input program that you need is not available, look for suitable BAPIs or IDocs, which you can also integrate with the LSM Workbench.

8.2.2 Quality of the Legacy Data

High Data Quality
If you can assume a high degree of data quality, there is only a low—or even negligible—risk that incorrect data records will be created. Because error handling plays only a subordinate role in such situations, you can use procedures with limited support for error processing, such as the CATT and batch input procedures combined with call transaction.

Low Data Quality
However, if the data quality is low or unknown, the probability of errors is correspondingly high. In such cases, you will appreciate the benefits of the batch input procedure, especially the error sessions and their easy-to-use correction options.

8.2.3 Data Volume

Small Data Volume
If you have to migrate relatively few data records (less than around 10,000 transactions), the throughput of the batch input technique or the CATT should be sufficient.

High Data Volume
If you have to deal with 100,000 or more data records, the time factor is the central focus of your migration task. In such situations, the decision-making factors are reduced to a single question: How can you transfer the data to SAP R/3 as quickly as possible? The answer here is the direct input procedure, provided the SAP R/3 system supports it for the specific application. If so, you can combine it with the LSM Workbench.

If a BAPI exists for the application, you can also use it for the data migration, in combination with the DX Workbench (see Section 10.2).

8.2.4 The Importance of Data Security

If you require an extremely high degree of data security, you will have to rule out all data migration procedures that write data directly to the database. Even though the direct input procedure supports controlled writing to the database, the checks in such situations are insufficient. Instead, we highly recommend using the batch input procedure, with its sophisticated error detection and handling functions.

Security Before Speed

If you are certain that your data is of high quality and can therefore skip the time-intensive input checks that reduce throughput, you can consider the direct input procedure for large data volumes.

Speed Before Security

8.2.5 Reusability

Given efficiency and cost aspects, you should aim to reuse existing procedures for similar situations. Under no circumstances should an insignificant change to the task at hand require you to start over from scratch.

If you want to take a test case that you recorded with the CATT and use it for similar future migrations, you can do so by extensively parameterizing the fields. Moreover, if you link the CATT to Change and Transport Management, you can distribute test cases to several different SAP R/3 systems.

CATT

The LSM Workbench enables you to modify existing data migration objects at any time. Various constellations are imaginable here. On the one hand, there are several ways to copy a project (in the context of the LSM Workbench) from one system to another and modify it in the new system. On the other hand, you can also copy and alter a project within a single system.

LSM Workbench

In general, you can always edit recordings to make them reusable, either directly in the recording editor or in a file where you saved the recording. This procedure is not recommended, however, because it requires numerous manual changes to the recorded information.

Batch Input Recording

8.2.6 Restrictions

The CATT is not capable of processing transactions that are based on the *SAP GUI control technology*. Furthermore, you have to exclude all *non-SAP GUIs* from the test cases (also see Section 10.1).

CATT

Because all test cases are based on recordings, the general restrictions associated with recording (see Section 8.1.1) also apply here. For information on dealing with incorrect data records, see Section 8.1.2; notes on performance appear in Section 8.2.3.

LSM Workbench As described in detail in Chapter 6, the LSM Workbench provides powerful tools for processing various file formats and converting structures and field contents. Chapter 7 discusses its limitations. If the structures in the legacy system have a greater hierarchy depth than do the structures in the SAP R/3 system, for example, the LSM Workbench will not be able to deal with them (at least not without additional tricks). Complex conversions, such as converting two source fields to a single target field as described in Chapter 7, also require additional effort.

Batch Input Two primary restrictions apply to the batch input procedure: Custom-recorded functions are incapable of dealing with transactions that have variable screen sequences, and the procedure does not have sufficient throughput to support large data volumes.

8.2.7 User-Friendliness

LSM Workbench If you define user-friendliness as the degree to which the requirements of a migration procedure are fulfilled, the LSM Workbench with its numerous design options is clearly superior to the other procedures. Nonetheless, the complexity associated with this flexibility may frighten potential users at first. Still, we hope that this book has reduced—if not eliminated—such uncertainties, enabling you to apply the full spectrum of options supported by the LSM Workbench to your specific migration task.

CATT The attraction of the CATT is that the procedure is identical for all data migration tasks. Another advantage is that only a relatively small number of steps are required for a given migration task. If you define user-friendliness as ease of learning, then these two factors speak clearly in favor of the CATT.

Mail Merge Processing Although combining batch input recording with Word mail merge processing requires more steps than the CATT, the procedure is the same for every migration task here as well. Your additional preparation work is rewarded with an easy-to-use option for handling incorrect error messages: the batch input error session.

8.2.8 Summary

Ranking in Terms of Functionality The migration techniques can be clearly ranked according to their functional scope:

1. LSM Workbench

2. Batch input recording/call transaction

3. CATT

This ranking means that everything you can do with the CATT is also possible with the batch input recording or call transaction methods. In turn, the latter two techniques represent only a fraction of the options available in the LSM Workbench.

Because you should always select the simplest possible procedure for a data migration project, first examine whether a CATT can help you to achieve your migration objectives. If not, examine a more complex procedure — batch input recording or call transaction method. If these methods do not achieve the desired results either, you will have to use the most powerful procedure — the LSM Workbench.

Complexity and Functionality

Table 8.1 shows a decision matrix that takes the various decision-making factors into account.

		Complexity		Data quality		Data volume	
		High	Low	High	Low	High	Low
Data quality	High	LSM	CATT, CT				
	Low	LSM	BI				
Data volume	High	LSM	LSM + DX	LSM + DX	LSM		
	Low	LSM	CATT, BI, CT	CATT, BI, CT	BI		
Reusability	Important	LSM	CATT	CATT	LSM	LSM	CATT
	Unimportant	LSM	BI, CT	CT	BI	LSM	BI, CT
Key:							
BI = Batch input recording, possibly combined with mail merge processing in Microsoft Word							
LSM = LSM Workbench (with standard batch input, batch input recording, direct input, BAPI, IDoc)							
CT = Call transaction							
DX = Data Transfer Workbench (see Section 10.2)							

Table 8.1 Decision Matrix for Data Migration Procedures

Example
Assume that you have to deal with the following situation: The *complexity* of your migration task is relatively low, and you have a medium-sized *data volume*. Because you don't have any information about the *data quality*, you will have to assume that a high probability of errors exists. As far as efficiency is concerned, you are very interested in *reusing* the procedure to deal with similar situations in future.

By applying the decision matrix (displayed above) to this set of factors, you can derive the following information:

▶ Reusability important → CATT

▶ Low data volume → CATT

▶ Low data quality → BI

▶ Low complexity → CATT

Always Use the Simplest Procedure
Typically, you should always use the simplest available procedure to solve every partial problem. Because you have to solve the overall problem, however, and not just partial problems, you must select the procedure that takes into account all the different aspects of the problem at hand. For the preceding situation, batch input recording is the right choice, especially when combined with Word mail merge processing in order to avoid programming. Note that in the above example, the objective of reusability is sacrificed in favor of the other objectives.

Decision Matrix
If you apply the above decision matrix logically to your own migration projects, you will be able to identify the procedure that best meets your needs.

9 Migrating Fixed Assets with Microsoft Excel

In the previous chapters, you learned about migration techniques that can be used equally for all SAP applications. In this chapter, we will briefly compare the specific techniques for migrating fixed assets, before introducing you to a technique for migrating data with Microsoft Excel—a procedure that enables you to do away with ABAP programming altogether.

9.1 Assessment of Procedures for Migrating Fixed Assets

The migration of fixed assets is characterized by the fact that the data has to be transferred from an upstream system or from a manually managed fixed asset card file. This is usually the first activity after configuring Asset Accounting and classifying the assets. In this context, data migration refers to both migrating the asset master records and transferring the corresponding transactions, such as depreciation and acquisitions.

Migrating Master and Transaction Data

SAP R/3 provides several options for migrating fixed assets, which are listed and assessed briefly below:

▶ **Automatic migration using direct input**

This procedure is recommended for very large asset portfolios (more than 100,000 fixed assets) when you have to transfer the data to SAP R/3 as quickly as possible. The speed of this method comes at the expense of the data quality, however, as only rudimentary checks are performed during the import process. Furthermore, this method does not support asset retirements that have already taken place, nor group assets with asset subnumbers. The corresponding SAP R/3 program is called RAALTD11 and can also be run in combination with the LSM Workbench (see Chapter 6).

Very Large Asset Portfolio

▶ **Automatic migration using batch input**

Batch input is generally safer than direct input. Under the batch input procedure, comprehensive checks are performed during the data import, minimizing the risk of incorrect data records. But these additional checks create a load on system performance. This procedure is recommended for transferring large asset portfolios (between 50,000 and 100,000 fixed assets). Depending on the installed hardware and the system configuration, the batch input interface transfers between

Large Asset Portfolio

10 and 40 asset master records (including transactions) to the sub-ledger in Asset Accounting each minute. Conversely, the direct input procedure can process 10 times this number. Another advantage of the batch input procedure is that it supports asset retirements, as long as the legacy data transfer is performed at the end of the fiscal year. The corresponding R/3 program in this case is called RAALTD01, which you can integrate with the LSM Workbench similarly to RAALTD11.

Medium-to-Large Asset Portfolio ▶ **Automatic transfer using BAPI**
In contrast to the procedures described above, this procedure also supports the transfer of asset retirements when the legacy data transfer is performed in mid-year. We recommend using the BAPI method in combination with the LSM Workbench whenever you have to migrate medium-to-large asset portfolios (between 50,000 and 100,000 assets). Please note, however, that this method does not support asset groups or investment support.

Medium-Sized Asset Portfolio ▶ **Automatic transfer using Microsoft Excel**
You should use this procedure whenever you have a medium-sized num-ber of legacy assets to transfer (less than 50,000 assets) and want to avoid ABAP programming. Because an asset record usually requires at least five rows in Excel, as you will see below, and an Excel worksheet contains only a limited number of rows, you may have to distribute the assets to be migrated among several Excel files and then import them into SAP R/3 one after another. The Excel procedure offers similar performance to the batch input procedure. Please note, however, that the Microsoft Excel method cannot be used to migrate asset retirements, group assets, asset subnumbers, or investment support.

Small Asset Portfolio ▶ **Manual transfer transaction/CATT**
If only a few assets (less than 100) have to be migrated, you should consider whether automatic migration techniques are required at all, or whether it might not be more efficient to use a specific data transfer transaction (AS91) to migrate the legacy data manually. None of the restrictions described for the other procedures apply to manual migra-tion.

CATT Test Case ▶ If you have to migrate more than 100 fixed assets, entering the data manually in Transaction AS91 can be arduous. Because this transaction offers useful support, however, you should consider integrating trans-action AS91 in a CATT test case, which does not require any ABAP pro-gramming. In this context, Transaction AS91 is also suitable for migrat-ing medium-to-large data volumes. You can read more about the CATT in Chapter 5.

This brief comparison shows the strengths and weaknesses of the individual methods. Therefore, before you choose a procedure, you should know exactly which data you want to migrate to SAP R/3 and how important the factors of performance and data security are in your specific situation. Once you have clarified these criteria, you can choose the method you deem most appropriate to perform the legacy data transfer. It also shows, however, that the requirements of a data migration project can become so complex that they cannot all be satisfied by a single procedure. In such cases, look for a *combination of procedures*. Consider a situation, for example, in which the number of assets to be transferred is so large that only the direct input procedure and its high performance can be considered, but at the same time involves asset retirements, which direct input does not support. In such cases, you have to define which procedure you will use to migrate which assets.

Selecting the Migration Procedure

Regardless of which data transfer method you choose, your first step is to configure the SAP R/3 system to enable the transfer of legacy data. To do so, choose **Financial Accounting · Asset Accounting · Asset Data Transfer · Set Company Code Status** in Customizing (see Figure 9.1).

R/3 Customizing

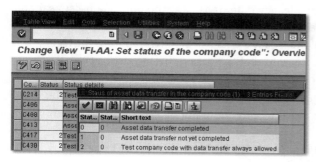

Figure 9.1 Setting the Status of the Company Code

We differentiate between three system states:

► **Test status = 2**
If this status is set, you can both enter postings in Asset Management and migrate legacy data.

System States in Asset Accounting

► **Transfer status = 1**
This status supports only the legacy data transfer, which means the postings to Asset Management are blocked in the SAP R/3 system.

► **Production status = 0**
Set this status when you have completed the legacy data transfer successfully. No further transfers of legacy data are allowed. Postings are required to implement any future changes in values.

You must set the company code status to either 2 or 1 to transfer the legacy data.

At this juncture, we should mention that the G/L accounts in Financial Accounting are not updated in any of the preceding procedures; only the corresponding asset master data and line items in Asset Management are updated. Therefore, the legacy data transfer does not support automatic integration between the general ledger and the subledger, as is normally the case for subledger postings. You must reconcile the balances manually with the particular G/L accounts in an additional step.

If Financial Accounting is already live in your SAP R/3 system before you implement Asset Accounting, however, the balance sheet accounts for the fixed assets and the corresponding depreciation accounts will already be up-to-date. This means that you don't have to transfer the balances from Asset Accounting to the general ledger (see Section 9.4).

9.2 Types of Legacy Data Transfer

End of Fiscal Year
or Mid-Year

Depending on when the assets are transferred to the SAP R/3 system, you can choose between a legacy data transfer at the end of a fiscal year and a mid-year legacy data transfer. The data transfer date is the date on which the posting status of the legacy assets will be migrated from the legacy system to SAP R/3. Please note that the data transfer date is generally different from the time the data is physically recorded in SAP R/3. The physical recording of the legacy data often takes place after the data transfer date, because various closing activities are required in the legacy system.

9.2.1 Legacy Data Transfer at End of Fiscal Year

Master Data, APC,
and Accumulated
Depreciation

If the legacy data transfer date is the end of the last closed fiscal year (usually December 31, YYYY), the master data, acquisition and production costs, and accumulated depreciation are transferred to the R/3 system in their values from end of the last closed fiscal year (31.12.YYYY). In this case, no mid-year depreciation or transaction postings can be included in the legacy data transfer.

To configure the necessary Customizing settings, choose the following menu path: **Financial Accounting · Asset Accounting · Asset Data Transfer · Parameters for Data Transfer · Date Specifications · Specify Transfer Date/Last Closed Fiscal Year** (see Figure 9.2).

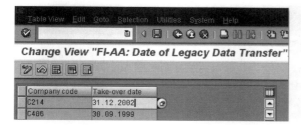

Figure 9.2 Legacy Data Transfer at End of Fiscal Year

You specify the last fiscal year before the transfer.

9.2.2 Legacy Data Transfer in Mid-Year

In a mid-year legacy data transfer, the transfer date is after the end of the last closed fiscal year. Under these framework conditions, the master data and accumulated values are transferred at the beginning of the year (usually 01.01.YYYY + 1). Also, you must migrate all the depreciation and transaction postings that have occurred during the current year (that is, in YYYY + 1). Configure the Customizing settings required to transfer the assets—as of March 1, 2003, for example—analogous to the procedure described in Section 9.2.1 (see Figure 9.3).

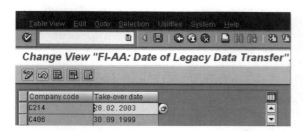

Figure 9.3 Mid-year Legacy Data Transfer on March 1, 2003

In addition to the data transfer date, you have to record the period when the last depreciation was posted in the legacy system. You configure the necessary Customizing settings under **Financial Accounting · Asset Accounting · Asset Data Transfer · Parameters for Data Transfer · Date Specifications · Specify Last Period Posted in Prv. System (Transf.During FY)** (see Figure 9.4).

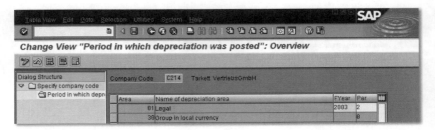

Figure 9.4 Specifying the Period of the Last Depreciation Posted in the Legacy System

Depreciation in the Current Year

You can differentiate your handling of depreciation postings in the current year (YYYY + 1):

▶ **Transfer of depreciation posted in the current year**
One alternative is to transfer all the depreciation posted in the legacy system up to the transfer date. In the last example, this means transferring the depreciation posted in the legacy system up to 28.02.YYYY + 1. Accordingly, the new system—SAP R/3 in this case—posts the first scheduled depreciation on 31.03.YYYY + 1.

▶ **No transfer of depreciation posted in the current year**
The other option is to not transfer the depreciation posted in the current year at all. The total depreciation from the current year that has accumulated up to the transfer date is duplicated as extraordinary depreciation, which occurs after the legacy data is transferred to SAP R/3. In this example, you also have to start an extraordinary depreciation posting run on 31.03.YYYY + 1. Therefore, all depreciation accumulated in YYYY+1 is posted in March. You can then start the scheduled depreciation posting runs in April.

9.2.3   Other Options for Transferring Asset Data

You can use the parameterizations described below (see Figure 9.5), but they are by no means required.

▶ **Recalculate depreciation for previous years**
If you want to define a new depreciation area in SAP R/3 that did not exist in your legacy system, such as book valuation or tax-based valuation of the fixed assets, you can have the SAP R/3 system recalculate the accumulated depreciation for this depreciation area up to the last closed fiscal year. You can use the depreciation parameters defined in SAP R/3. You can use this option only when the company code is set to test status (2).

- ▶ **Recalculate replacement values and base insurable values**

  If you activate this option, the system assumes that the acquisition value has been fully posted at the time of capitalization.

- ▶ **Specify the sequence of depreciation areas**

  This option has a direct impact on performance when you use the batch input method to migrate the legacy data. In this context, you must enter the independent depreciation areas first. Dependent depreciation areas whose values are derived from the independent depreciation areas should be named last.

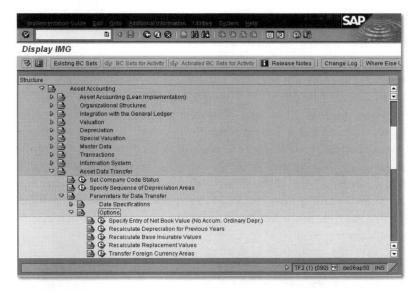

Figure 9.5 Other Options for Transferring Asset Data

Note that the order of the depreciation areas in the data transfer file can differ from the sequence defined in Customizing.

9.3 Case Example: Migrating Fixed Assets with Microsoft Excel

Now that you have learned about the Customizing settings that are required regardless of which migration method you use, we will describe the migration of asset data with Microsoft Excel in more detail.

This method is useful particularly when you have to migrate only small or medium-sized data volumes. Because the number of rows is finite in Microsoft Excel worksheets, an Excel file can process only a limited number of fixed assets. If you run out of lines in a Microsoft Excel worksheet,

Small and Medium-Sized Asset Portfolios

you can simply split the data among several Excel files and then import the files into the SAP R/3 system in sequence.

The next section describes how to use this method, based on a brief case example.

9.3.1 Which Data Should You Transfer?

As we mentioned in Chapter 2, "Which data should you transfer?" is the first question that you must address in any data migration project. Only after you answer this question can you consider the best migration method to use and compose the team necessary to support the data migration project.

Assumptions   In this example, you assume that the user department responsible for asset accounting already uses the correct SAP terminology. This means that translation of field texts in the legacy system to the corresponding field texts in the SAP R/3 system—a process that may require a great deal of coordination and system demonstrations—is not necessary. Moreover, the user department must be able to provide an Excel file that contains the asset values to be migrated in table form (one complete data record in each row; see Figure 9.6). Extracting the data from the legacy system is not always a simple task, either. You may have to refer to external consultants to accomplish this task, a fact that you will have to address when assembling your project team.

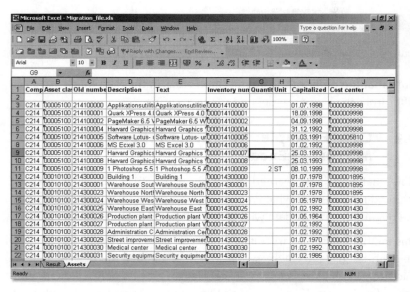

Figure 9.6 Fixed Assets to Be Transferred to Microsoft Excel (Not Formatted)

The Excel file contains one complete data record in each row, consisting of master data information such as the company code, asset class, (legacy) asset number, and cost center, along with transaction data such as the accumulated Acquisition and Production Costs (APC) and accumulated depreciation for each depreciation area (the latter of which does not appear in Figure 9.6).

9.3.2 Data Format for the Transfer to SAP R/3

The SAP R/3 system expects the data transfer file in a specific format. As a result, even if the Excel file provided by the user department contains all the relevant information, the file still cannot be imported into SAP R/3 in this format. To be transferred correctly, the structure of the Excel file must resemble the structure displayed in Figure 9.7.

	A	B	C	D	E	F	G
1	0	Identifier					
2	1	Company code	Asset class	Description	Text	Quantity	Base unit of meas
3	2	Cost center	Business area	Location	Manufacturer	Property indicator	Type of insurance
4	3	Depreciation area	Depreciation key	Useful life in years	Useful life in periods	Depreciation calculatio	Cumulated APC
5	4	Sequential number	Real depreciation area	Transaction type	Amount	First acquisition on	
6							
7	0	214100000					
8	1	C214	00005100	Application utility D	Applikationsutilitie D (Ekström)		
9	2	0000009998	0014	FTSO00		1	02
10	3	01	LING	003	000	01.07.1998	6.820,67
11	3	30	LING	003	000	01.07.1998	6.820,67
12							
13	0	214100001					
14	1	C214	00005100	Quark XPress 4.0 V	Quark XPress 4.0 Win95/NT multilingual		
15	2	0000009998	0014	FTSO00		1	02
16	3	01	LING	003	000	01.09.1998	1.388,16
17	3	30	LING	003	000	01.09.1998	1.388,16
18							
19	0	214100002					
20	1	C214	00005100	PageMaker 6.5 Wir	PageMaker 6.5 Win95/NT dt.		
21	2	0000009998	0014	FTSO00		1	02
22	3	01	LING	003	000	01.09.1998	896,26

Figure 9.7 Fixed Assets to Be Transferred to Microsoft Excel (Formatted)

Rows 1 to 5 of the Excel file form the *header section*. You use them to determine which asset information (company code, asset class, cost center, accumulated APC, accumulated depreciation, and so on) you want to migrate. The remaining rows, starting from row 6, determine the *asset section*. The values for the individual assets to be migrated are entered here. Note that a blank row appears between the header section and the asset section. Furthermore, the individual assets in the asset section are each separated by a blank row.

Minimum Data for Transfer	At the minimum, the Excel file must provide placeholders (fields) in the header section for the identifier—that is, the asset number from the legacy system—the company code, the asset class, and the capitalization date of the asset. You have to supply these fields with values for every fixed asset in the lower asset section. If you have defined required entry fields for certain asset classes in Customizing for Asset Accounting, you will also have to reserve fields for these required entry fields in the header section, as they also have to be assigned values in the asset section.
Relationship Between Header Section and Asset Section	Aside from the minimum requirements that you defined in the header section, you do not have to fill all the fields in the asset section with values. The header section merely represents the maximum set of fields that can be transferred. You can decide whether you want to use all the fields for each individual asset.
Data Structured by Record Type	The asset values to be transferred are organized in *record types*. You enter the record type in the first column of the Excel file. The subsequent columns contain the fields that are assigned to each record type. A maximum of five record types is supported, but not all record types are required.

▶ **Record type 0**
Contains only the identifier, the number of the fixed asset in the legacy system. This identifier is required to assign any errors that occur during the data migration to a specific asset. The error log that is generated during the data migration is described in Section 9.3.5.

▶ **Record type 1**
The asset master data is entered here, along with general data and inventory data.

▶ **Record type 2**
Contains posting information and time-dependent data.

▶ **Record type 3**
The depreciation areas are defined here, along with accumulated and posted values. Please note that the depreciation area always has to be named first.

▶ **Record type 4**
Contains all asset transactions. The sequence number and depreciation area have to be entered in the first two columns. The sequence number differentiates the various postings in the current year. Therefore, you can use record type 4 whenever you want to transfer data in mid-year (see Figure 9.8).

Record type	Seq. number	Area	Transaction Type	Amount	Posting date
4	1	01	100	5000	01/01/97
4	1	02	100	4900	01/01/97
4	2	01	100	1000	01/01/97

Figure 9.8 Asset Transactions in a Mid-Year Data Migration

If certain record types are not required to transfer the data—such as record type 4 in the previous example—you don't have to include them in the structure of the Excel file (in either the header or asset sections).

As mentioned above, the asset values are listed below the header section. You enter them in the Excel file according to the structure of the header section.

Assume, as shown in Figure 9.7, that you have defined the header section for record type 1 such that the company code appears in column B and the asset class appears in column C. In this case, the field contents of all record type 1 fields will be interpreted as the company code in column B and as the asset class in column C. Accordingly, you must ensure for every asset that all the rows that are identified as record type 1 have the company code in column B and the asset class in column C. The procedure is similar for the other record types.

Dealing with Leading Zeros

Remember that fields that are displayed with *leading zeros* in the SAP R/3 system have to have this same format in the Excel file. Accordingly, the company code must always have four places and the asset class must have eight.

Using Place-holders

When you start preparing for the legacy data transfer, it is entirely possible that the enterprise structures have not all been defined yet. If the name of the company code has not been defined yet, for example, you can define a variable for it (e.g., CoCd = X). You can then use the Excel **Search and Replace** function to set the company code to the desired values prior to the data transfer.

Formatting the Data Transfer File

Now that you are familiar with the data transfer format used by SAP R/3, the next step in the case example is to take the Excel file that was provided by the user department and format it according to the requirements of the SAP R/3 system (see Figure 9.7). Because formatting the data manually is an onerous task, even if only a small number of assets have to be transferred, you can use the small macro described below to format the Excel file automatically.

9.3.3 Formatting Data with Visual Basic

Purpose of a Macro

Macros are useful whenever you have to perform an activity repeatedly in Microsoft Excel. Instead of performing this activity manually each time, you can automate the process. In this example, this means that you can automatically format the file provided by the user department in order to prepare it for the upload to SAP R/3. This automation involves a number of commands and functions that are saved in a Visual Basic module and can be performed at any time—to format the data, for example.

You have to use Visual Basic to write this macro, which represents a custom data formatting program in Microsoft Excel. Because the procedure is not particularly complicated and can be used as a template for transferring all assets with the Excel procedure, it is described below.

Assumptions

The macro is based on the following assumptions:

▶ The assets to be transferred are available in table-like form in a worksheet of an .xls file (see Figure 9.6).

▶ Record types have been assigned to the asset values to be transferred.

▶ The macro adds an additional worksheet, which formats the asset values appropriately for the data transfer to SAP R/3, to the .xls file.

Creating the Macro

To create a macro, open the file that your user department provided in Excel and choose **Tools · Macro · Macros ...** The dialog box shown in Figure 9.9 opens.

Figure 9.9 Creating a Macro in Microsoft Excel

Enter a name for your macro and click on **Create**. An editor appears, in which you must enter the following program coding in Visual Basic:

```
 1 Sub NewStructure()
 2
 3    Dim vRow As Variant, vResRow As Variant
 4    Dim MaxRow As Integer
 5    Const kOriginalSheet = "Assets"
 6    Const kResultSheet = "Result"
 7    vResRow = 1
 8    vResCol = 1
 9    MaxRow =
        Worksheets(kOriginalSheet).UsedRange.Rows.Count
10 With Sheets(kResultSheet)
11 For vRow = 3 To MaxRow
12        .Cells(vResRow, 1).Value = "0"
13        .Cells(vResRow, 2).Value =
          Sheets(kOriginalSheet).Cells(vRow, 3).Value
14     vResRow = vResRow + 1
15        .Cells(vResRow, 1).Value = "1"
16        .Cells(vResRow, 2).Value =
          Sheets(kOriginalSheet).Cells(vRow, 1).Value
17        .Cells(vResRow, 3).Value =
          Sheets(kOriginalSheet).Cells(vRow, 2).Value
18        .Cells(vResRow, 4).Value =
          Sheets(kOriginalSheet).Cells(vRow, 4).Value
19        .Cells(vResRow, 5).Value =
          Sheets(kOriginalSheet).Cells(vRow, 5).Value
20        .Cells(vResRow, 6).Value =
          Sheets(kOriginalSheet).Cells(vRow, 7).Value
21        .Cells(vResRow, 7).Value =
          Sheets(kOriginalSheet).Cells(vRow, 8).Value
22        .Cells(vResRow, 8).Value =
          Sheets(kOriginalSheet).Cells(vRow, 6).Value
23     vResRow = vResRow + 1
24        .Cells(vResRow, 1).Value = "2"
25        .Cells(vResRow, 2).Value =
          Sheets(kOriginalSheet).Cells(vRow, 10).Value
26        .Cells(vResRow, 3).Value =
          Sheets(kOriginalSheet).Cells(vRow, 12).Value
27        .Cells(vResRow, 4).Value =
          Sheets(kOriginalSheet).Cells(vRow, 13).Value
28        .Cells(vResRow, 5).Value =
          Sheets(kOriginalSheet).Cells(vRow, 14).Value
```

```
29        .Cells(vResRow, 6).Value =
          Sheets(kOriginalSheet).Cells(vRow, 15).Value
30        .Cells(vResRow, 7).Value =
          Sheets(kOriginalSheet).Cells(vRow, 16).Value
31        .Cells(vResRow, 8).Value =
          Sheets(kOriginalSheet).Cells(vRow, 9).Value
32        .Cells(vResRow, 9).Value =
          Sheets(kOriginalSheet).Cells(vRow, 17).Value
33        .Cells(vResRow, 10).Value =
          Sheets(kOriginalSheet).Cells(vRow, 18).Value
34        .Cells(vResRow, 11).Value =
          Sheets(kOriginalSheet).Cells(vRow, 19).Value
35        .Cells(vResRow, 12).Value =
          Sheets(kOriginalSheet).Cells(vRow, 20).Value
36     vResRow = vResRow + 1
37        .Cells(vResRow, 1).Value = "3"
38        .Cells(vResRow, 2).Value =
          Sheets(kOriginalSheet).Cells(vRow, 21).Value
39        .Cells(vResRow, 3).Value =
          Sheets(kOriginalSheet).Cells(vRow, 22).Value
40        .Cells(vResRow, 4).Value =
          Sheets(kOriginalSheet).Cells(vRow, 23).Value
41        .Cells(vResRow, 5).Value =
          Sheets(kOriginalSheet).Cells(vRow, 24).Value
42        .Cells(vResRow, 6).Value =
          Sheets(kOriginalSheet).Cells(vRow, 25).Value
43        .Cells(vResRow, 7).Value =
          Sheets(kOriginalSheet).Cells(vRow, 26).Value
44        .Cells(vResRow, 8).Value =
          Sheets(kOriginalSheet).Cells(vRow, 27).Value
45     vResRow = vResRow + 1
46        .Cells(vResRow, 1).Value = "3"
47        .Cells(vResRow, 2).Value =
          Sheets(kOriginalSheet).Cells(vRow, 28).Value
48        .Cells(vResRow, 3).Value =
          Sheets(kOriginalSheet).Cells(vRow, 29).Value
49        .Cells(vResRow, 4).Value =
          Sheets(kOriginalSheet).Cells(vRow, 30).Value
50        .Cells(vResRow, 5).Value =
          Sheets(kOriginalSheet).Cells(vRow, 31).Value
51        .Cells(vResRow, 6).Value =
```

```
                Sheets(kOriginalSheet).Cells(vRow, 32).Value
52              .Cells(vResRow, 7).Value =
                Sheets(kOriginalSheet).Cells(vRow, 33).Value
53              .Cells(vResRow, 8).Value =
                Sheets(kOriginalSheet).Cells(vRow, 34).Value
54          vResRow = vResRow +2
55  Next vRow
56  End With
57  End Sub
```

Listing 9.1 Visual Basic Macro for Data Formatting in Excel

Remarks on Programming

We do not intend to deal with the syntax of Visual Basic at this point. Not only would this exceed the scope of this book, it would detract from our main focus of this book—avoiding programming wherever possible. You should consider programming only as a last resort, when your specific situation does not permit any other solution. We have provided an explanation of the coding in the text that follows. This should be sufficient to enable you to transfer the legacy data using the Excel procedure. This means you can use the above macro as a template for your migration activities, making only minor changes to reflect your specific requirements. The program sections you have to modify are described in detail further below. If you would like to learn more about Visual Basic, please consult the specialized literature on this subject.

Sub/End Sub

Every macro created in Visual Basic starts with Sub ⟨name⟩()—Sub New-Structure() in this case—and ends with End Sub (see program lines 1-57). Visual Basic creates this frame automatically as soon as you create a macro. The statements required for the formatting are specified in between them.

Declaration of Variables

As is the case in most programming languages, you first declare your variables and constants (see program lines 3-6). You declare variables with Dim ⟨name⟩ As ⟨data_type⟩ and constants with Const ⟨name⟩. Accordingly, the macro consists of the variables vRow, vResRow, and MaxRow, where vRow and vResRow have data type *variant*, which allows any characters. In contrast, MaxRow has data type *integer*, which means this variable can process only whole numbers.

Declaration of Constants

You declare kOriginalSheet, the original worksheet provided by the user department (see Figure 9.6), and kResultSheet, the worksheet formatted by the macro, as constants. These constants are assigned the values Assets and Result. If you want to name your worksheets differently, you merely have to change the values assigned to the constants in the dec-

laration section, without having to change the placeholders for the constants—kOriginalSheet and kResultSheet—in the program.

Initializing the Variables
Once you have declared the variables and constants, you can initialize the variables, or set them to initial values (see program lines 5-9). MaxRow is set to the number of rows in the original worksheet. If you want to migrate 1,000 legacy assets, for example, and the data record of your first asset appears in line 3 of the original worksheet—as in the above example— MaxRow is set to 1002.

Formatting
Once the variables and constants have been declared and initialized, you can begin formatting the worksheet for upload to SAP R/3, kResultS-heet. This formatting begins at With Sheets (kResultSheet) and ends at End With (see program lines 10-56). In between is a loop (see program lines 11-55), which is increased incrementally from row 3 of the original worksheet—where the first data record is located—until its end. This is achieved with the Next vRow command, which is located in program line 55. This guarantees that all the data records from the original worksheet can be processed and transformed to the correct format.

Simulating the Loop
The first time you run the loop, cell A1 of the formatted worksheet, which is addressed in Visual Basic with Cells(1,1), is set to the value 0 (see program line 12). This means record type 0 of the first data record appears in the upper-left corner of the worksheet, which corresponds to the required format. The cell to the right—Cells(1,2)—is set to the identi-fier of the original worksheet, which is located in Cells(3,3)—in cell C3 (see program line 13). All the information for record type 0 of the first asset has now been entered.

Addressing the Cells
Note that you can address the cells of the formatted worksheet with .Cells(x,y).Value, while addressing the cells of the original worksheet requires a preceding Sheets(kOriginalSheet). This is due to the parameter of the With Sheets statement, kResultSheet. In all cases in which no Sheets (worksheet) appears before the cell address, the system assumes that the worksheet in the parameter of the With Sheets state-ment—also kResultSheet in this case—is involved (see program line 10).

Formatting Record Types 1 and 2
The variable vResRow is now increased by 1, resulting in the new value 2 (see program line 14). This means the row changes, with the result that the next cell addressed in the formatted worksheet is Cells(2,1), which is set to the value 1, which once again identifies record type 1 (see program line 15). The next statements supply the cells of the formatted worksheet to the right of Cells(2,1) with the records for record type 1 from the original worksheet. These are contained in row 3 for the first asset to be

migrated and are addressed accordingly with `Cells(3,1)`, `Cells(3,2)`, and so on (see program lines 16-22). Once all the information for record type 1 has been set, the next row change takes place in the formatted worksheet, which means the preparation for record type 2 can begin (see program lines 23-35).

Formatting Record Type 3

The procedure for record type 3 is different. Because two depreciation areas have to be transferred, two rows have to be provided for this record type. Accordingly, the information for the first depreciation area is saved in `Cells(4,x)` and the information for the second depreciation area in `Cells(5,x)`. In this example, `x` can assume values between 1 and 8 (see program lines 36-53).

Because the transactions from the current year are not relevant for the data transfer, the information for record type 4 is not needed. Formatting of the first data record is now complete.

Processing the Subsequent Records

As mentioned above, a blank row must be inserted between the individual assets to ensure an error-free data transfer. This is achieved with the `vResRow = vResRow + 2` statement, which is located in program line 54. After `vRow` has also been increased by 1 and is now set to 4 (see program line 55), the second asset from the original worksheet, which is contained in row 2, can be formatted in a similar fashion. This process continues until `vRow = MaxRow`—that is, until the last row of the original worksheet is reached and all the assets have been converted to the data transfer format. Figure 9.10 shows the result of the macro.

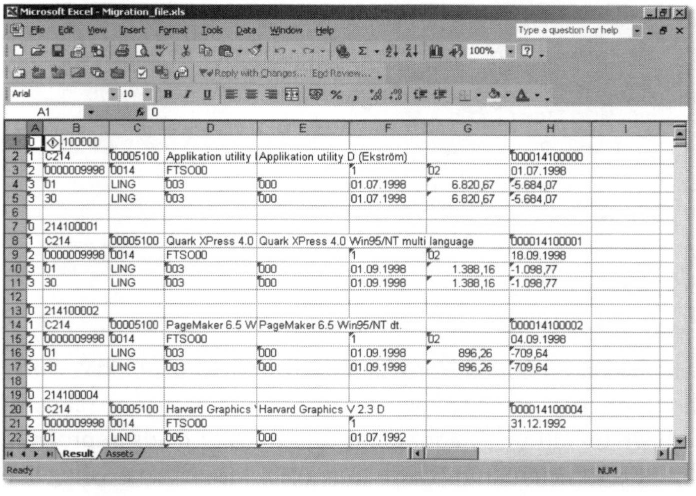

	A	B	C	D	E	F	G	H
1	0	100000						
2	1	C214	00005100	Applikation utility	Applikation utility D (Ekström)			000014100000
3	2	0000009998	0014	FTSO00		1	02	01.07.1998
4	3	01	LING	003	000	01.07.1998	6.820,67	-5.684,07
5	3	30	LING	003	000	01.07.1998	6.820,67	-5.684,07
6								
7	0	214100001						
8	1	C214	00005100	Quark XPress 4.0	Quark XPress 4.0 Win95/NT multi language			000014100001
9	2	0000009998	0014	FTSO00		1	02	18.09.1998
10	3	01	LING	003	000	01.09.1998	1.388,16	-1.098,77
11	3	30	LING	003	000	01.09.1998	1.388,16	-1.098,77
12								
13	0	214100002						
14	1	C214	00005100	PageMaker 6.5 W	PageMaker 6.5 Win95/NT dt.			000014100002
15	2	0000009998	0014	FTSO00		1	02	04.09.1998
16	3	01	LING	003	000	01.09.1998	896,26	-709,64
17	3	30	LING	003	000	01.09.1998	896,26	-709,64
18								
19	0	214100004						
20	1	C214	00005100	Harvard Graphics	Harvard Graphics V 2.3 D			000014100004
21	2	0000009998	0014	FTSO00		1		31.12.1992
22	3	01	LIND	005	000	01.07.1992		

Figure 9.10 Fixed Assets to Be Transferred to Microsoft Excel (Formatted, Without Header Section)

To avoid misunderstandings: The macro does not yet provide the file that you can upload to SAP R/3. It merely formats the asset section. Therefore, to create a file that the SAP R/3 system can read, you have to add the header section. To do so, copy the worksheet from Figure 9.10 that you just formatted to a new file called *Upload.xls*, and insert the header section accordingly (see Figure 9.7).

If you want to use this macro to format your data, you do not have to worry about the correct assignment between the header and asset sections in advance. Instead, you simply let the macro generate the asset section and then append the header part later at the top of your final *Upload.xls*, in line with the result of the asset part. You should also understand the second assumption of the macro in this context. You merely have to take the data from the worksheet provided by the user department, assign it to record types in your mind, and note the corresponding columns. If you identify columns 1, 2, and 4 as columns that have to be assigned to record type 1, for example, you can leave program lines 16 to 18 unchanged. However, if the identifier, which belongs to record type 0, is located in column 1 instead of column 3, and column 3 contains information for record type 1, you have to change the statement in program line 13 from

```
.Cells(vResRow, 2).Value =
Sheets(kOriginalSheet).Cells(vRow, 3).Value
```

to

```
.Cells(vResRow, 2).Value =
Sheets(kOriginalSheet).Cells(vRow, 1).Value
```

Program line 16 would change accordingly, from

```
.Cells(vResRow, 2).Value =
Sheets(kOriginalSheet).Cells(vRow, 1).Value
```

to

```
.Cells(vResRow, 2).Value =
Sheets(kOriginalSheet).Cells(vRow, 3).Value
```

Additional changes are needed, for example, when your original worksheet contains more data transfer fields for record type 1. In these circumstances, you have to add these additional data transfer fields in program lines 16 to 22. It is sufficient in this case to make a copy of an existing line and modify the copy accordingly. In contrast, if you want to transfer less information for each asset, you can simply delete the unnecessary lines in the formatting blocks.

As you can see, only minor modifications to the above macro are required to deal with specific situations. In this context, it is an excellent template for transferring legacy data, as long as you have to migrate only small to medium-sized data volumes.

Macro Can Be Used as a Template

9.3.4 Assigning the Data to R/3 Fields (Mapping)

Now that your data is available in the format expected by the SAP R/3 system, you can assign the fields in your *Upload.xls* file to the corresponding fields in the SAP R/3 system. Assign the R/3 **Company Code** field to field BUKRS in your Excel file, for example. This procedure is called *mapping*.

To conduct the mapping, choose menu path **Financial Accounting · Asset Accounting · Asset Data Transfer · Legacy Data Transfer using Microsoft Excel** or enter transaction code AS100 (see Figure 9.11).

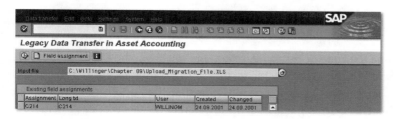

Figure 9.11 Initial Screen—Legacy Data Transfer with Microsoft Excel

In this initial screen, which starts the legacy data transfer using the Excel procedure, you first have to specify the path of the *Upload.xls* file. You can then choose whether you want to use an existing mapping or define a new one. One alternative is to select the corresponding mapping and click on the **Start Mapping** button. The second alternative requires you to click on the **Create Mapping** button and then enter a name for the mapping and an explanatory long text (see Figure 9.12).

Upload.xls

In this table, the system lists only the field texts that are defined in the header section of your *Upload.xls* file. They are sorted by record type 0, 1, 2, 3, and 4. The potential fields of the asset master records in the SAP R/3 system are distributed among different tab pages. The potential R/3 fields for record types 0 and 1 are located in the **Header Data** tab page. The fields from record type 2 are distributed across several tab pages. They range from time-dependent data to leasing. The same applies to the fields of record type 3, which are located in the tab pages **Depreciation Areas**,

Performing Mapping

Accumulated Values, and **Posted Values**. All fields from record type 4 are located on the **Transactions** tab page.

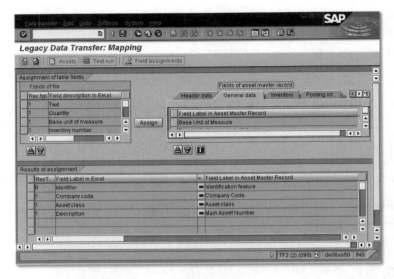

Figure 9.12 Legacy Data Transfer—Mapping

SAP R/3 Validation Checks

To define the specific mapping, select one row from the **Fields of file** table and fields of the asset master record in the **General data** tab page, and then click on the **Assign** button. Note that the system does not check whether this mapping makes sense. It merely verifies that each field from the *Upload.xls* file is assigned to exactly one R/3 field. As mentioned previously, you have to assign the identifier, the company code, the asset class, and the description, along with any defined required entry fields.

Saving the Mapping

The system asks whether you want to save the mapping prior to the data transfer. You can also save the mapping after the data transfer, however, with the **Saved Assignments** button. Consequently, you can reuse defined mappings for similar migration processes.

Checking the Date Format

Before you start the data transfer to the SAP R/3 system, you have to ensure that the date format in your *Upload.xls* file agrees with the date format configured in the SAP R/3 system. To check or change this setting, choose **Settings · Date Format**. SAP R/3 supports the following date formats: North American format (MM/DD/YY or MM/DD/YYYY), European format (DD.MM.YY or DD.MM.YYYY), ISO format (YYYY-MM-DD), and SAP format (YYYYMMDD).

9.3.5 Uploading the Data to SAP R/3 and Log File

You upload the assets to SAP R/3 in the same transaction where you defined the mapping previously. You can choose between a *test run* and an *update run* of the asset migration program.

If you perform the migration as a test run (with the **Test Run** pushbutton), the system lists completion confirmations without creating the assets in the database. Accordingly, the test run is equivalent to a simulation of the data migration, creating a comprehensive log for every fixed asset (see Figure 9.13).

Test Run

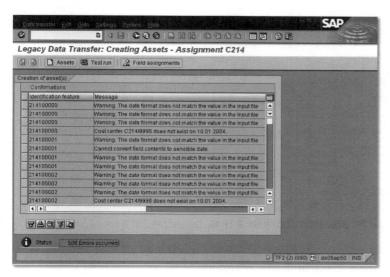

Figure 9.13 Log from Simulation of the Legacy Data Transfer

You can double-click on an entry in the log to display detailed information for the selected asset (see Figure 9.14).

The most frequent cause of errors is a discrepancy between asset values in the *Upload.xls* file and the R/3 Customizing of the corresponding asset class. Once you have changed the Customizing accordingly, you can start a new test run. We recommend repeating this iterative process until the test run ends free of errors. You can then start the update run by pressing the **Create Assets** button (see Figure 9.13).

Cause of Errors

During the update run, the system uses the values from the *Upload.xls* file to create new fixed assets; the fields in SAP R/3 are assigned values according to the defined mapping. To display the master records for successfully created assets, click on the **Details for Confirmation** button. A

Update Run

log of incorrect assets that could not be created is also displayed here. You can also download the error file to Microsoft Excel by clicking on the **Export Errors to File** button. You can now analyze and correct the errors, eliminating the last obstacles to a final upload.

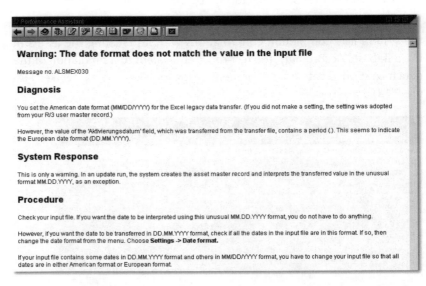

Figure 9.14 Error Log—Details

9.4   Preparing to Go Live

Now that you have successfully transferred the assets into SAP R/3, several concluding activities are always required, regardless of which data transfer method you used.

9.4.1   Setting Reconciliation Accounts

Balance Sheet Asset Accounts

Once you implement Asset Accounting, you can no longer post directly to the balance sheet asset accounts defined in the general ledger. Because the general ledger is integrated with the Asset Accounting subledger, however, the balance sheet accounts are updated automatically whenever a transaction takes place for an asset. Therefore, the subledger is the leading system, while the general ledger is the receiving system.

Manual or Automatic Setting of Reconciliation Accounts

As an alternative to setting reconciliation accounts manually in Financial Accounting, SAP R/3 provides a report that you can use to define G/L accounts for reconciliation accounts in Asset Accounting. In the process, the report selects the G/L accounts that are defined as balance sheet accounts under account determination in Asset Accounting. To do so, choose menu path **Financial Accounting · Asset Accounting · Preparing for Production Startup · Production Startup · Set Reconciliation Accounts**.

If you accidentally defined an incorrect account in account determination for Asset Accounting, or you have to make subsequent adjustment postings to Asset Accounting, you can use the following menu path to reset the reconciliation accounts: **Financial Accounting · Asset Accounting · Preparing for Production Startup · Production Startup · Reset Reconciliation Accounts**.

Resetting the Reconciliation Accounts

In this case, however, please note that consistency is no longer guaranteed between the subledger and the general ledger, because the balance sheet accounts can once again be posted to directly—without subledger integration.

Data Consistency

9.4.2 Transferring Balances

As mentioned above, this means the legacy data transfer does not support automatic integration between the general ledger and the subledger, as is normally the case for subledger postings. You therefore have to reconcile the balances manually with the involved G/L accounts in an additional step. You can omit this step if Financial Accounting was already active in your SAP R/3 system prior to implementing Asset Accounting. In this case, the balance sheet accounts for the fixed assets and the corresponding depreciation accounts will already be up to date. Accordingly, you only have to define the balance sheet accounts for the fixed assets as reconciliation accounts (see Section 9.4.1).

Reconciliation Between General Ledger and Subledger

If you have to transfer the balances, you will have to synchronize the balance sheet values from Asset Accounting with both the balance sheet asset accounts and the corresponding depreciation accounts in the general ledger. To do so, use menu path **System · Services · Reporting** to call Report RABEST01, which generates an asset list with a reporting date of January 1 of the current fiscal year. It is identical to the corresponding asset list from December 31 of the previous year, which means no depreciation from the current year is included. You now have to compare the asset list with the corresponding account balances from Financial Accounting, dated December 31 of the previous year.

Transferring the Balances

Because transferring the balances requires postings to reconciliation accounts, which is not supported in the Financial Accounting application menu, you must enter this posting in Customizing for Asset Accounting.

To do so, choose menu path **Financial Accounting · Asset Accounting · Preparing for Production Startup · Production Startup · Transfer Balances**.

The offsetting postings are generally made to an account that is set up especially for the data transfer (see Section 2.2.5).

9.4.3 Activating the Company Code

This is the last activity involved in the legacy data transfer. As previously mentioned, legacy data transfer is possible only when the company code is set to test or transfer status. Because the many change options available in test status make it unsuitable for long-term use in a production client, and the transfer status does not allow any postings to Asset Accounting aside from the asset migration, you have to set the company code to **Productive** status after the migration. Consequently, values can be changed only through new postings.

10 Outlook and Related Areas

This chapter deals with several issues that are not directly related to the core subject of this book, but which can help expand your overall understanding of the data migration area.

10.1 eCATT—extended Computer Aided Test Tool

The *eCATT*, or *extended Computer Aided Test Tool* (transaction code SECATT) is an enhancement to the CATT tool introduced in Chapter 5, and is available in every SAP R/3-based system with a Basis Release 6.20 and later. The primary motivation behind the enhancement was the limited functionality of the Computer Aided Test Tool (CATT), which was originally developed in Release 3.0. Despite all its advantages—which were discussed in detail in Chapter 8, along with an assessment of each individual migration technique—there are some situations that the CATT is simply not equipped to address.

Purpose of the eCATT

For example, the CATT technique enables you to process only transactions that are based on the standard SAP GUI. Figure 10.1 shows an example screen template that satisfies this requirement.

Standard SAP GUI

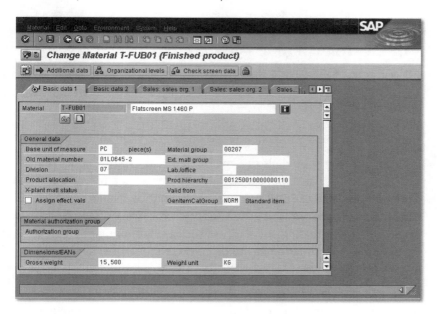

Figure 10.1 Example of a Standard SAP GUI Transaction Without GUI Controls (MM02—Change Material)

As a result, none of the transactions that employ the GUI control technology can be used for automated tests with the CATT. Accordingly, the following activities are not supported:

▶ Expanding a tree and selecting a node

▶ Calling the context menu with the right mouse button and selecting an entry

▶ Clicking a hyperlink

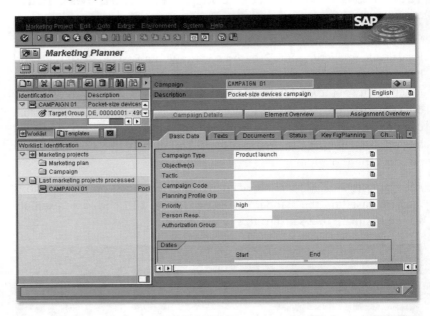

Figure 10.2 Example of a Standard SAP GUI Transaction with GUI Controls (CRM Marketing Planner)

Figure 10.2 shows a transaction based on the GUI control technology.

In this context, it should also be mentioned that external applications—such as Internet-based applications that are started in a browser and that communicate with the SAP R/3 system—cannot be included in test scenarios, because the CATT does not support processing of non-SAP GUIs. Because of the increasing popularity of such applications (see Figure 10.3, for example), this situation has to be corrected.

With this in mind, a new procedure was needed that maintained the proven advantages of the CATT, yet also supported all SAP transactions—regardless of whether they used GUI controls or not—and moreover could integrate external applications as part of the process chain in test scenarios. The eCATT not only has greater functionality than the CATT, it also has an improved user interface, which boosts ease of use as shown in Figure 10.4.

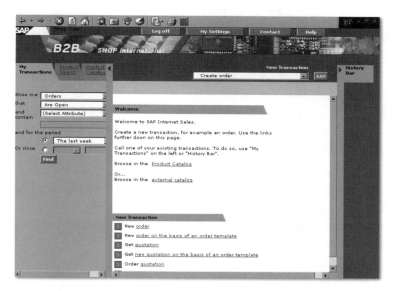

Figure 10.3 Example of an Internet Application: CRM E-Selling

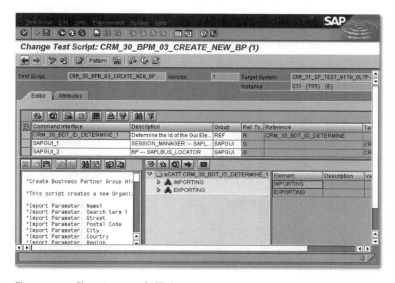

Figure 10.4 Changing an eCATT Script

Even though the described advantages and functions of the eCATT make it the preferred test tool for mySAP solutions, it can also be used for migra-

Test Tool for mySAP Solutions

tion projects like the CATT. Experienced CATT users should have no problems learning how to use the eCATT.

10.2 Data Transfer Workbench

Transaction SXDA The *Data Transfer Workbench* (or *DX Workbench*) is a standard tool in your SAP R/3 system. The corresponding transaction code is SXDA.

Managing Data Migration Projects The DX Workbench helps you manage and organize your data migration projects. It provides tools for analyzing the corresponding SAP structures and gives you an integrated view of the standard SAP data transfer programs. It also allows you to register your own data transfer programs and auxiliary programs and use them as needed.

From a functional perspective, there are overlaps between the DX Workbench and the LSM Workbench. The combined use of both tools can be extremely helpful in practice. One recommended procedure is described later on in this chapter. But first, let's get a detailed view of how the Data Transfer Workbench works.

10.2.1 Features

Project, Subproject, Run Definition, Task The Data Transfer Workbench supports the following organizational units: *Project*, *subproject*, *run definition*, and *task* (see Figure 10.5). A project contains one or more subprojects. Each subproject is assigned exactly one business object and one import technique—for example, customer master (business object) and batch input (import technique). Each subproject also contains one or more run definitions, and each run definition consists of one or more tasks. Examples of typical tasks include:

▶ Exporting legacy data

▶ Cleaning up legacy data

▶ Converting data (using the LSM Workbench, for example)

▶ Checking converted data

▶ Importing data into the SAP R/3 system

Data Transfer Workbench Framework Nonetheless, you cannot expect that the DX Workbench will automatically supply suitable programs for every possible task. Instead, this tool is really a *framework* in which you can integrate your own programs.

Run Once you have created a run definition, you can run it in dialog or in the background as often as you want. Each such *run* is logged in the Data Transfer Workbench.

Data transfer workbench

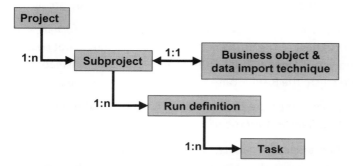

Figure 10.5 Organizational Units in the Data Transfer Workbench

The following postprocessing options are available for runs that were not completed successfully:

Postprocessing a Run

▶ The run can be continued or cancelled.

▶ A specific task that has not been fully completed can be set to "completed."

▶ The run can be deleted.

A particularly useful function in the Data Transfer Workbench is the ability to generate test data automatically. You can generate a file, even with sample data in some cases, that the data import programs (e.g., standard batch input programs such as RFBIDE00) can process. This type of file can help you recognize the mapping of fields to data transfer structures (such as BKNA1).

Generating Test Data

Please note, however, that this function requires specific programs that are not available for all business objects.

The Data Transfer Workbench also has functions for editing files. For example, you can split a large file into several smaller ones. Conversely, you can also merge several small files to create one larger file.

Splitting and Merging Files

10.2.2 Particular Strength: Data Import via BAPI

The particular strength of the Data Transfer Workbench becomes evident when the BAPI technique is used to import the migration data. As you learned in Chapter 6, the LSM Workbench uses IDoc inbound processing to import legacy data using the BAPI import technique. While this technique is very safe and easy to use, its benefits are offset by its long runtimes and low throughput. In addition, it involves creating IDocs in the SAP R/3 system, which require an archiving run to delete them. This is compounded by the fact that only successfully processed IDocs are archived.

Greater Throughput Than the LSM Workbench The Data Transfer Workbench expects the import data in IDoc format, just like the LSM Workbench. The difference here is that the data is not passed on to inbound processing, as it is in the LSM Workbench. Instead, it is transferred directly to the BAPI. Consequently, throughput is much higher.

Separate Error Handling Due to this approach, separate error handling functions had to be developed for the Data Transfer Workbench:

▶ You first define a specific *package size*. The package size defines the number of transactions that are passed on to the BAPI in one *LUW* (*Logical Unit of Work*). You have to select the package size carefully. The larger the packages, the smaller the load on the database, which, in turn, increases throughput. If an error occurs within a package, however, none of the transactions contained in that package will be updated.

▶ You now must decide where to store the transactions that couldn't be imported. There are two alternatives.

    ▷ The transactions can be saved in a separate error file.

    ▷ The transactions can be saved as IDocs and then processed using the standard inbound processing functions.

The interaction between the Data Transfer Workbench and the LSM Workbench is described in the next section.

10.2.3 Combination with the LSM Workbench

Starting the LSM Workbench When you create a run definition in the Data Transfer Workbench, you can start the LSM Workbench to process the task "Map the Data"—that is, convert the data to the SAP format (assuming the LSM Workbench is installed in your SAP R/3 system and your SAP R/3 system is Release 4.6C or later).

To do so, you must define the corresponding project, subproject, and object from the LSM Workbench in the DX Workbench.

When you start a run in the DX Workbench, the data import program runs first, followed by the data conversion program from the LSM Workbench.

Recommendation If you use the DX Workbench and the LSM Workbench in combination, the DX Workbench is always the "leading" workbench. This means the Data Transfer Workbench calls the functions of the LSM Workbench.

Depending on which import technique you select, we recommend the following procedure for combined usage:

▶ **Batch input or direct input import technique**
In this case, the "value added" by the Data Transfer Workbench consists of the generation of test data described above. All other functions are covered by the LSM Workbench.

▶ **BAPI or IDoc import technique**
Due to the particular strength of the Data Transfer Workbench in importing data via BAPI, we recommend using the Data Transfer Workbench for the data import in this case. Use the LSM Workbench for all the other steps.

These recommendations are summarized in Table 10.1 below.

	Batch input, direct input	BAPI, IDoc
Data Transfer Workbench	Generating test data	Importing the data
LSM Workbench	Loading, converting, importing the data	Loading and converting the data

Table 10.1 Procedure for Combination of DX Workbench and LSM Workbench

10.3 Data Migration Between R/3 Systems or Within an R/3 System

There are situations in which an SAP R/3 system has already been successfully installed and is used for production, but where the IT department and user departments are still confronted with data migration requirements. Typical situations include changes resulting from business reengineering or the consolidation of two SAP R/3 systems due to a takeover or merger. Regardless of your underlying motive, all of these scenarios have one thing in common: You have to extract and reallocate data within one or more production systems. If the system in question is an SAP R/3 system, you can extract the data rather easily—as long as you know in which SAP R/3 table the necessary data is stored (after all, there are over 25,000 R/3 tables in the system). To help you find the right table, Appendix A lists the R/3 tables that are used most frequently in data migration projects, however, this list is by no means complete.

When Do You Have to Extract Data?

If you want to extract *profit center master data*, for example, and you know the structure of the relevant table, CEPC, you could proceed as follows: When you choose menu path **Tools · ABAP Workbench · Overview · Data Browser** or Transaction SE16 and enter the name of R/3 table CEPC,

Extracting Profit Centers

the corresponding fields and their contents appear, as shown in Figure 10.6.

Field Selection
You can configure the view shown here with **Settings · List Format · Choose Fields ...** to display only those fields that are relevant to the data transfer. You can simply hide the unneeded fields, as shown in Figure 10.7.

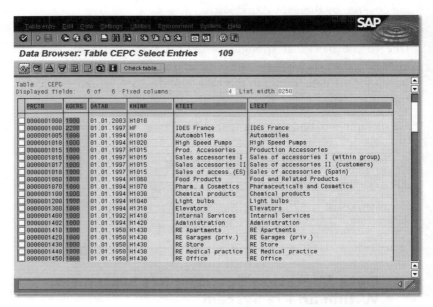

Figure 10.6 Profit Center Master Data, Displayed in the Data Browser (Transaction SE16)

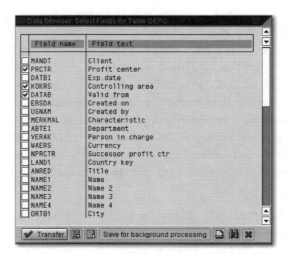

Figure 10.7 Data Browser—Select Fields

Once you have selected the fields that you want to display, you can choose **Edit · Download …** to make the dataset available in a spreadsheet program such as Microsoft Excel. See the dialog box in Figure 10.8.

Figure 10.8 Data Browser—Download

All you have to do now is enter the path where you want to save the extracted dataset. Note that you always have to assign a format to the file name, which determines the program you will use to open the file later. If you want to process the file with Microsoft Excel, for example, choose file extension *.xls*, as shown in Figure 10.9.

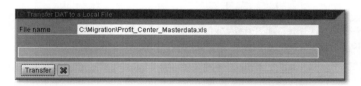

Figure 10.9 Data Browser—Download—File Format

Once you have postprocessed it, you can use this file as the foundation for data migration using the procedures introduced in Chapters 4, 5, and 6.

10.4 Migration Workbench

There are also situations in which the procedures described previously will not meet your requirements, for example:

▶ You want to consolidate two or more live SAP R/3 systems in a single SAP R/3 system.

▶ You want to transfer a company code from one SAP R/3 system to another SAP R/3 system in order to model a changed group structure.

In both cases, you must set up a new SAP R/3 system, either partially or completely, and transfer large sections of data from one SAP R/3 system to the new system—including the complete change history.

SAP has developed a special tool for such situations. It is called the *Migration Workbench* and is currently available only via SAP consulting services.

The functionality of the Migration Workbench is shown in Figure 10.10. Its basic structure will not surprise you:

▶ Structure information in the ABAP Dictionary is used to define mappings and data conversion rules.

▶ This structure information is used to generate programs for extracting, converting, and importing data.

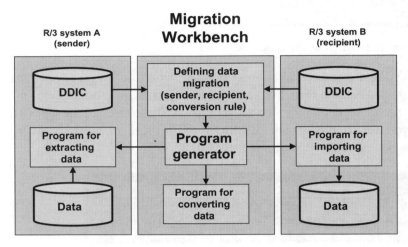

Figure 10.10 Migration Workbench

You already know this as the foundation of the LSM Workbench. However, the Migration Workbench differs from the LSM Workbench in the following aspects:

▶ The Migration Workbench specializes in extracting data from an SAP R/3 system and also provides functions that generate data extraction programs.

▶ The Migration Workbench has more powerful and flexible data conversion tools than the LSM Workbench.

▶ While the LSM Workbench uses standard SAP interfaces to import the data, the Migration Workbench takes the "direct route," writing the data directly to the SAP R/3 database. As a result, the Migration Workbench achieves a throughput that is far greater than all the other procedures described in this book.

- The Migration Workbench can also transfer data between SAP R/3 systems with different releases. In addition to application data (master data, transaction data), you can also use this tool to transfer organizational units (client, company code, plant).

10.5 Data Migration in SAP CRM

CRM (*Customer Relationship Management*) is another software product from SAP. In many cases, the SAP CRM solution is used in combination with an SAP R/3 system. The latter is often called the "R/3 backend system," indicating that the SAP CRM system, with all its "channels" (Internet applications, mobile applications, call center), is focused on the customers, while the SAP R/3 system is aimed at the "back office" and takes care of execution—that is, order processing and all the downstream processes.

Customer Relationship Management

If you operate an SAP CRM system with integrated SAP R/3 system, the SAP CRM system already contains all the necessary features for exchanging data between the two systems. In particular, SAP CRM has special functions for the initial load of the SAP CRM system with data from the SAP R/3 system.

SAP CRM systems with a Release 3.0 and later can be operated independently of an SAP R/3 system. Any other backend system can be used in place of the SAP R/3 system, or you can do without a backend system altogether. In either case, you have a "standard" migration task, which involves transferring the data required in the SAP CRM system (such as customer data, product data, orders, conditions, and prices) from the non-SAP system.

CRM Independent of R/3 Since Release 3.0

To achieve this, the SAP CRM system provides *external interfaces*, which have IDoc format for "external" systems, which brings us back to the LSM Workbench. You can use the LSM Workbench with or without the Data Transfer Workbench (see Section 10.2.3) to transfer the data from a non-SAP system to a SAP CRM system. The process flow—illustrated schematically in Figure 10.11—is as follows:

External Interfaces

- You first transform your data from the non-SAP system to the suitable SAP IDoc format, as usual.

- You then submit the converted data to IDoc inbound processing, which takes care of all the further steps: The data is converted to *BDoc format*[1] and passed on to the CRM Middleware[2] for distribution to all the involved components.

As a result, you use the familiar IDoc import technique with the LSM Workbench.

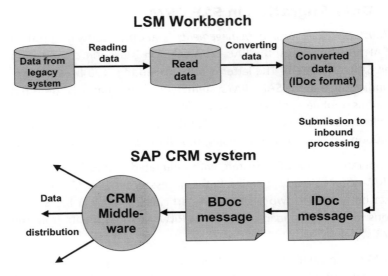

Figure 10.11 LSM Workbench and SAP CRM System

To select one of these external interfaces from the SAP CRM system in the LSM Workbench, select import method **IDoc (Intermediate Document)** and an IDoc type whose name starts with "CRMXIF" in the data migration step **Maintain Object Attributes**. CRM 3.1, for example, provides IDoc types for business partners, products, pricing conditions, orders, and invoices. For more information, go to the SAP Service Marketplace at *https://service.sap.com/crm-ci*.

---

1 *BDoc* stands for *business document*. This format is used exclusively in the SAP CRM system.
2 CRM Middleware is a component of the SAP CRM system, and controls the distribution of data between the individual components.

Appendix

This appendix contains an overview of R/3 tables that you will frequently encounter during R/3 internal data migration.

A   R/3 Tables for Selected Master and Transaction Data

A.1   Financial Accounting

- ▶ General ledger accounts
  - ▶ SKA1: G/L accounts—chart of account
  - ▶ SKB1: G/L accounts—company code-specific data
  - ▶ GLT0: G/L accounts—transaction figures
- ▶ Customers
  - ▶ KNA1: Customers—general data
  - ▶ KNB1: Customers—company code-specific data
  - ▶ KNC1: Customers—transaction figures
- ▶ Vendors
  - ▶ LFA1: Vendors—general data
  - ▶ LFB1: Vendors—company code-specific data
  - ▶ LFC1: Vendors—transaction figures
- ▶ Secondary index for document data
  - ▶ BSIS: Secondary index for G/L accounts
  - ▶ BSAS: Secondary index for G/L accounts—cleared items
  - ▶ BSID: Secondary index for customers
  - ▶ BSAD: Secondary index for customers—cleared items
  - ▶ BSIK: Secondary index for vendors
  - ▶ BSAK: Secondary index for vendors—cleared items
- ▶ Document header
  - ▶ BKPF: Document header for accounting
- ▶ Document lines/line items
  - ▶ BSEG: Document segment for accounting
  - ▶ BSEC: Document segment for one-time data
- ▶ Tax data
  - ▶ BSET: Document segment for tax data

A.2   Controlling

▶ Cost centers

  ▶ CSKS: Cost center master record

  ▶ CSKT: Cost center texts

  ▶ CSSK: Cost center/cost element

  ▶ CSSL: Cost center/activity type

▶ Internal orders

  ▶ AUFK: Order master data

▶ CO production orders

  ▶ AFKO: Order header

  ▶ AFPO: Order item

▶ Settlement rules

  ▶ COBR: Settlement rules

▶ Profit centers

  ▶ CEPC: Master data table for profit centers

  ▶ CEPCT: Profit center master data texts

  ▶ CEPC_BUKRS: Company code assignment of profit centers

A.3   Logistics

▶ Material master

  ▶ MARA: General material data

  ▶ MARC: Plant data for material

  ▶ MARD: Storage location data for material

  ▶ MARM: Units of measure for material

  ▶ MARV: Material control record

  ▶ MAKT: Material short texts

  ▶ MVKE: Sales data for material

▶ Bill of materials (BOM)

  ▶ STKO: BOM header

  ▶ STPO: BOM item

  ▶ STPU: BOM subitem

- **Sales document**
  - VBAK: Sales document—header data
  - VBAP: Sales document—item data
  - VBEP: Sales document—delivery scheduling data
  - VBKD: Sales document—business data
  - VBPK: Sales document—product proposal header
  - VBPV: Sales document—product proposal
  - VBUV: Sales document—incompleteness log

B   Glossary

This glossary contains the main terms that you encountered in this book.

ABAP Advanced Business Application Programming. A fourth-generation programming language developed by SAP for application development.

ABAP Dictionary Describes the logical structure of application development objects, as well as their representation in the structures of the underlying relational database.
All the components of the runtime environment, such as application programs and database interfaces, retrieve their information for these objects directly from the ABAP Dictionary.
The ABAP Dictionary is fully integrated in the ABAP Workbench.

Account Structure that records value transactions within a company code. The account contains transaction figures, which contain the changes to the values in a summarized form per posting period.

Account determination Automatic procedure for locating the accounts for postings transactions in Financial Accounting without requiring user intervention.

Account group Object whose attributes determine the creation of master records. The account group determines the data that is relevant for the master record, and determines a number range from which numbers are selected for the master records. An account group must be assigned to each master record.

Account type Key that specifies the accounting area to which an account belongs, such as asset accounts, customer accounts, vendor accounts,

or G/L accounts. In addition to the account number, the account type is required to identify an account, because the same account number can be used for each account type.

Acquisition and Production Costs (APC) Upper limit for valuation of an asset in the balance sheet.

Asset Accounting Subsidiary ledger accounting module in Financial Accounting. All business activities for fixed assets are recorded in Asset Accounting.

Asset class Main criterion for classifying fixed assets according to legal and management requirements. For each asset class, control parameters and default values can be defined for depreciation calculation and other master data. Each master asset record must be assigned to one asset class.

Asset subnumber Unique number that, in combination with the main asset number, identifies an asset in the SAP R/3 system. Using the asset subnumber, you can represent complex fixed assets in the SAP R/3 system. The fixed asset is identified by the main asset number. Each individual part of the asset, or subsequent acquisitions, can be represented by a subnumber. You must enter separate master data for each subnumber.

Balance Amount resulting from the difference between the debit and credit side of an account or document. If the credit side is larger, it is called a credit balance; if the debit side is larger, it is called a debit balance.

Balance sheet account Account on which the debit and credit entries resulting from business transactions are recorded.
The balance of a balance sheet account is carried forward at fiscal-year end and is identified in the balance sheet at all times.

Balance sheet asset account General ledger account in Financial Accounting on which asset transactions are recorded. It is the account to which acquisition and production costs are posted, as opposed to the accumulated depreciation account. Both of these accounts are asset accounts, however.

BAPI Business Application Programming Interface. A standardized programming interface that facilitates external access to business processes and data in the SAP R/3 system. You define Business Application Programming Interfaces (BAPIs) in the Business Object Repository (BOR) as methods of SAP business objects or SAP interface types. BAPIs offer an object-oriented view of business components in the SAP R/3 system. They are implemented and stored as RFC-enabled function modules in the Function Builder of the ABAP Workbench.

Batch input Interface that enables you to transfer large volumes of data to an SAP R/3 system. You can use batch input for both the initial migration of legacy data and the periodic import of external data.

Batch input session Sequence of transactions supplied with user data by a program. The SAP R/3 system stores these transactions in a stack until you decide to process them. No database updates are performed until the session has been processed. Using this technique, you can transfer large amounts of data to the SAP R/3 system in a short time.

Business data object → Data object

Business object → Data object

CATT Computer Aided Test Tool. A tool in the SAP R/3 system for testing business processes.

Chart of accounts Classification scheme consisting of a group of general ledger (G/L) accounts. For each G/L account, the chart of accounts contains the account number, the account name, and technical information that controls the function of the G/L account and the creation of the G/L account in the company code.

Client In commercial, organizational and technical terms, a self-contained unit in an SAP R/3 system with separate master records and its own set of tables.

Company code Smallest organizational unit for which a complete, self-contained set of accounts can be drawn up for purposes of external reporting.

Constant Named data object that is declared statically in a program and cannot be changed at runtime. In ABAP, you declare constants with the CONSTANTS statement.

Conversion → Data conversion

Cost center Organizational unit within a controlling area that represents a defined location of cost incurrence. The definition can be based on functional requirements, allocation criteria, physical location, or responsibility for costs.

Customer account Structure that records value movements in a company code that affect receivables or payables against a customer.

Customizing Settings that a system administrator has to configure during system implementation. The procedure aims to adjust the company-neutral and industry-specific delivered functions to your company's business requirements. Customizing is required prior to commissioning the system. You use the Implementation Guide (IMG) to customize the SAP R/3 system.

Data conversion Involves modifying the structure or values of data according to defined rules.

Data migration The transfer of business data (master and transaction data) from any external system to an SAP R/3 system.

Data migration object Describes a data object and other attributes that are relevant for data migration: The structure of the data object in the legacy system and the SAP R/3 system, along with the mapping that connects the two structures.

Data object Business data unit, such as customer master, material master, and financial document.

Data transfer → Data migration

Data Transfer Workbench Tool for managing and organizing data transfer projects. Can be used in combination with the LSM Workbench.

Data transformation → Data conversion

Depreciation Reduction of the asset book value because of decline in economic usefulness or because of legal requirements for taxes. Ordinary depreciation provides for the planned distribution of the acquisition and production costs over the useful life of the asset. Unplanned depreciation is justified by a foreseeable, lasting reduction in the value of the asset because of unplanned circumstances.

Depreciation area Area showing the valuation of a fixed asset for a particular purpose (for example, for individual financial statements, balance sheets for tax purposes, or management accounting values). Along with "real" depreciation areas, you can define derived depreciation areas. The values for these derived areas are calculated from those of two or more real areas.

Depreciation posting run Depreciation is posted in Financial Accounting by starting the depreciation posting run. This program creates a batch input session that contains all the posting information for Financial Accounting. The corresponding posting documents are created as the session is processed.

Direct input Data migration technique in which the data for migration is checked directly—avoiding the dialog transaction—and written to the database of the SAP R/3 system.

Document Proof of a business transaction. A distinction is made between original documents and data processing (DP) documents: Original documents include incoming invoices, bank statements and carbon copies of outgoing invoices. DP documents include accounting documents, sample documents, and recurring entry documents. Whereas accounting documents are a representation of the original document in the SAP R/3 system, sample and recurring entry documents are simply templates to simplify entry of accounting transactions.

Document header Object that contains information that applies to the entire document, such as the document date and document number.

Document type Key used to differentiate the various business transactions to be posted. The document type controls how the document is stored and defines the account types to which it will be posted.

Domain Object that describes the technical attributes of a data element, such as the data type and length. A domain can also define a value range containing the valid values for fields that refer to that domain. You can group fields that have similar technical or business purposes under a single domain. All fields based on a domain are updated automatically when you change the domain. This ensures that the fields are consistent.

DX Workbench → Data Transfer Workbench

Dynpro DYNamic PROgram. A dynpro consists of a screen template and the underlying structure logic. The main components of a dynpro are attributes (such as screen number, next screen), layout (arrangement of texts, fields, and other elements), field attributes (definition of the attributes of the individual fields), and the flow logic (calls of relevant ABAP modules). Used synonymously with *Screen*.

eCATT extended Computer Aided Test Tool. An extended version of the CATT that can also control non-SAP GUIs and transactions containing GUI controls.

Elementary data type ABAP data type. ABAP supports eight predefined elementary data types:
C (character strings), D (dates), F (floating point numbers), I (integers), N (numeric strings),
P (packed numbers), T (times), and X (hexadecimal). Data types D, F, I, and T are predefined in all aspects, while data types C, N, P, and X can be post-defined as well as predefined.

Field mapping The assignment of source fields to target fields and the corresponding conversion rules.

Fiscal year Period of usually 12 months, for which the company produces financial statements and takes inventory.

Frontend The workplace computer—usually a PC.

Function module Function for general use. Function modules are external subroutine written in ABAP that are developed in the Function Builder. They are managed in a central function library, and can therefore be called from any ABAP program. This helps to avoid redundant code and makes the programming process more effective. In contrast to FORM routines, function modules have the same standard interface.

G/L account Structure that records value movements in a company code and represents the G/L account items in a chart of accounts. A G/L account has transaction figures that record changes to the account during a posting period. These figures are totals that are used for G/L reporting.

General ledger Ledger designed to present the values used in creating financial statements. It records values at company code level.

Group asset Combination of a number of assets for the purposes of a common, summarized calculation of depreciation. A group asset is represented in the SAP R/3 system by a separate master record.

IDoc Intermediate document. SAP format in which business messages are exchanged. The term *IDoc* (or *IDoc message*) specifies the specific message, while *IDoc type* refers to the structure.

Internal table Data object that exists only at program runtime. An internal table consists of any number of identically structured table rows of the same data type, with or without a header line. The header line is similar to a structure and serves as the work area of the internal table. The data type of the lines can be either elementary or structured.

Legacy data Business data that is to be transferred from the legacy system to the SAP R/3 system.

Legacy system Business IT system that is to be replaced partially or completely within the course of an R/3 implementation project. As part of the replacement process, data will be migrated from this system to the SAP R/3 system.

Legacy System Migration Workbench Tool based on the R/3 technology that supports single and periodic data transfers from legacy systems to SAP R/3 systems.

Line item Individual line of a document.

Loop Sequence of program statements executed repeatedly. A loop is executed either a fixed number of times or until a certain condition becomes true or false.

LSM Workbench → Legacy System Migration Workbench.

LSMW → Legacy System Migration Workbench.

Mapping The assignment of fields between a legacy IT system and a successor system. This step is required to transfer field contents from the legacy system to the successor system during the data migration process.

Master data The information that remains the same over a long period of time. Master data contains information that is needed often and in the same form. Example: The master data of a cost center contains the name of the cost center, the person responsible for the cost center, the corresponding hierarchy area, and other information.

Migration Used synonymously with *data migration*.

Migration Workbench Tool developed by SAP especially for migrating data between SAP R/3 systems. Currently only available in combination with SAP consulting services.

Non-SAP system → Legacy system

Object → Data migration object

Optional entry field Input field in which data entry is optional. In contrast to required entry fields, processing continues if you don't enter data in optional entry fields.

P&L account All business transactions that result in a change of stockholders' equity, and therefore the overall company result, are posted to P/L accounts, which are a component of the profit and loss statement. Typical examples include sales revenues, personnel expenses, and costs of materials.

Parameters Data required to execute a function module or subroutine (import parameters) or returned by the method or subroutine after it is called (export parameters). The interface of the method call is determined when the parameters are defined.

Posting key Two-digit numeric key that determines the way line items are posted. This key determines several factors, including the account type, the type of posting (debit or credit), and the layout of entry screens.

Primary window Main window of a task. Primary windows are the windows where the main action of a task is performed. Within each session, there is always one primary window on the screen. Primary windows can call secondary windows, or be replaced by another primary window.

R/3 standard interface Interface to the R/3 system with type batch input, direct input, BAPI, or IDoc.

R/3 system SAP's enterprise resource planning (ERP) software. General term for any system based on the R/3 technology, such as SAP R/3, SAP APO, and SAP CRM.

Reconciliation account G/L account to which transactions in the subsidiary ledgers (such as in the customer, vendor, or assets areas) are updated automatically. Typically, several subledger accounts post to a common reconciliation account. This ensures that the developments in the subledger accounts are accurately reflected in the general ledger (that is, in line with balance sheet conventions).

Replacement value The current valuation of an asset, which is different from the acquisition and production costs. The replacement value of an asset can result, for example, due to price changes because of inflation or price changes because of technical advancements.

Required entry field Input field in which data entry is mandatory. Required fields are generally indicated by a question mark. Such screens cannot be processed successfully unless you enter data in all required entry fields. You can leave optional fields blank.

SAP application server Part of the SAP client/server architecture. Describes the computer where the application logic of the SAP R/3 system is running.

SAP Basis release Release of the SAP Basis component of the SAP R/3 system.

Sequential file File with sequential organization. The records in a sequential file are saved consecutively without a keyword.

Status bar Element of the graphical user interface (GUI). The SAP R/3 system uses one of the output fields of the status bar to display messages issued by the primary window. Other fields in the status bar provide information on the system status. The status bar extends along the entire width of the lower edge of the primary window.

Subledger Ledger whose purpose is to represent business transactions with customers and vendors. Subledgers in assets accounting are ledgers that represent the development of asset values.

Subledger accounting Accounting at the subsidiary ledger level, such as customer, vendor, or asset. Subledgers provide more details on the postings made to the reconciliation accounts in the general ledger.

Subroutine Module of a program that can be called by multiple programs. You use subroutines to avoid having to write frequently used program components more than once. Data can be passed explicitly from and to subroutines.

Table-like file File in which all the records possess the same structure.

Test case Testable entity in an SAP R/3 system. A test case frequently models a specific business process or process chain.

Text file File with text information whose records are separated by end-of-record indicators.

Transaction Describes an application. To reach the initial screen of an application, you can navigate through the menu hierarchy or enter a transaction code in the command field. Using the transaction saves you from having to navigate through the various menus, leading you directly to the initial screen.

Transaction code Sequence of alphanumeric characters that identifies a transaction in the SAP R/3 system. To call a transaction, you enter the transaction code in the command field and click on **Enter**.

Transaction data Transaction-specific data that is short-lived and assigned to certain master data. Individual posting documents are called transaction data. For example, transaction data relating to sales development can be assigned to a vendor's master data. The total sales of a vendor consist of the data of the individual business transactions, the transaction data.

Transaction figures Sum of all postings to an account, separated by posting period and credit/debit.

Translation Manipulating the values of field contents, based on a table that specifies which old values are to be replaced with which new values.

Transport request Document for copying corrections between different system types. A transport request records released corrections. When the request is released, the transport is performed. For example, you can transport corrections from a development system to a consolidation system.

Variable Placeholder used to store and address data under a particular name in a particular format. You can distinguish variables by their name, type, length, and structure.

C   About the Authors

Michael Willinger was born in 1971 in Heidelberg, Germany. He studied business administration at the University of Mannheim from 1990 to 1996, focusing on bank management, financing, auditing, fiduciary structures, and statistics. He first encountered SAP R/3 during his graduate studies in business data processing; it has had a major impact on his career path ever since. From 1998 to 2001, Michael Willinger worked as an SAP consultant (focus: Financial Accounting) at Bilfinger & Berger AG, a construction firm, before he moved to Tarkett AG, an internationally active manufacturer of flooring. At present, he is the project manager for the global implementation of the R/3 Financial Accounting and Controlling modules.

Johann Gradl was born in 1961. He studied mathematics and computer science at the Technische Universität München (Munich Polytechnic University) from 1980 to 1986 and—after a hiatus during which he performed his civil service duty—he completed his doctorate in mathematics from 1988 to 1990. Johann Gradl joined SAP in 1993. He initially worked in the R/2 Services department, and then turned his attention to the area of data migration. He was a driving force behind the development of the Legacy System Migration Workbench described in this book. He subsequently performed various tasks related to the development of Customer Relationship Management (CRM). In his current position of Vice President for Installed Base Maintenance & Support, he is responsible for the products CRM and BW, among others.

Index

Practical solutions to streamline 24/7 operations Service Level Agreements, disaster recovery, security

355 pp., 2004, US$ 79.95
ISBN 1-59229-025-8

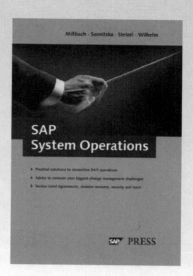

SAP System Operations

www.sap-press.co

M. Missbach, R. Sosnitzka, J. Stelzel, M. Wilhelm

SAP System Operations

With system landscapes becoming increasingly more complex, administering them efficiently is proving equally difficult. This unique new book provides you with concepts and practical solutions that will enable you to optimize your SAP operations. Get in-depth information to set up a viable Standard Operation Environment (SOE) for SAP systems, as well as time-saving tips for certification and validation of your system landscape. Plus, benefit from and customize the numerous examples and case studies extracted from the worldwide operations of many large SAP customers.

Unlock the full potential of your SAP systems!

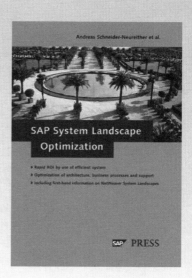

220 pp., approx. US$ 79.95
ISBN 1-59229-026-4, May 2004

SAP System Landscape Optimization

www.sap-press.com

A. (Ed.) Schneider-Neureither

SAP System Landscape Optimization

This reference book serves as an essential collection of insights, procedures, processes and tools that help you unlock the full potential of your SAP systems. First, hit the ground running with a detailed introduction to SAP NetWeaver and the mySAP Business Suite. Then, elevate your mastery of key concepts such as system architecture, security, Change and Transport Mana- gement, to name just a few. All of the practical advice and detailed information provided is with a clear focus on helping you guide your team to achieve a faster return on investment.

Authorization concepts for SAP R/3 and Enterprise Portals!

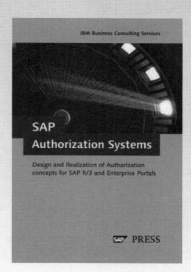

284 pp., 2003, US$ 59.95
ISBN 1-59229-016-7

SAP Authorization System

www.sap-press.com

IBM Business Consulting Services GmbH

SAP Authorization System

Design and Implementation of Authorization concepts for SAP R/3 and SAP Enterprise Portals

This practical guide offers you a detailed introduction to all the essential aspects of SAP Authorization management, as well as the necessary organizational and technical structures and tools. Take advantage of a proven Phase Model to help you navigate through all of the stages leading up to the implementation and deployment of an authorization concept, from the procedural steps required to design the concept, to the production phase, and lastly, to the supervision phase. In addition, you'll quickly learn how to set up authorization via the SAP R/3 Profile Generator.

Take full advantage of Employee Self-Service (ESS).

352 pp., 2003, US$ 59.95
ISBN 1-59229-021-3

mySAP HR Technical Principles and Programming

www.sap-press.com

E. Brochhausen, J. Kielisch, J. Schnerring, J. Staeck

mySAP HR Technical Principles and Programming

Finally, a technical reference book that gives you an in-depth, firsthand look at the data structures of SAP HR. You can greatly advance your key projects with detailed insights for analyzing and working with this mission critical data, and much more. First, gain a thorough understanding of the concept of information models, through which the master data in HR is structured. Then, learn about the individual information models of personnel administration and time management. Special features of HR role and authorization concepts are clearly defined-from both the functional and technical perspectives.

- Detailed guidance on SAP Web AS architecture, tools, and functionality - Comprehensive practical examples including a complete BSP application

528 pp., 2003, US$ 69.95
ISBN 1-59229-013-2

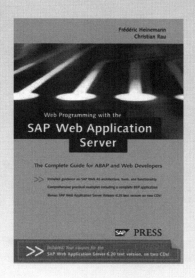

Web Programming with the SAP Web Application Server

www.sap-press.com

F. Heinemann, C. Rau

Web Programming with the SAP Web Application Server

The complete guide for ABAP and Web developers

The SAP Web Application Server (Web AS) is the latest evolutionary stage of the SAP Basis System. The book provides a step-by-step introduction to web development using Web AS. The first section focuses on the key components of Web AS for web development using standards such as XML and HTTP. By using a variety of examples, the second part of the book shows you in detail how to program with Business Server Pages. This must-have resource is written not only for ABAP programmers who need more information on these essential new concepts, but also for web developers interested in Web AS programming with JavaScript.

New Third Edition -- completely revised! Now includes: How to speed up your BSP applications

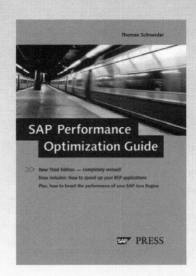

494 pp., 2. edition 2003, US$ 59.95
ISBN 1-59229-022-1

SAP Performance Optimization Guide

www.sap-press.com

T. Schneider

SAP Performance Optimization Guide

Analyzing and Tuning SAP Systems

Optimize the performance and economical running of your SAP-System - the new edition of this book shows you how! Whether you administer an R/3 or one of the newest mySAP-Solutions, you learn how to syste- matically identify and analyze performance problems. Another focus is the adaptation of appropriate tuning measures and verification of success. Performance optimization includes the technical side as well as the analysis of applications. For the new edition the book has been thoroughly revised and brought up to date. A new chapter provides insight into the connection of the system to the Internet with the help of Web AS.

Tips and tricks for dealing with SAP Business Information Warehouse

450 pp., 2004, US$ 69.95
ISBN 1-59229-017-5

SAP BW Professional

www.sap-press.com

N. Egger

SAP BW Professional

Tips and tricks for dealing with SAP Business Information Warehouse

Learn the ins and outs of SAP Business Information Warehouse (BW), and gain the knowledge to leverage the full potential of this key technology. Whether it's in terms of project management, data modeling or reporting, you'll benefit from volumes of basic and advanced information. All content is presented in an easy-tofollow format, illustrated by proven examples, sample solutions and clear graphics and screen shots.

The official guidebook to SAP CRM 4.0

450 pp., approx. US$ 59.95
ISBN 1-59229-029-9, May 2004

mySAP CRM

www.sap-press.com

R. Buck-Emden, P. Zencke

mySAP CRM

The Official Guidebook to SAP CRM 4.0

Discover all of the most critical functionality, new enhancements, and best practices to maximize the potential of mySAP CRM.

Learn the essential principles of mySAP CRM as well as detailed techniques for employing this powerful SAP solution in all customer-oriented business processes. Practical examples highlight important functional aspects and guide you through the complete Customer Interaction Cycle. Plus, you'll also discover the ins and outs of key functional areas and benefit from expert advice illustrated throughout with mySAP CRM business scenarios. A fully updated presentation of the implementation methodology, as well as the technical fundamentals of SAP CRM 4.0, serve to round out this formidable resource.